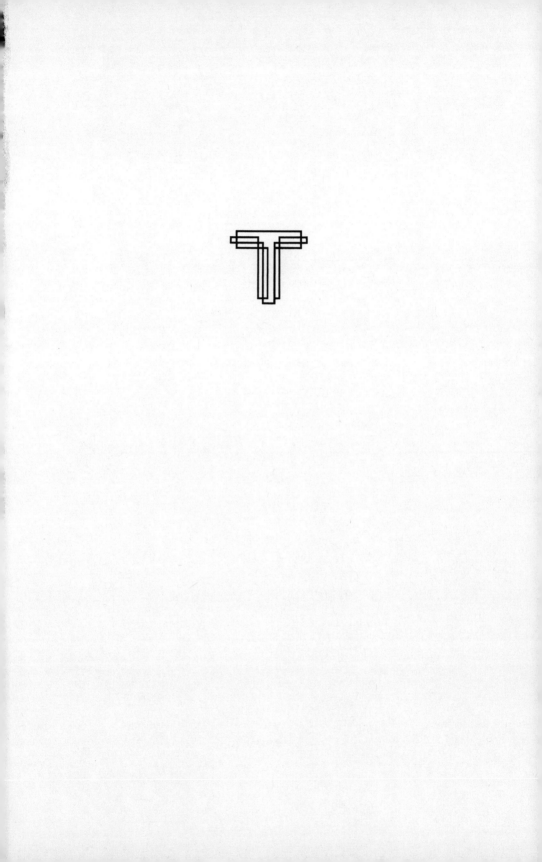

A BODY OF WORK

DANCING TO THE EDGE AND BACK

DAVID HALLBERG

WITHDRAWN

TOUCHSTONE

NEW YORK   LONDON   TORONTO   SYDNEY   NEW DELHI

Touchstone
An Imprint of Simon & Schuster, Inc.
1230 Avenue of the Americas
New York, NY 10020

The dancers and stage managers appear through the courtesy of
The American Guild of Musical Artists, AFL-CIO.

Certain names and characteristics have been changed.

First Touchstone hardcover edition November 2017

For information about special discounts for bulk purchases,
please contact Simon & Schuster Special Sales at 1-866-506-1949
or business@simonandschuster.com.

The Simon & Schuster Speakers Bureau can bring authors to your live event.
For more information or to book an event, contact the Simon & Schuster
Speakers Bureau at 1-866-248-3049 or visit our website at www.simonspeakers.com.

Interior design by Kyle Kabel

Manufactured in the United States of America

10 9 8 7 6 5 4 3 2 1

Library of Congress Cataloging-in-Publication Data

Names: Hallberg, David, author.
Title: A body of work : dancing to the edge and back / David Hallberg.
Description: New York : Touchstone, 2017.
Identifiers: LCCN 2017031000 (print) | LCCN 2017042462 (ebook) |
    ISBN 9781476771175 | ISBN 9781476771151 (hardback) |
    ISBN 9781476771168 (trade paperback)
Subjects: LCSH: Hallberg, David. | Ballet dancers—United States—Biography.
    | BISAC: BIOGRAPHY & AUTOBIOGRAPHY / Entertainment &
    Performing Arts. | BIOGRAPHY & AUTOBIOGRAPHY / Personal Memoirs. |
    PERFORMING ARTS / Dance / Classical & Ballet.
Classification: LCC GV1785.H258 (ebook) | LCC GV1785.H258 A3 2017
    (print) | DDC 792.8092 [B] —dc23
LC record available at https://lccn.loc.gov/2017031000

ISBN 978-1-4767-7115-1
ISBN 978-1-4767-7117-5 (ebook)

For Mom and Dad,
who never doubted and always nurtured my passion.

For Mr. Han,
whose tireless commitment shaped that passion.

INTRODUCTION

I *remember what it feels like to dance. To move so freely that my body releases and creative intuition takes over, leading me beyond the worry of executing technique to a realm where nothing exists but the movement, the music, the emotions. I miss those memories of freedom, but they are embedded in my mind and body. I can replay them whenever I wish.*

I think of the ballroom scene in Romeo and Juliet. *She is seated, plucking a lute, while I dance for her, spinning, boldly flirting, an unapologetic intruder at the ball, unable to contain my magnetic attraction to this enchanting stranger as destiny binds us. Finally, the other guests leave the ballroom and we are alone, face-to-face, longing, gazing. We dance, playfully and innocently for the moment, but with an undercurrent that will soon reveal itself as tempestuous passion.*

When the scene is over, I dash offstage. I pant in the wings, out of breath. I slip out of the heavy, sweat-drenched velvet tunic I've danced in for the past forty-five minutes and wipe my face on a towel to remove what is left of my stage makeup. I put on a flowing white shirt, which clings to my still-damp body. My dresser drapes a floor-length brown cape over my shoulders. My lungs burn; I desperately fill them with air in preparation for bounding onstage again.

All around me, the anticipation is palpable. I feel it backstage: from the dancers watching in the wings, from the stage manager cueing the lights in a hushed tone, from the musicians in the orchestra pit caressing their instruments as they play the hypnotic Prokofiev score.

The scene changes. Juliet's balcony appears in the distance. The audience waits in the piercing silence. The stillness, the soundless stage shrouded in dim lights, creates an atmosphere that is alien, unique, almost unearthly.

I stand there, awaiting my entrance, eyes closed, seeking to break free from nerves.

When the first notes of the pas de deux begin, I open my eyes. My Juliet is there, on her balcony, bathed in moonlight. The sight of her gives me strength, arouses me emotionally and physically. Erases all doubt and fear. I move toward her, beckon to her, enfold her, as we speak with our bodies in ways far more profound than mere words. It is love, I am convinced. Both real and staged. The lines are blurred. There are no boundaries. We dance as one person, one thought, nothing held back. No gesture ruled out, as long as it is truthful.

Moments like this are worth it all. The doubt. The sacrifice. The injuries. The scrutiny. The burden of expectation. Those moments of living so intensely and fully on the stage are why I danced. Now, each day, I face one towering question: will I ever experience that euphoria again?

AT THIS POINT, the lengthy time I've been injured seems like a purgatorial dream from which I cannot wake. My life as a dancer seems distant, like another lifetime. Moscow. The stages I danced on. The partners I loved. The prime shape I was in. Circling the world once, twice, three times each year. I can't let myself remember too much; when I do, it invokes despair and a knife-sharp pain of loss. It forces me to face what still seems unthinkable: that I no longer have the ability to be the dancer I was, the person I am meant to be. To answer my calling.

Dancers say, "Our bodies are our instruments." We know we must take care of them. Not abuse them and wrongly assume they will always be at the ready.

But when you are healthy, you have no way to imagine how it would feel to be stripped of your art, your means of expression.

I'm locked in a desperate fight. A fight with my body, which does not work for me anymore. And the longer I go on fighting, setback after setback, month after month, I lose, in a very slow but inexorable way, the ability to envision myself back on the stage.

It's been more than two years since my life became divided into two distinct parts: before the injury, and after. Before, I was dancing at full force, in one grand opera house after another. But I began to sense something was wrong. It was a gradual, encroaching sensation, barely noticed at first. In any case, I had a lot at stake and couldn't be bothered. I danced in pain because I had to.

MRIs, X-rays, CAT scans later it was determined that my injured foot needed to be surgically reconstructed. Wear and tear. A bone embedded in my deltoid, slowly fraying the ligament. No massage therapy, no acupuncture, no other known treatment could help. An operation would be a radical move; making the decision to do it left me anxious. But soon after that, I felt calm. Or was it simply resignation? Or immobilizing fear? In any case, I was desperate to be well, to fix the problem that had plagued me. Nearly two years after that initial operation, and the rehabilitation process that followed, I still had not returned to dancing and had a new and different cause for anxiety: the fact that everyone knew how wrong everything had gone.

And so there was a second operation. The morning it took place, I walked into the hospital as a normal person, relatively free of pain (it was dancing that induced the unbearable pain). I left there an invalid, hardly able to put one crutch in front of the other. I was officially "out." That's the word the dance world uses to signify that someone is injured. "Is he out?" they ask. So there I was: "out" and aching and trying my best to crutch ahead. Anyone who has been on crutches knows the feeling. That feeling of being totally helpless. You can't carry a glass of water to the couch. Middle-of-the-night negotiations to the toilet in the dark. Wanting to get out of the apartment; unable to go anywhere. A constant negotiation: the

3

reactions of others. The gawking eyes when you are finally able to crutch down the sidewalk. Especially if they know you from the stage. As a dancer.

Rest is the physical and mental devil. But rest is the healer. With idle time come the waves. Waves of elation and positivity followed by waves of depression. A wave of people come to wish you well. Keep you going. Bring you soup or flowers. Have a chat. The feeling is light; you are thankful to have the support. They try to make you believe you'll get better.

But the visits tail off and time alone becomes more and more frequent. I have always thought that if I had a stretch of free time I would use it to the fullest advantage. Learn the piano. Improve my Russian. Read War and Peace. *God knows I have enough books. Their collection has been an obsessive pastime. But as the days slip by, I remain unproductive, shadowed at first by the stupor of oxycodone, then by the paralyzing reality of the long road ahead, a road that seems to lead far away from the stage.*

It's the uncertainty that has killed me the most. The inability to say for sure whether I will ever be back on the stage, where everyone expects me to be. As the months crawl on, my ambition to get there never wavers, but the dream of being there seems exactly that: a dream. I wear emotional armor, necessary protection against the thoughtless things otherwise kind people say. Even my mother, who is only well-meaning, asks, "Well, honey, what if this doesn't work? What will you do then?"

As if the thought hadn't crossed my mind that maybe I am on the road to not recovering.

I go to see a dance performance in New York City. Someone spots me, yelling across the aisle at intermission, "David, is there any hope?" I look at him, stunned, and say, "Of course there is hope. There is always hope." What else could I say?

In fact, there are many hopes. The hope that I will be able to jump again. The hope that the simplest steps won't cause me pain. The hope that I can dance a show I committed to a year and a half before. The hope that I will not disappoint the ballet companies that rely on me.

Thick in my disquieting haze, before I realize it, three more months have passed. Then another month. And another. The goal remains as distant as ever. Even the smallest goal becomes a long shot. A proper tendu. One pirouette. A bend or stretch of the leg that does not cause pain.

And so I am faced with the truth: the power of my will is all I have at this desolate time.

CHAPTER 1

Morning class was an essential daily task. Like making that pot of coffee first thing in the morning. Out of bed, half-asleep, and straight to the coffee machine. Filter. Water. Coffee grinds. On switch. Every day. Day in. Day out.

By nine thirty a.m. I would shuffle into a worn studio that was always empty and silent. The only light came from the morning sun edging in through huge windows. Outside, one floor down, the streets and noise of New York City.

At first, my body resisted the task at hand, especially when I was drained from the previous night's performance. But the work continued the following morning, as if no exertion occurred, as if I hadn't given to the performance every ounce of my emotional and physical energy.

I started with what I often dreaded: that first small physical movement that would call me to attention, easing me out of my slumber into another day. I would always begin with the same exercises. Done at my own pace and with the understanding that if I skipped them, I would not be set up well for later, when I would need to push my body in order to transform ballet's absurdly difficult steps into seemingly effortless movement onstage. I began with small, basic movements, continuing on to those that are more advanced and complicated, each of them essential to achieving huge jumps and whiplash turns. People often wonder why we need daily ballet class when we are already professionals. But it is when we are performing virtuoso moves that we need those classes more than ever.

The deeper I went into the movements, the further I escaped into thought. The exercises slowly became a meditative experience. My mind would wander to last night's show, my coming travels, the day's rehearsals, a project I wanted to develop, a choreographer I needed to contact, emails I needed to write.

As the start of class drew near, other dancers trickled into the studio, shuffling in just as tired as I was. Everyone spoke in hushed tones. The lights would be turned on by someone who needed to feel they were officially starting class. As more dancers arrived, the volume and energy picked up. Some chatted about the show the night before, about what they did after it. Others discussed the new ballet they were learning, talking as they stretched or strengthened. A few, with headphones on, weren't yet awake enough to discuss anything. We all wore different "uniforms." Mine was Nike sweatpants, tights underneath, a cotton T-shirt, an insulated track jacket. Traditionalists wore nothing but tights and a T-shirt or leotard, as we all did when we were training and weren't allowed to wear "junk": the sweatpants, leg warmers, and baggy clothes that obscure the body and keep it from being exposed to the teacher's critical eye. But I like junk. It's comfortable.

Fads in dance attire come and go. In the 1970s and '80s the more tattered and ripped your practice clothes were, the better. Maybe the wear suggested the dancer was working harder than others or was too dedicated and rehearsing too hard to take the time to buy new clothes. That has changed. I've gotten flak from my colleagues for having holes in my dancewear. When I was promoted to Principal Dancer a friend said, "Now you're making Principal salary, so you can afford some better-looking clothes."

But class is not a catwalk. The important thing is not how good the clothes look on the dancer; all that matters is what's being danced in those clothes.

Moments before class was to begin, the teacher and accompanist would enter the studio, the former standing in the front of the room, the latter taking a seat at the grand piano.

"Are we ready?" the teacher would ask, "or do we need five more minutes?"

Always five more minutes. Compulsory for dancers to do their last stretches, yoga positions, exercises with weights. Or merely to delay the recognition that the day's responsibilities were calling.

Grace period over, the talking ceased. We assumed our usual places at the barre. These barre spots are not free for the taking. There is, in every ballet company in the world, a pecking order. All the spots—by the piano, by the mirror, at the end, in the center—are accounted for. Some are claimed by Principal Dancers, others by members of the Corps de Ballet who have stood in the same spot for years. When outsiders come to take class with a company, they know not to claim a place at the barre until class starts. And God help the new kid who takes a much-coveted spot.

With one hand placed on the barre, we began with pliés. The most basic of movements. A dancer's training commences at a very young age and starts with pliés at the barre. Whether you've danced once or a thousand times, it is the plié that begins your day.

A plié is a bending of the knees with the feet positioned in specific ways. This fundamental movement is the precursor to more advanced steps. Every turn and every jump—however high or low—starts with a plié. It's the essential taking-off point to things far more difficult and impressive. For so many years I did pliés every day with a mindless ease and agility gained through repetition. I had done this series of exercises daily for twenty years. That is what we do: repeat the same movements every day throughout the entirety of our careers. It never ceases. If we think we don't need class and the daily focus it provides, our work slips and that slippage is eventually visible on the stage. The audience can tell; they may not know in technical terms what isn't working, but they know that something doesn't look right. "I can't put my finger on it," they'll say, "but it didn't quite do it for me."

So class is critical; if the basics go, the rest goes with them.

As we moved along to more strenuous movement, still holding on to the barre, my mind would drift again. At times I would become bored. Distracted. Want another coffee. I would look out the window, wishing I could take advantage of the beautiful day. Especially on Saturdays, when it seemed that everyone in New York City was just a few blocks away, leisurely strolling through the stalls at the Union Square Greenmarket. But class pushed on. That was a saving grace. You had to dive in and take motivation from other dancers in the room as you executed the familiar steps in their never-changing order: plié, tendu, dégagé, rond de jambe, fondu, frappé, développé, grand battements.

CLASS ALWAYS HAS the same structure: barre followed by center work, during which we execute combinations of steps, some in one place and some moving across the entire studio. As they increase in complexity, class becomes more like a performance, with dancers caught between two desires: to show off to colleagues and to dance for the sheer bliss of moving. As the dancers grow ever warmer, layers of clothing come off, one by one. The daily strip-down to a leotard and tights.

After a while, the windows would steam up from the body heat of eighty exhausted, sweating dancers. Inevitably someone would write on them in the same spirit that you'd write *Wash me!* on the dirty windshield of a car. Here, the words were always some variation of *I LOVE BALLET!*, in all their intended sarcasm.

Some dancers would trail out of the studio and leave class

early, saving their energy and bodies for the long rehearsal day ahead. But those who stayed would pull off stunning jumps and turns, soaring higher and higher across the studio, unleashing a whirlwind of grand leaps and fleet turns in the air. The pianist's music would propel us as we sought to one-up each other with every successive combination.

And the music . . . ah, the music! An essential aspect of dance. The skill and enthusiasm of the pianists and what they choose to play is paramount. Their music could take me beyond where I stood. It could take me into the melody, into the small accents of the downbeat, in front of the phrase, or behind it just a bit. Or, if they were uninspired, their lack of enthusiasm could make the steps seem more grueling, deepen my fatigue, make me momentarily hate my profession. But music, as a whole, allowed me to envisage new ways of inventing my work. Lengthen where I once tightened, ascend more slowly where I once rushed. When I heard something I loved, the steps were forgotten and I just danced. Around me, others would be dancing too, all of us engulfed in the beauty that comes from the fusion of music and movement.

That euphoria occurred for me on an early morning in a nondescript daily class years ago. The first chords of Schubert's Moment Musicaux No. 2 took me somewhere beyond my place at the barre. I was simply doing pliés, but as I heard the first chords of the No. 2 opening, I became lost in its simplistic perfection. Suddenly, I felt I embodied the music. Bending and stretching my legs, coordinating my arm movements, this everyday exercise became something ethereal, heightened, spiritual. There was godliness in the movement. Meaning and purpose. It wasn't the pliés that changed me. It was the beauty of Schubert that possessed me. This is what music can do to a dancer, if one is open to listening.

In such moments of transcendence I was doing what I aspired to do, and loving it in the purest and most primitive way.

*   *   *

MY MEMORIES OF morning class bring to mind the eternal interplay among dancers that veers between intense competition and mutual support. The extreme physicality and grueling nature of ballet create unusually close attachments. We feel part of a special tribe, drawn together by shared dedication, experience, and the understanding that dance possessed us all at a very young age. Because ballet demands and consumes so much energy and time, for many dancers the world begins and ends with dance. They proceed from class to rehearsal to performance and back to class again, year after year, barely noticing life passing beyond the studio and stage. To fulfill what's asked of us, in a physical sense, we feel that we don't need to interact with the "real world." Many of us never do, despite the fact that a knowledge of art and music, literature and poetry provides powerful enhancements to anyone's dancing.

Though we become professionals at an early age, we paradoxically remain juvenile in many aspects of our lives. Our schedules are dictated to us, our ballets are chosen for us, our touring schedules are arranged by others. Our conversation revolves, for the most part, around the ballet we're learning, the ballet master we'd rather not work with, the performance we wish we could give or the one we already gave. Our colleagues are not only our friends; they become our husbands, wives, one-night stands, occasional enemies, enduring affairs. For dancers throughout the world, all of life seems encapsulated within the confines of their own companies.

But unity of the tribe also has a dark side: our devotion to one another is inevitably trumped by our individual desire to succeed. A group of dancers drinking at a bar at night can revert to bitching about other dancers like a clique of chatty schoolgirls ensconced at the popular table. I have been subject to my own demons of jealousy when someone else got a role instead of me, or when I danced the second performance instead of opening night, or when someone else was invited to a ballet company I hadn't yet danced for. All of us are extremely vulnerable, which leaves us craving support from our peers and opens us to moments, in class and rehearsal, when we can laugh together about the silliest, most ridiculous things. We encourage each other through those rehearsals that run late into the evening when we're delirious from the long day's work. We share collective discovery in rehearsals that are euphoric; we remain united through rehearsals that are a living hell. I miss the way that, on an opening night, we huddle together onstage just before the curtain rises and share a moment of "we did this together." Even when we hate the ballet we have created with a choreographer, we still stick together, soldiering on to make the experience something constructive. It's a remarkable and invaluable intimacy.

SOMETHING ELSE I miss: the routine that characterized every performance day. Each dancer has his or her own preshow rituals. No matter where in the world I danced, mine started invariably with morning class, with setting up my body. Then home, or to my hotel, where I'd have a relatively large lunch. Chicken, rice, salad. Not too many carbs, no sugars. Filling enough to last me through the performance but light enough to not feel like a weight in my stomach.

Soon after eating, full of food and feeling dozy, I would take a nap. One of the ballerinas I have partnered, Gillian Murphy, is famous for her two-hour sleeps. But sleeping for that long before a show would make me too groggy. So my naps lasted half an hour, or an hour at most. The moment I woke to the sound of the insistent alarm, the anxiety and stress of the show rushed into my mind. *It's happening,* I would think. *The wait is over.*

In the shower, hot water warmed me as I mentally reviewed the steps I would soon dance. After the shower, always a shave. I have a superstition that if I don't shave before the show, it means I have slacked off somehow and am not fully committed to the performance. I normally dressed nicely: suit, good shoes, all intended to emphasize the evening's event, the sense of occasion. Usually there was a dinner afterward with family or friends, or a special treat when I could slip away with my manager and have a couple of drinks and dinner alone at our usual place.

I always packed clothes to sweat in when I warmed up before the show, and a greeting card for my ballerina in which I would write a *merde* note. "*Merde*" is the word dancers use when wishing each other good luck. Obviously, we're not going to say "break a leg," as actors sometimes do, but that we came to settle on the unlikely "*merde*" still amuses me.

Before I left the apartment, my feelings were a jumble of anticipation, excitement, and dread. Yet nothing compares to it. The nerves you feel with the show fast approaching. The pressure to dance your absolute best. Troublesome questions would seep in at the last moment, attacking my mind like some plague I didn't know I'd contracted. I would careen between confidence and fear.

I can do this, let's conquer this!

What if I miss this turn? Mess up that lift? Do I have enough stamina? Will I get it right? I have to get it right. I cannot miss this lift! It will all be over if it goes wrong!

No matter how much I'd prepared, the performance was always a risk. Anything can happen on that stage. Ballets have passages that are incredibly tricky, even potentially dangerous. One misplaced step of the foot and it can painfully twist. One slightly off-kilter landing from a high jump and something can crack that shouldn't. Dancing virtuoso steps can feel like traversing a darkened room trying to avoid a trip wire.

*   *   *

I'VE ALWAYS DREADED that moment when the show is over and the coaches, director, and staff come onstage to talk to the dancers. I'd look into their eyes as if to say, "Was it good? Did I do okay?" When you perform, you subject yourself to judgment and criticism from everyone.

And when people who attended the show would praise a performance, I often suspected they were lying. I knew they felt the need to be complimentary and I understood why. They know you've given everything you've got onstage, and not to say something nice would be rude. But most times their praise produced one reaction in me: I wanted to hide. Which is perverse, considering that dancers who can't take a compliment annoy me.

Still, their well-meant words would make me want to run up to my dressing room and see no one. To be alone with a beer. I could even feel guilty about drinking that beer. I'd think, *I don't deserve it. I didn't dance well enough. I only deserve to work harder. Or give up.*

After more than two years of not having felt that vulnerability, it strikes me that I could have been less harsh in my judgment. I wish I had focused on the sheer enjoyment of dance that I felt as a child. Accepted that nothing is ever perfect.

Yet I also believe that my harsher judgments had value. Because unless I kept questioning and recognizing my shortcomings, I couldn't learn and I couldn't evolve. The trick is to be realistic, balanced: to not overpraise or be easily pleased yet not judge myself too harshly, as others often tell me I do.

Once, in a rehearsal with the prima ballerina Diana Vishneva for American Ballet Theatre's *Sleeping Beauty*, I danced my variation while she looked on. As I toiled away at the jumps and turns, incorporating notes from our coach, I could feel Diana peering at me from the side of the studio.

Finally she said, "You have everything ballet needs of a dancer, but you don't know it."

Her comment left me speechless. I will never forget those words. They made me realize that not acknowledging your own potential or talent isn't modesty. It's a disservice to yourself and your art form.

THESE DAYS, I am consigned to watch from the sidelines. As I try to recover, my daily routine of rehabilitation places me in the building during rehearsal hours, peeking in on a studio where a new ballet is being created or an old one is rehearsed. I take company class with the other dancers. But the difference is that I am in a cocoon, healing. After class, I watch them head off to rehearsals that I no longer have the privilege to participate in. They complain just as I did. They stress just as I stressed. But they also feel the happiness and satisfaction of having a purpose. Their goal is the final product onstage. My goal is to be able to call my dancing my own again. To execute steps proficiently enough to rehearse, let alone perform.

So what keeps me going even now, when the path is so rough and uncertain? Hunger. Since childhood I have had an insatiable hunger for dance. I cannot control it. It controls me. And it has set me on a path dictated by one essential principle: never be afraid to go where your passion leads you.

CHAPTER 2

The drive that spurred me on was not forced into me. It was never someone else's dream. I didn't have stereotypical stage parents pushing me to work, insisting I take class, telling me I needed to make something of myself. It was my own dream and I was fortunate that, although my parents had never been involved in the arts, they came along wholeheartedly for the ride.

I GREW UP in a typical suburban household. My mom and dad were hardworking Americans trying to create a harmonious home for me and my older brother, Brian. We lived first in the small town of Rapid City, South Dakota, where my parents owned three restaurants, all of which eventually closed. After that we moved to the suburbs of Minneapolis.

My mother went back to nursing and worked her way up the corporate ladder to become CEO of a hospital. She is a born leader, democratic and fair.

My dad had a number of professions: he was a clothing salesman, a food broker, a real estate agent, and finally the owner of a used appliance store. One thing I inherited from him was his visually creative sensibility, which you could witness throughout our houses. We lived in seven different ones over the course of my childhood. It wasn't that we needed to move; my dad just got bored with spaces quickly and would seek out new renovation projects to tackle. Each of our homes was decorated with original taste and flair. My dad's favorite hobby was to rearrange the furniture, and pieces would come in and out: couches, paintings, lamps, chairs, everything. It was a constant rotation to fit the mood of the month, coinciding with the changing color of paint on the walls, which went from eggplant to burgundy to azure to gold.

On weekends he blasted loud music throughout the house, anything from Dire Straits to Beethoven. My mother loved it; my brother and I tolerated it.

Brian and I were polar opposites from the starting line. Very close in age, we fought constantly. He had little tolerance for my annoyances, which made me enjoy them even more. I knew exactly how to make him explode. My favorite way was to sing a song. He would then ask me to stop. I'd hum a few more notes.

He'd look at me contemptuously and say, "I asked you to stop singing."

"I had to finish my song," I'd reply.

When I had exhausted his patience he would punch me and I would cower away in tears. We each had our own ammunition. I would annoy. He would hit.

MINE WAS A true American childhood, at least for a while. In the first years of elementary school I went to classes, came home, did my homework, and played with friends in the backyard, riding my bike with a pack of other kids, building forts with them in the woods. Summer evenings were idyllic, long events when we would run all over the neighborhood until the escaping sun put an end to that day's activities.

All of that was changed one evening by a mysterious man gliding across our TV screen. His name was Fred Astaire. His talent and effortless charisma ignited a flashing spark within me. I stared at the screen, unsure of what he was doing but certain of its significance. I was mesmerized. I wanted to *be* him. Move the way *he* moved. He skimmed across the stage smoothly, calmly, effortlessly. It was so clear to me that *that* was what I wanted to do.

Fred's dancing was the birth of it all for me. He became an obsession. With that obsession came the vision of myself dancing. Jumping, turning, gliding across the floor. Dance is a force that has always been stronger than myself. Even when I was eight years old, that force pulled me into its world. I knew nothing about it but wanted to know everything. And from that moment of seeing Fred on the screen, dance has stayed with me every day of my life.

I BEGAN DANCING in my family's basement in Minneapolis, in the long rectangular laundry room, which had a door that closed off the music and noise. I started alone: no class, no peers, just me on the cold concrete floor next to the washer and dryer and shelves of detergent and bleach, lightbulbs hanging over me.

For tap shoes, I had my Sunday-school penny loafers, some duct tape, and a handful of nickels from my mom. I looped the duct tape around to make double-sided tape and stuck it to the bottoms of the shoes. I carefully lined up the nickels one by one, row by row, and affixed them to the soles and the heels. I had tap shoes.

The nickels were heavier than pennies and made more noise, replicating (to my naive standard) the tapping sounds Fred's shoes made on the TV. I paced back and forth, alone in the laundry room, making up the steps as I saw fit. No technique, no names for steps, just the joy of moving and the sound my feet made when I struck them on the concrete.

As Halloween approached, I pulled together what was then my sartorial ideal: a bowler hat, a white shirt, and black pants. And my makeshift tap shoes. I was officially Fred, if only for a day.

Dancing came to me naturally. Like eating or sleeping, it felt like second nature. It was simply a part of me. I answered its call because I had no other choice. Ignoring it wasn't an option. The force was too great. I never imagined in those early days that dancing would become my profession. I didn't even know that dancing *was* a profession. I just knew I had to do it.

WHEN CHRISTMAS ROLLED around, my parents got me a pair of proper tap shoes. It was by far the most exciting gift under the tree. Even better than the Nintendo that Brian and I had begged them for.

Opening that rectangular package, seeing the red shoe box and, inside it, the black patent leather Capezios, was the official starting point. No more nickels on the bottoms of my penny loafers, but true sound, from true shoes. No more imitating Fred, but *being* Fred.

My parents enrolled me in an after-school tap program. Once a week, a noncommittal forty-five minutes, just a class where I could express my desire to dance with like-minded kids.

I could not have pursued that desire without my parents' support. They had no idea where it would lead. They didn't know if I had "talent." All they wanted to do was show their love for their son and help him fulfill his desire to dance like Fred. From the very start, they were on board, never asking me if I wanted to play T-ball like the other boys. They took the road that parents often do not take. I hear frequently from young boys who have the exact passion I had when I was their age. They just have to move. They fall in love with dancing, with its beauty and athleticism and rigor. But their parents think a dancing boy does not fit society's norm, the role of a normal boy. They don't want their kid to endure the pains of teasing and being the outcast. They figure sports are the better option. The road more traveled.

I understand the predicament parents face when their son wants to do something they know nothing about and no other boy in their neighborhood is doing. But kids' natural inclinations are what they are. When I played sports I would make excuses to go to the bathroom in the middle of games, my disinterest showing in my lack of motivation. I knew these sports—soccer, baseball, basketball—weren't for me. But dance was my outlet, my purpose, my joy. And my parents could see that in me. Which is exactly why they nurtured it.

How lucky I was that my parents chose to help me pursue what made me blissfully happy. That it didn't matter to them that my happiness started with putting on tap shoes and eventually led to ballet shoes and tights.

THE FIRST PERSON to teach me proper dancing technique was a tapper named Maxine Vashro. She was a spitfire, energetic and lively. Her class was held in the basement of the local community college. Maxine would demonstrate and we would follow: shuffle, ball change, flap (learning it sounds more like *fa-lap*, striking the floor twice). Then picking up the pace, flap ball change, shuffle ball change, flap heel, all in repetition. I remember the students going "across the floor" one by one, and seeing my reflection in the mirror as I made my way. I was not terribly focused at the beginning. I was still a kid who liked to hang with neighborhood friends, and at times I would call my mom at work to ask her if I "have to go to tap today."

Nevertheless, my interest grew into intense fascination. I would show people my tapping skills without apprehension or self-consciousness. When I was at the grocery store, I would tap down the long aisles, a perfect length of space to try newly invented moves. I was never ashamed of or embarrassed by what I wanted to do. I never felt I needed to hide it or lie to friends about what

I was doing after school. It came so naturally to me that I naively assumed everyone had a similar desire and passion.

My third-grade crush was a girl named Amanda. To express my devoted affection I gave her a photo of myself dancing in the basement. It was maybe a tad unique to give my crush a picture of myself tapping away, arms swung to one side of my body, smiling at the camera. Unfortunately, my little present provoked a mildly horrified response from her and her friends.

I QUICKLY CAUGHT on that the boys in my class didn't approve of my passion. But it was hard to understand why they wanted to pick on me. A couple of them would regularly chase me around the classroom and act as though they were going to do something far worse. I was never a kid who fought back, nor did my dad ever give me that traditional talk: "Stand up for yourself, boy. Come on, punch me! Let's see what you got!"

So when bullies approached me, I had no idea what to do. My instinctive reaction when facing danger is to run, and I did exactly that. It didn't work. I suppose I could have just ignored them, but it's different in the moment when you're a little kid being taunted by your contemporaries. They seemed to get pleasure out of my inability to fight back.

I just wanted to fit in. Like every kid, I wanted to be accepted by my peers. But there was a fundamental difference that made me a target. A weak target, at that. I was effeminate. I wasn't wearing sparkly shoes and prancing around the classroom (which is perfectly acceptable)—I was just different. My best friends were girls. I could always hang out with them more easily than with boys. I had a constant flow of girl friends, so many that my fourth-grade teacher took me aside one day and said they were distracting me from my schoolwork. Other boys would be trying to gain attention from the girls, and I was seen as the effeminate roadblock to their desires. They didn't want me in their way.

TEACHER APPRECIATION WEEK came once a year, and while other students dutifully wrote to teachers they liked, I used the opportunity to write to the school counselor and let him know I was being harassed daily by a group of persistent classmates.

Though I needed to share what was happening, being forthcoming with that information made me feel even more vulnerable. Next thing I knew, I was in the counselor's office giving the names of my taunters. Then my parents were called in. They wanted to take me to a child psychiatrist who could teach me how to deal with bullies. I told them I didn't want to go, but they insisted, saying it would do me good to "just talk about what was bothering me." I could tell it killed them to know I was being demoralized by other kids.

A week later, despite my protests, I walked into the psychiatrist's office in a high-rise building in downtown Minneapolis. I hated the idea of talking about an emotional issue for which I wasn't even seeking advice. The thought of verbalizing my problems to an adult made me feel even weaker, like I couldn't do anything myself.

Despite my reluctance, we finally spoke about what was happening at school. The psychiatrist suggested I develop an alter ego who could help me stick up for myself. We named him "Tough Tom." The idea was that, when the bullies started to go at me, I would somehow work up the confidence to become my trusty and stronger other self. But Tom turned out to be less than trusty, because when I was being verbally assaulted I couldn't convince myself that an imaginary character would help me in any way.

The teasing followed me to Phoenix, Arizona, when my parents relocated there for work. It was an exciting move for a now ten-year-old boy, a fresh start and, potentially at least, a chance to make new friends.

I picked out my outfit for my first day of fifth grade. I was like every other kid, making a personal statement for the start of the school year. The prospect of new school clothes and the chance to show them off was thrilling. I chose a black T-shirt, black-and-white-checkered flannel shorts, and my favorite, coolest item: red high-top Converse sneakers, paired with white tube socks. As I walked to my classroom, some boys barked, "Nice shoes!" It stung.

After that the teasing escalated. It confounded me. I was just being myself. I couldn't act another way or put on another face. And I still couldn't stand up to them. It wasn't in my nature. I cowered in front of the bullies. It hurt to be made fun of and all I wanted when it was happening was to get away from it. Yet as much as I wanted to escape, I also wanted to fit in.

IN PHOENIX, THE pinnacle of my entire week was the dance class I began taking at a local jazz studio. With more formal training, I mustered up the courage to audition for my school talent show. A lot of kids would sing, some would dance, others did magic tricks or gymnastics. I was the only boy dancing. I didn't want to be teased, but when it came to dancing, I took every opportunity to do so, even if the entire student body would be watching and judging me. I decided on a few routines I had been working on at the studio: a tap solo, a jazz routine to an early nineties dance anthem, "The Hitman," and a top-hat-and-tails tap dance to "Sing Sing Sing." I was focused and nervous auditioning in front of my music teacher, Mr. Bernstein. I took my dances very seriously, so I was anxious while waiting to hear whether I made it into the show, and full of joy and excitement when I did.

It took some courage to dance in the talent show. But I didn't

K

for massacre when he

er peers.

er kids, each one ner-

Bernstein came over

, David," he said. "Ig-

on you by other kids.

lance."

hat I had something

d, nodded, and then

at was the first bit of

ateful to him, for he

a that anyone—even

as the right to follow

see it as such. Every student set himself up for massacre when he went out on that stage in front of his or her peers.

As I sat in the music room with the other kids, each one nervously awaiting his or her turn to go on, Mr. Bernstein came over to me and sat down.

"You must follow your passion to dance, David," he said. "Ignore the nastiness and the teasing heaped on you by other kids. All you need to do is explore your love of dance."

Never before had someone suggested that I had something worth nurturing. At the time I simply listened, nodded, and then went onstage to perform my routine. But that was the first bit of encouragement I received. I'll always be grateful to him, for he was the first to instill in me the crucial idea that anyone—even a tap-dancing boy in suburban America—has the right to follow his dreams.

CHAPTER 3

Increasingly I became everyone's favorite target at school. I was the class punching bag for the other boys' entertainment. One day, as I waited quietly outside the classroom for school to commence, four guys approached me and formed a half circle around me. I tried to prepare myself for whatever was coming.

"Hey, girl," one taunted.

I was used to hearing this, but that didn't keep it from stinging; it was becoming just as familiar as my real name.

"You know you're a girl, right?" another said. "And what do girls do? Huh? Do you know? Girls wear perfume!"

Before I could react they drained an entire bottle of cheap drugstore perfume all over me. Every last drop. In seconds. On my shoulders. My face. My hands. My arms. My clothes. I had done nothing to them. I stood there frozen, in shock and disbelief. Embarrassed and empty and alone.

They had purchased that bottle of perfume for the very purpose of humiliating me. Most of the boys were not in my class, so they'd have made a special trip around the grounds to find me. Mission accomplished. I reeked of perfume. I officially smelled like a girl.

From that scarring moment on I built a shell around myself. I was miserable and scared—scared of the bullies who seemed to take such pleasure in hurting me; scared of what they planned to do and say. The more the bullies went after me, the more I withdrew. And the more I withdrew, the deeper I sank into the reality that I honestly didn't fit in and felt like I never would.

THE RELENTLESS BULLYING I received at school prompted me to find refuge in dance. Dancentre, my jazz studio, was my safe haven, where I had friends with whom I shared the love of movement and who saw me as the person and the dancer I was, not as a freak outcast.

I thrived on the physical and emotional release that came through the movement of jazz, tap, hip hop. Any form of dance fed my craving. I was never judged negatively. The opposite. I was encouraged to be the dancer I wanted to be. I wasn't the girl or the faggot. I was free, my true self, and comfortable in my skin.

In jazz classes, form and technique mattered less than style and attack, and jazz gave me freedom to express myself so long as I knew the combination. I needed this expression. It helped me blot out the horrible teasing that went on during the day.

MY FIRST BALLET class was at Dancentre when I was eleven. Ballet was not popular with the jazz students, who viewed it as boring, a waste of time, and too stiff. I also felt that way. Jazz teachers would tell us about the importance of ballet, saying that it's the foundation of every other form of movement. But of course we never listened. We would all make excuses to skip ballet class, giving lame reasons for why we couldn't take class that day.

"I have too much homework and need to study."

"My toes hurt."

When I did take a ballet class I would wear baggy sweatpants and a T-shirt. I couldn't in my wildest dreams imagine wearing tights! The girls would dispiritedly put their hair in a bun and maybe wear pink tights. The ballet studio was, to put it mildly, a very unmotivated atmosphere.

One day, not long after I started my feeble attempt at ballet, I saw, posted on the front door of the studio, an invitation for kids to try out for Ballet Arizona's version of *The Nutcracker.* Instantly, I thought, *I want to audition.* Thinking back, that spark of sudden interest perplexes me. Why was I so attracted to the idea of auditioning for *The Nutcracker* when I only halfheartedly studied ballet? I knew a total of three steps in the classical idiom. Yet reading about that audition ignited a curiosity to explore the unknown that would guide me throughout my career and, on more than one occasion, lead me in an unexpected direction.

BECAUSE I WAS scheduled to compete in an afternoon jazz competition on the weekend of the audition, Ballet Arizona agreed to meet me for a private audition on Saturday morning.

At their studio I was tentative, quiet, intimidated. There were kids my age sprawled in every part of the reception area, all waiting for their chance to prove they could be part of *The Nutcracker.* I was met by Katharine Frey, the company's ballet mistress (a term used in the ballet world for the rehearsal director). She led me past groups of eager kids into an empty studio. My eleven-year-old eyes had never seen a studio that big. It was a vast, run-down empty space, equally intriguing and intimidating.

THE AUDITION LASTED less than fifteen minutes. I was trying out for the coveted role of the Nutcracker Prince, who saves Clara from the evil Rat King and leads her to the Kingdom of the Sweets. This was the best role a boy could get in the production. The ballet mistress started to teach me the intricate mime scene at the beginning of Act II, in which the Prince recounts his battle with the Rat King. I had never even seen mime, much less performed it. She would show me a mime passage and then sit down quietly in her chair and watch me demonstrate it. But I couldn't get past more than the first few gestures. I was in completely over my head. This was my first attempt at portraying the Prince, and deservedly, I got the far lesser role of the Nutcracker in the battle scene, during which my entire face was obscured by an enormous foam head.

DESPITE THE DOWNGRADE, it was during the eight performances of *The Nutcracker* that I became irretrievably enthralled by ballet. I was mesmerized. Once I took my foam head off after the battle scene each night, I would phone my mother and beg, "Can I stay and watch?"

Nurturing my newfound obsession, she usually obliged. I would stand quietly in the wings, transfixed by everything I saw and sensed. The dancers seemed suffused with a purpose bigger than themselves. They were like worshipers devoted to a religion. It was as if the stage itself were holy ground. I could feel the energy, the nerves, the reverence. The lead man dancing the Cavalier, in his tunic and white tights, took such care to support his beautiful ballerina onstage.

I was so taken by these professional dancers, by the focus it took to perform. The attention to preparing their shoes by dipping them in the rosin box just before they went onstage. That final practice of a difficult step just before the curtain went up. The call of the stage manager to "Places" right before the orchestra sounded. The muffled applause of the audience through the closed curtain as the conductor came out to the podium. And the dancers' swift intake of breath as they moved onto the stage and their struggle for breath when they came off it.

Ballet seemed important. It had purpose. It was serious, weighty, a force stronger than any individual dancing it. I couldn't help but inch as close as I could to witness this new world. I felt equally comfortable and enthralled. It was a brilliant new feeling. Ballet had captured me, never to let go.

CHAPTER 4

The division between my two worlds became more defined. As my dancing life after school flourished and became more and more of a haven, my life at school sank into a hell as the bullying escalated.

The extreme highs of expressing my calling as a dancer were consistently offset by the extreme lows of being everyone's targeted "faggot."

In my suburban school district in Phoenix, 1,500 kids came together for seventh and eighth grades at Desert Shadows Middle School. A completely new experience: new classes, new friends, and a new sense of freedom.

At Desert Shadows, I didn't disappear into the mass of teenagers as I'd hoped I would. I was immediately singled out. The new faces from other elementary schools saw me as fresh prey: an effeminate blond boy who took dancing classes with girls after school and didn't hide it.

Puberty was still far on the horizon for me, so I had a high-pitched voice and a very slight, skinny wire of a frame. The inevitable physical changes that other boys were experiencing were a big deal, and they would brag about who was shaving already, who had hair in their armpits. I didn't even see peach fuzz on the top of my lip, let alone the need to shave anything off. I also still had a slew of girl friends.

Because I found it so easy to connect with girls, talking to them wasn't an awkward event like it seemed to be for the other boys. As it had when I was younger, this made other boys jealous and added fuel to an already blazing fire. Once again, the two words I became very accustomed to hearing were "girl" and "faggot."

But I had trouble with some girls too. One day, on the bus ride home, I could sense, across the aisle, two girls whispering about me. I was sitting there, waiting for my stop, when one of them turned to me.

"Say 'hello'!" she demanded as the other looked on.

I knew exactly why she said it. I looked her dead in the eyes. Cold. Enraged. Hurt.

I said, "Why? So you can hear how much I sound like a girl?"

They both looked back at me in shock. I had totally caught them off guard. A thick, tense silence ensued. The only answer they could muster up was a feeble "No."

I looked away. I didn't make a scene; instead I stared out the window, my face hidden from theirs, and cried quietly. I couldn't help myself. I had never felt so bereft. If I couldn't fit in, then all I wanted was to be left alone.

TO MY DISAPPOINTMENT, things were no better at Sunday school. Once, on a forced weekend retreat with my Lutheran church, the other boys honed in on me. None of them went to my school, so this was yet another crop of taunters. They didn't want me sleeping in the same room with them because I was a faggot. I might "try something in the middle of the night." Their unwarranted fear was matched by my own anxiety.

There was no other cabin to stay in, so while the other boys chummily piled into bunk beds and giggled themselves to sleep, I slept in a bed by myself in the corner.

Church was supposed to be the most accepting, inclusive environment. It was where people worshiped something greater than themselves and where kids could learn about the beauty, forgiveness, and acceptance of God. I imagined religion to be a refuge from the judgments and confusions of everyday life. A sort of utopia. At least that's what they told me it should be at my suburban church, La Casa de Cristo.

Later, I would be disappointed, to say the least, when I learned that my own church regarded homosexuals as sinners.

AS SEVENTH GRADE moved on, I became more and more depressed. I started to write in the back of my school notebook about how much I hated school and wanted to escape. I dreaded leaving home to head to the bus stop. The teasing started and ended there every single day. Once I joined the kids in line for the bus, my guard was up, like a shield in battle. When the day was over and I was dropped off at the same bus stop, I could finally transform back into my true self.

I realize now how incredibly lucky I was to find both escape and a form of salvation in dance. I always make a point of that very thing to boys who reach out to me to tell me about the teasing they endure in school. I tell them to be grateful that they have an outlet that is as unique as being a dancer. The kids taunting you should only be so lucky to have a passion equal to yours. And by no means should teasing and verbal abuse be an excuse to give up what you love. I make the point that I never considered quitting dance because the teasing was so relentless. When I hear of other young people considering that option, I give my most impassioned reasons why that is a mistake. You cannot give in to the bullies and detractors. You cannot let them win the fight. They will say whatever they like, but you always have something stronger than they do: The courage to do something different. And the passion to equal that courage.

*　　*　　*

DURING MY JAZZ years I auditioned for a small TV pilot called *Kid Tech*. It told the story of a group of kids who lived in a world of war and conflict and had magic powers that could bring world peace. Six young dancers were chosen to be in it. We came to the project with equal commitment and enthusiasm. As we rehearsed, we experienced that collective euphoria found in the simple bliss of movement. Dancing hours on end in a small studio, I felt at home with them.

Among the six kids was Jack. A year younger than me, he danced at a different jazz studio. I had never seen him at competitions, where you normally encountered the same group of dancers. He came from a poor family and lived in a rough part of Phoenix known for its crime and violence. His mother worked night shifts as a nurse, so he took care of himself most days, getting from school to the dance studio by city bus. You could see instantly that he wasn't spoiled like some of us kids. Whereas we came in with new clothes and the latest gadgets, he dressed simply, appreciating what he did own.

He was also the most arresting dancer in the group. Sharp, confident, edgy. He had a spark that no one else possessed. Your eye was just drawn to him and his mesmerizing raw energy. He upstaged everyone.

Jack and I got along instantly. We bonded over our mutual love of dance and had enough different interests to be immediately fascinated by each other. Physically, we were complete contrasts. I was blond; he was dark. I was lanky; he was compact. He was a huge Paula Abdul fan and schooled me in which pop stars were worth listening to. I took in every word he said, transfixed by his confidence and cool, brash demeanor. He was true to himself in front of others, unapologetic and proud. While I was getting made fun of on all fronts and cowering under the pressure, Jack would never take abuse from other kids. He would fight back. I was in complete awe of him.

As our friendship developed, we started to talk on the phone every day. At school, I constantly looked at the clock, anticipating the moment when I could call Jack. We would both rush home for our daily phone call, which took place just before we went off to our separate dance studios. I savored anything he had to say.

"I've been counting the hours till we could talk again," I'd tell him.

"I know," he'd say, "I couldn't concentrate all day."

Our friendship, we agreed, was the very best thing in our lives.

On weekends we'd spend the entire night on the phone, from six p.m. until six a.m. He would play me dozens of songs and I would reciprocate. One of us would doze off holding the receiver and the other would wake him. Together we watched the sun rise, me at one end of Phoenix, Jack at the other.

I finally mustered the courage to tell him that I couldn't stop thinking about him. I waited on the phone, holding my breath until he broke the silence and said the same thing.

AS MOST COUPLES did in middle school, we selected "our" song, making our connection official. The song was "Sometimes It Snows in April" by Prince, a ballad about someone whose best friend dies and is looking back on their intensely unique connection.

We would play that song for each other, think about the lyrics, and cry.

"You can never leave me," I'd say.

"I'll never leave you and you'll never leave me," he'd reply.

WE FINALLY MADE a date for Jack to sleep over at my house. I was consumed with anticipation. I obsessed over what we could possibly do in those many private hours together. Would we go to sleep early or talk until the sun came up? Would we listen to music? Would we kiss? When he arrived I met him and his mother at the front door. After niceties were exchanged between our parents, we escaped into my bedroom.

With the door locked behind us we stood face-to-face, uncertain of what to say or do next. Spontaneously, like two magnets, we wrapped our arms around each other and held on tightly for what seemed like minutes. It felt like an electrical surge to have his arms around me.

"I couldn't wait to see you," I whispered.

"I know, me too," Jack said.

We stayed up all night in a blissful stupor, listening to music, looking at magazines, talking, and cuddling.

FALLING FOR EACH other was never a choice. It felt so natural and unforced. Through this first sleepover and others to follow, we discovered what intimacy is like with someone you care about so deeply. I had fallen in love with Jack and he had fallen in love with me. We became obsessed with one another. Dance was our shared passion. But our mutual love—pure and honest—was the warmest sensation yet. Throughout the summer, we would fall asleep together in my twin bed, clinging to each other. My parents set up a second bed for him to sleep in, but we never used it. In the mornings, my mom would come in and say goodbye before she left for work and see us sleeping side by side in my tiny bed. She never said anything about it, so I could only guess what she was thinking. I didn't care what it looked like to my parents, or to my brother, who caught us, on several occasions, holding hands or hugging. Someday, I assumed, I would have to let them know the truth. But, dreading their reaction, it was a lot easier to opt for silence instead.

CHAPTER 5

At school, the bullying continued unabated and unmonitored by the teachers. These days, I hear of antibullying campaigns at schools and of kids being suspended for taunting others. I wish that had been the case when I was struggling to fit in. Back then, bullying was not an issue to be taken seriously. The prevailing attitude was "kids will be kids."

Eventually the abuse I absorbed caused me to crack. The issue that was the ultimate breaking point wasn't a kid tormenting me. I accidentally missed a rehearsal at my jazz studio. There was a policy that if you failed to show up for a rehearsal you were cut from the number for the upcoming competition. I wasn't there, so I was out. I called the studio in a panic. Rehearsal had started. One missed rehearsal signified that the one place I knew I belonged had ousted me. In rehearsal I was happy, confident, assured. I couldn't lose that.

Suddenly all the pain I'd held in after being called a faggot for so long bubbled up and flooded out of me. The facade I had built up no longer worked. The armor no longer shielded me. I couldn't allow myself to be pushed anymore. Or called a girl. Or have perfume poured on me. Or be singled out and mocked for just being myself. I sobbed uncontrollably. I called my mom in a panic. She was on her way home from work. I tried to tell her what had happened but was barely able to speak or breathe. She tried desperately to calm me down, but I was hysterical. It all came out in heaving sobs.

I had never told my parents that I was the punching bag at school. I had kept it all a secret, knowing they would make a bigger deal out of it than I could stomach. I certainly didn't want to be sent to see another psychiatrist. But now the words came pouring from me. I told my mom that I had no friends. That I was taunted daily. I was constantly called a girl and a faggot and everyone made me the butt of their jokes. I told her how miserable and depressed I was. There was silence on the other end as she listened in shock.

When she finally arrived home I had stopped crying, embarrassed by my uncontrolled outburst. But the words had been spoken, the pain exposed. She drove me to rehearsal an hour late. My teacher graciously decided not to take me out of the piece, but I knew what was waiting for me when I returned home. My parents wanted to hear all about the bullying, the depression. How long had it been going on? Why hadn't I said anything?

THE NEXT MORNING my parents insisted on meeting with my principal to ask him what the school's responsibility was in regard to constant bullying. The principal's attitude was that neither he nor the teachers could control every word students said. My parents looked at him, aghast and confused at this admission of impotence.

They stormed out. That afternoon they assured me that I would not have to spend another year at Desert Shadows Middle School.

The looming question was where to go. Surely every other school would be the same. The same jocks and cool crowd. The same girl friends of mine that would make the guys jealous. Where could I possibly seek refuge and start anew?

*   *   *

JACK HAD HEARD that the city's first art school was opening the following year in downtown Phoenix. As soon as he told me the name—Arizona School for the Arts—I knew it was the answer for a lanky suburban boy obsessed with dancing.

So I finished off my seventh-grade year in hell, surviving the name-calling until the bitter end. Then I emerged, making my pilgrimage to my new school, where I joined two hundred students in grades five through twelve from all around Phoenix. Dancers, singers, actors, musicians. And Jack.

The entire student body at ASA immediately bonded over our distaste for "normal schools." We dismissed things as "so public school": sports teams, varsity jackets, proms, cliques, bullying. And while we all commiserated over our inability to fit in elsewhere, ASA offered us a haven where we could be ourselves. Jack and I could walk around the school holding hands. Kids could play the piano and sing during lunch break. No form of expression was taboo. No one made fun of anyone else for their taste in clothes, artistic inclination, or sexual orientation. I had found my daytime nirvana, to complement my equally gratifying evening utopia. At last my two worlds were one.

ON WEEKENDS, I would, at times, accompany my mom to the market. After one uneventful Sunday trip, just after I turned fifteen, we headed back home with a car full of groceries. It was a day like all the others until I called out, "Mom, you just missed the turn to our street!"

"I know, honey," she said dryly. "There's something I need to talk to you about."

What had I done? When had I lied? I couldn't think of anything I'd done wrong. At least nothing from my own perspective.

She slowed the car and pulled over. We were on a quiet street in the suburban complex we lived in, where every house looked identical. No cars or people in sight. We were all alone.

She lowered the radio to a hum and turned to me.

"Honey, I want you to know that anything you say, your father and I will support. Okay?"

"Yes," I answered with trepidation.

"We want to know if you have had any experiences with other boys."

I was frozen. Floored. Before this moment I had pictured how my parents might react to me telling them that I was gay. I imagined my father actually taking it quite well. But a vision burned in my mind of my mom not accepting it, and kicking me out of the house. I had heard of scenarios like this, of other gay boys living through that sort of nightmare. My overwhelming fear of their reaction meant I'd never even considered telling them the truth.

"What do you mean 'experiences'?" I asked as I sheepishly gazed at her from the passenger seat.

"Well . . . have you had any experiences with other boys in a sexual way?"

This was my fork in the road. I saw it clearly in front of me. I could continue to live my reality in secret and not tell her. Just say no. It would then be a question of her believing me or not.

Or I could tell her exactly what had been happening for two years with Jack. The fact that I had fallen in love for the first time. A pure, innocent, honest love. And how that love happened to be shared mutually. I guessed she must have had more than an inkling.

So I took the riskier path of the two and responded with one word.

"Yes."

Her manner remained cool and calm. I searched deep in her eyes for any shred of disapproval, but she seemed unfazed.

"Okay," she said. "Since when?"

"Since I met Jack."

"Well, honey, we both want you to know we will always support you and love you. No matter what happens. But most importantly," she went on, "we want you to be safe."

I vaguely knew what she was talking about. In the wake of the 1980s AIDS epidemic, as I was discovering my sexuality in the 1990s, we were taught in school about the dangers of unprotected sex. It had been branded in my mind. With complete fear of the consequences.

"We can't see our son die of a disease he could have potentially prevented."

That one sentence hit the perfect chord for a fifteen-year-old. I imagined my parents reacting to my death: my mother sobbing at the kitchen table, my dad hovering over her, both of them bowed by the weight of a sorrow they would carry the rest of their lives. So I understood that, in their desire to protect me, they were also protecting themselves.

She went on, "If you ever want to talk to me or to Dad about anything, just know that you can."

I wasn't sure how to respond. "Okay," I finally said.

I remember looking around at the houses that replicated ours, hearing the low hum of a pop song from the radio in the awkward silence. Our conversation had lasted about thirty seconds yet changed everything. I didn't have to sit them down and "confess," as I had feared I would. I didn't have to see my mom cry or contend with the drama I had assumed would ensue if I ever came out to them. It had happened in the simplest, easiest way: my mother asked me and I said yes.

Then she shifted the car into drive and we rode home in

silence, the not-so-secret "secret" revealed and a huge weight removed and set aside.

I DON'T KNOW what gave me the courage that day to be honest with my mom. I could have more easily denied my relationship with Jack despite the fact that I had given her plenty of reasons to assume its existence. But it was the right time. As the weeks marched on and we settled into a newfound truth, I saw a book on my parents' bedside table titled *Now That You Know: A Parents' Guide to Understanding Their Gay and Lesbian Children.* I didn't believe that raising a gay child should be any different from parenting a son who is straight. Still, it was comforting to have this further proof that both my mother's and father's inclination was to be understanding rather than judgmental.

Getting used to the truth turned out to be a little more difficult for my older brother. We never got along, back then, at the best of times. He was the physically stronger of us two, stockier in build and more masculine. We had completely different tastes in everything. He listened to Metallica. I listened to Prince. He played drums. I danced. That, mixed with adolescent angst, didn't produce a harmonious brotherly love. When Jack and I started to discover our mutual affection, Brian was at times in his bedroom, next to mine. Sometimes Jack and I forgot to lock my bedroom door and Brian would walk in on us. He saw us lying together, holding each other, and I tried to pass it off as "we just fell asleep like that." Brian didn't believe a word I said. At first, Jack and I were panicked about being caught but after a few times we didn't really care. And once it was all out in the open, Brian settled into the idea that his younger brother was gay. In time, he not only accepted it; he made it clear that he loved me for who I was.

*   *   *

IF MY SEXUALITY ever discomfited my parents, they kept it to themselves. In time, they became fervent supporters of the gay community, donating time and money to local and national equality groups. When people ask how I came out to my parents and what their reaction was, I'm proud to be able to say that they wholeheartedly accepted me from the beginning.

To this day I jokingly say that, thanks to their continued advocacy in support of LGBTQ rights, at times they're gayer than I am.

AT HOME AND at school I had, at last, stepped fully and permanently into my own skin. I was regarded with respect and given encouragement to be the dancer I dreamed of being, and above all, to be my honest self. Though I finally met friends who understood and accepted me, Jack remained my closest ally, at least for a time. Ultimately, we drifted apart, and went from being lovers to mere acquaintances. I mourned the fact that the most solid relationship in my life was gone. We could never again experience what we knew as kids. It was hard to accept that the love we shared, for all its power, was a first love but not the last.

Still, Jack remained paramount in my adolescent development. Our relationship established my sense of how anyone should love and be loved.

CHAPTER 6

At Arizona School for the Arts, the entire student body had four hours of academics every morning. After lunch we flocked to our elected arts programs; the dancers were bused to the School of Ballet Arizona. With no proper dance studios on school grounds, we made our way to the best ballet school in the state.

The dance program offered just one option: we would all take ballet from the school's director, Kee Juan Han. I didn't like the prospect of taking only ballet. Though I had been enchanted by the performances of *The Nutcracker* that I watched from backstage, I had decided that I was not interested in studying ballet. Too strict. Too formal. I was fully immersed in the jazz and competition worlds and couldn't imagine having to wear black tights and a tight white T-shirt, the prescribed uniform in the ballet studio. On the daily bus to the ballet school, my stress level would build. As the girls put the last touches on their buns and gabbed away, I would look out the window, immersed in anxiety about the class to come. I was in over my head. I barely knew the steps let alone the combinations. On top of that, I had never been more petrified of a teacher than I was of Mr. Han.

Kee Juan Han was a young-looking man in his midthirties who easily commanded respect from his students. As the school's director he was clearly our superior, and we always called him

Mr. Han. Never by his first name. This set the tone immediately. He was preternaturally focused and demanded the same from us. He'd had a very strict upbringing in Singapore, sharing a small one-bedroom apartment with his parents and six siblings. He left home at a young age to study on a much-needed scholarship at the Australian Ballet School. He joined the Sydney Dance Company and later danced with Indianapolis Ballet Theatre and Boston Ballet. He learned early on what it means to work hard, make the most of what you have, and not make excuses for yourself. He brought that intense mind-set into the studio, where, at times, it was too much for certain kids who wanted to take ballet "because it's pretty." Mr. Han had no patience for that mentality.

He would hush the studio with his arrival, call roll, and gaze intently around the quiet room. We all stood at attention by the barres lining the perimeter of the studio, in our uniforms, waiting. He would tell one student that his uniform wasn't quite right, ask another if she was ready to work harder today than she had the day before. He was aware of everything and we got away with nothing.

At the beginning, my relationship with Mr. Han was distant. He didn't attempt to stop me from competing in jazz competitions or push me into ballet. But I did my best in class and observed him for a while. Clad in crisp white socks and ballet shoes, he would demonstrate each step to show us exactly what he wanted. He moved with precision and fluidity, a lasting effect of his distinguished career as a dancer. He gave every step and position absolute importance. Each lengthening of the foot, every stretch of the leg was done meticulously.

"Peel your toes off the floor before the tendu."

"Use the head in complete unison with your arms."

His constant corrections and dry sense of humor would hit their mark when he threw them your way. He would walk up to someone and poke the soft spot under their butt, asking, "What flavor Jell-O are you today? Raspberry?"

Or when a boy dripped sweat profusely into little puddles on the floor, Mr. Han would look at him and say, "Oh . . . are you singing in the rain?"

Although he was strict and demanding, he took every student at face value. He never discriminated based on body type or whether someone was a serious ballet student or not. He worked everyone with the same intensity. There were no favorites; approval was conferred on those who were the most focused and worked hardest.

Mr. Han made it clear that he would not tolerate anyone who thought they were better than others or had an air that demanded premature respect. The only respect given in the classroom was to be given to the teacher and the work.

All of his students regarded him with a mixture of fear and reverence that propelled us to push harder in each class. On those occasions when we weren't working hard enough to pick up the combinations or were blankly staring at him when he was demonstrating a step, he would simply walk out. As he was leaving the studio, he would say, "Come to me when you are focused and can remember what I am showing you. When you are ready to work."

The fifteen or so of us would look at each other, dumbfounded and petrified, trying desperately to remember the last combination he had given. We would work on the exercise feverishly, thrown into order by the shock that, once again, he was upset enough to leave the studio. Minutes later we would negotiate who would be the sacrificial lamb, the one designated to walk to his office and tell him, "We are ready to work."

Whenever I was selected, I sheepishly entered his office and told him we were focused enough to begin again.

"Are you sure?" he would ask.

"Yes," I'd say under my breath before racing back to the studio to join the rest of the nervous students.

He would then return at his leisure and resume his class. You could have cut the tension with a knife. There were no lazy mistakes after he returned. Walking out on us invariably gave him the results and attention he demanded.

I WAS ALWAYS nervous about going to class. The vast vocabulary of steps was entirely new to me and I imagined myself the only one who couldn't pick them up. That feeling of being left behind, flailing about in my desperation to keep up, would plague me. But in fact, as the year progressed, I absorbed the combinations like a thirsty sponge. My new uniform, tight as it was, started to fit like a second skin.

It was a gradual transition but a major shift in my mentality and focus. In the jazz world, individual expression is rewarded more than technique and perfection. I could express myself completely, and doing so had helped me find the confidence I desperately needed. Yet now I was intrigued with this classical art form, and increasingly devoted to classes with Mr. Han. I had no belief that my work displayed talent. That I was any good at all. The year before, a teacher from another jazz studio had told my parents that I had more talent than any kid in her school. I didn't believe her and thought she was just trying to get me to train at her dance studio. But I really didn't care whether I had any talent. It wasn't my focus to be the best. I was simply obsessed.

So the day came when I was sitting across from Mr. Han in his office, ready to shed the jazz world I was so comfortable in. I was eager to begin training more seriously with Mr. Han. If he was happy that I finally had taken the plunge to work with him full-time, he hid it well. He looked at me dryly and explained that, yes, I had talent, but I was starting a serious study of classical ballet a lot later than most dancers did. I was still growing, and was all legs and no muscle or real strength. I was nowhere near the level that other boys my age were in the rest of the country.

I never forgot those few words, which gave me the impetus to propel myself into hours on end of sweat-filled work in the same studio I had stepped into years before for my botched *Nutcracker* audition. It was time to play catch-up. I was thirteen at the time.

AFTER I FORMALLY joined the ballet school, I worked privately with Mr. Han six days a week. Classical ballet was like my black hole, a gravitational force pulling me in deeper and deeper. I was attracted to the idea of perfection, to the fact that there are precise ways to execute every turn, jump, and step. I savored the nonnegotiable structure of the work. I couldn't get enough.

I always felt a sense of dread coming into the ballet studio at night, knowing what taxing work was ahead of me. Mr. Han would look at me and say simply, "Let's go." No smile, no question of whether I was tired, no small talk. Down to business straightaway. There was no pianist, not even any recorded music. There was just Mr. Han's voice commanding me. The only distraction was the low, constant buzz of the cheap fluorescent lights flickering high above on the ceiling.

We would start at the same exact point every time. The en dehors pirouette: a stretch of the foot to the side, plié, raise the foot to the knee, and turn outward, away from the leg you're standing on. I would push for five or six rotations each time, and every time I was corrected.

After about twelve repetitions on each side, we would move on to en dedans pirouettes: stretch of the foot to the front, plié, foot to the knee, and turn inward toward your standing leg.

I would do that twelve times each, right and left, and we would move on again. Attitude pirouettes: stretch of the foot to the front, plié, leg raised to the back, knee bent, and turn. Seven times each, right and left. This would go on until I completed almost all styles of pirouettes in the classical idiom.

Mr. Han would stand five feet from me and pick me apart. I absorbed all of his criticism. I never questioned a correction or new approach. I had total trust in what he asked of me. I would never make excuses or complain about fatigue. I would have felt weak if I did, like I had failed him. My only goals were to execute the steps perfectly and to please him, which I believed I rarely did.

WE WOULD METHODICALLY progress from small turns to bigger turns, from small jumps to bigger jumps. Every private lesson was almost exactly the same. At times another teacher would pass by and watch for five or ten minutes from the doorway, interested in the progress being made. But most of the time it was just Mr. Han and me.

When I began this serious training, I was totally uninformed about the ballet world: steps, great dancers, ballets, choreographers, the history of classical ballet. I didn't know a good dancer from a bland one, or a mediocre physical build from a perfectly proportioned one. As I worked more and more intensely with Mr. Han and saw how hard he pushed me, I knew that I needed to meet him on equal ground. I had to push myself just as hard. Nothing was good enough in his eyes; therefore nothing was good enough in my eyes. There were always nuances of the work to dissect and analyze.

From time to time my parents would come early to pick me up and tiptoe into the studio, silently settling themselves in two chairs in the corner. They were always welcome to watch. I specifically remember one time when my parents were there and I was executing a manèges around the room. For a manèges, a dancer performs virtuosic steps in a huge circular pattern around the studio or the stage. I would start in one corner of the room, leap and split my legs, then land and turn and leap again as I made my way around the studio's perimeter. Mr. Han would make me do this over and over, correcting the smallest details. After the seventh time, I was bent over, gasping for air. I couldn't go on anymore, or sweat off one more ounce of body weight, or conjure up energy for one more series of jumps. So Mr. Han pushed even harder.

And when I had gone beyond my limit and hit the maximum level of fatigue, he slyly looked over to my parents, grinned, and asked, "How's Mommy and Daddy doing?"

"About to call Child Protective Services," my mother joked.

She and my father were stunned and wide-eyed as they watched, sitting on the edges of their chairs. What was happening in this studio? Why was all this self-inflicted pain something their son craved and couldn't get enough of? They didn't know what to say or do other than what they had always done: nurture my passion. And trust the man guiding it.

They saw the happiness I felt when I was dancing. They never asked Mr. Han to treat me more gently. Because they cared deeply about me, they said that if I ever wanted to stop I could. But the fact that I came back for more, again and again, was their indication that something was working. So they never objected when Mr. Han was putting me through his tough regimen. And they trusted him completely to guide me properly through the work.

THE PRESSURE THAT I put on myself both physically and mentally certainly had its rewards. My obsession with dancing was fed six days a week. But I needed a release from the extreme stress accumulated during those long hours of sweating away in black tights.

In those days, I was skinny, with short, spiky blond hair. I dressed like a raver kid in enormously baggy jeans paired with patent leather skater shoes and tight-fitting thrift store T-shirts. I had grown from being the depressed, desperate-to-fit-in kid in middle school to being a free-spirited beanstalk demanding attention with my clothing choices. I was constantly kicked out of class at ASA for laughing and encouraging my friends to pay attention to me and not to the teacher. I was the human equivalent of a golden retriever, begging to be liked.

The only times I was obedient were the six sessions a week when I worked in the ballet studio with Mr. Han.

And so, on as many weekends as possible, I would climb through my bedroom window and sneak out to raves on the outskirts of Phoenix, staying out until the early morning. The late nineties was the peak of the rave scene all over the country. The pulsing house music was a magnet for many people who craved the freedom that raves supplied. Getting my parents' approval was out of the question. Their answer, on the one occasion I decided to properly ask permission, was "No, honey." They were understandably and categorically opposed to late-night parties that crept into the wee hours and were packed with people high on drugs.

So there I was, covertly planning the getaway with two of my friends from school. The issues were always the same. Who would drive? When would we go? And most important, where would it be? Raves were always held in fairly distant, unfamiliar locations, the address given through a hotline that you called hours before the party started.

Abandoned warehouses were the most popular venues, and the three of us would head to a part of town we hadn't dared go to before, curious and unstoppable, like hungry little mice scampering for that perfect morsel of food. As we drove through the darkness of the night, we knew we were close when we heard the first faint sounds of the pulsing bass. *Boom. Boom. Boom. Boom.* The methodic pull of techno. We were immediately transported.

The crowd was a far cry from the group I usually associated with. The disciplined bun heads and ballet girls who never saw this hour of night were replaced by "candy kids" named Sparkle, Comet, and Sunshine, all draped in neon plastic necklaces and pacifiers. Ecstasy and Special K were the drugs of choice. I never even considered taking them, and oddly, given their widespread use, was never even offered any. My personal ecstasy was the music: the deep thumping bass, the extreme volume that negated the possibility of verbal communication. It was a realm that bore no relation to my everyday world and offered an absolute release from all forms of responsibility.

One popular venue was a place called the Icehouse, a former ice holding warehouse. I loved dancing in the cavernous rooms of that abandoned building, one of which had no ceiling so you danced gazing at the stars.

The smell was a mixture of perspiration, Vicks VapoRub, and cigarettes. I danced without a break for hours. I would leave the raves in the nascent glow of the morning light drenched in sweat. I crept back through my bedroom window undetected and would immediately fall, comatose, into my bed.

Come Monday, I would be totally rejuvenated and ready to return to the unforgiving regime of black tights and Mr. Han.

CHAPTER 7

As my ballet vocabulary broadened in those years with Mr. Han, I began to learn the basics of partnering a ballerina, a crucial skill for a male dancer. I started with the basics of holding a dancer as she balanced on one leg, promenading her around, and putting her into a small fish dive (basically a dip). These were just the baby steps of a career-long education in the subtle nuances of supporting a ballerina. But it was a bumpy road to begin with nonetheless.

For the year-end school performances I was given *The Sleeping Beauty* pas de deux with Brittany, one of my best friends. We were very close outside the studio, but as rehearsals inched on, we became each other's worst enemy. I had one opinion on how we should execute a step and she had an opposing one. We were angsty teenagers who didn't like to be proven wrong in front of our teacher. We both were convinced that we knew what we needed from each other. We had no idea what we were talking about.

Mr. Han put up with this behavior for about a week before he walked out, as abruptly as he had always done in class. "You need to learn to get along on your own," he said as he left. We looked at each other dumbfounded. What were we to do now? He wasn't going to help; he would come back when we'd had enough time to sort out our differences.

From then on, at the start of our rehearsal, he would come into the studio for mere seconds, make sure we had the music to rehearse to, and then leave us to our own strategies. We had no idea when he was coming back. We had been abandoned. There was no one in front of the room to tell us what to do or to mediate our passive-aggressive drama. We were forced to work together and communicate through our teenage self-righteousness. After a few days, those tiny things that had messed us up before became nonissues. We learned to admit mistakes and take responsibility when something went wrong. She made it work on her end, and I on mine.

In the process, we both learned an important lesson about how to enact a partnership. It was a key precursor to what I would need to implement when I became a professional.

MR. HAN TAUGHT the Vaganova method, which was created in the first part of the twentieth century by Agrippina Vaganova, a former dancer with the Mariinsky company. (It is still regarded as the foremost technique, and The Vaganova Academy of Russian Ballet in St. Petersburg is considered the greatest ballet school in the world.)

There is no positive reinforcement at that school. There are no parents calling the teachers and asking them to go easier on their child, or suggesting their kid be complimented once in a while. If a parent has an issue with the method of training or complains that their child should have a more prominent role in a school performance, the student will be shown the door.

Mr. Han was of this ilk. He did not offer celebratory congratulations for work well done. He went against most methods in America, where kids are doused with positive reinforcement, which makes them all too aware of their strengths and far too unaware of their weaknesses.

Though Mr. Han's method of training was ideal for me, it certainly wasn't for everyone. You would see, from time to time, a student deflate in a puddle of tears.

He would receive a flow of phone calls from parents who wanted him to go easier on their child who was complaining that he or she wasn't having any fun in class.

"Through hard work, you find joy," he would reply.

Ballet is hard. He was teaching his students discipline, focus, structure, and through those qualities, independence and self-assurance. If they didn't become dancers, they could implement the rigor his training required in other areas and professions. His goal was to teach, not coddle. If that was what they wanted, they would have to find it elsewhere.

I benefited greatly from this method of teaching and upheld its principles throughout my career.

"Hard work always pays off," I like to tell young aspiring students. "So be the hardest-working person in the room."

A crucial lesson Mr. Han taught me, which has stayed with me my entire career, was the value of self-criticism. He instilled in me the firm belief that whatever I did could always be done better. He taught me to question the work in front of me and strive for better results.

However, at times I can still confuse that with my dancing simply not being good enough. I need to remember that I can always learn from critique, but there does come a point where I need to trust that my performance is, in fact, good enough, even though I recognize that it could be better. This prompts me to keep striving as all dancers must do if they want to avoid becoming complacent or stale or, most dangerous of all, satisfied.

So I'm glad he never showered me with the compliments I would have liked to hear at that time. I was never even told that something I was executing was good. When it was good, he would say nothing and simply push me further, forcing me to go beyond my own ideas of what was possible. If he deemed my exercise worthy or at a level that momentarily pleased him, he would ask for more. More turns, more height in my jump, better quality.

I trusted him completely, and since I never knew what was good and what wasn't, I had to rely on that trust. I had no frame of reference, no one to whom I could compare myself. There were no other boys consistently in my class. Those who came in at one point or another would leave a few weeks or months later, either too bored or too challenged by Mr. Han's demands. And when I watched videos of male dancers whom I looked up to, I never imagined attaining their stature. They jumped too high and danced too well.

So I just worked. Nonstop. There was no other way. I went blindly into the ballet world, with 100 percent commitment. A commitment I never questioned.

AT SIXTEEN AND well into my third year of training with Mr. Han, I went away to my first summer intensive program, which was held for four weeks in Vail, Colorado. It would be attended by dancers from other schools around the country. I was a nervous wreck. The thought of dancing in the same class with other boys from professional schools terrified me. Could I execute the steps as well as they inevitably would? I was convinced they'd be dancing circles around me, that I'd be lost in the back of the studio. They would have huge jumps and soft landings and execute multiple pirouettes. Clean, crisp, masculine technique. I would be outdone in everything.

Again, I just worked as hard as I could. To my relief, I wasn't flailing about as I had imagined. The steps were manageable and I was on par with the other boys.

I was surprised to find that there was some attention paid to me in class by the teachers. They seemed to see something in me I didn't see in myself, and they made attempts to nurture whatever it was. This was my first indication that maybe I did have some talent for ballet. I was stunned. It was a significant milestone.

I'D ALWAYS HAD the greatest respect for Mr. Han and his taxing, relentless methods. After a month spent with other teachers, that respect deepened. For the first time, I had a clear sense of how far his rigorous teachings had brought me.

I'm still amazed by how I responded to Mr. Han's fierce method of teaching. He and I accomplished so much in the four years I worked with him. I never questioned any aspect of the training. I never defied him, stood up to him, or talked back to him. If he had complimented me I would have believed him and this would have created ego, an assumption that what I was executing was sufficient. The edge, the sharpness, the hunger I had when working in the studio with him would have diminished, and the relationship would have become more relaxed and therefore less effective.

But there was no relaxing with Mr. Han. And there were boundaries. He was my mentor; he wasn't my friend. His approach may seem old-school to some, but I cannot deny the results of those arduous years.

At times, I find myself longing for the days when I knew nothing, including the extent of my potential. When I was just a young boy working away with my demanding teacher late into the night. It was just work with no knowledge of what it might produce. Sometimes ignorance really is bliss.

THERE WAS EVENTUALLY a shift in my dynamic with Mr. Han. It happened after I became a professional, and he would come to see me dance at the Metropolitan Opera House. The first ballet he saw me in there was *Swan Lake*. I was cast as Prince Siegfried and it was my first major Principal role with American Ballet Theatre. With the knowledge that he was in the audience, the nerves I'd experienced during our private lessons flooded back to me. I was fourteen again, trying to execute those steps perfectly to please his critical eye. I wanted to make him proud, all the while knowing I could never do a performance that he would deem sufficient. Throughout the ballet my mind flashed repeatedly on the daunting fact that he was watching me. When I bowed after my solo, I bowed to my image of him sitting somewhere in the vast darkness of the audience. When the final curtain mercifully fell he came backstage to meet me in my dressing room. I waited nervously for him to pick the entire show apart, every move, jump, gesture. But that night he established the way he would react to all of my performances thereafter. Even if the show was excellent according to others, he would simply say, "Very good . . ." dryly, and in complete monotone.

"Thank you," I would reply, grateful and a little amazed that I got even that.

Then he would smile and add something like, "You had trouble with the turning in the Act three solo, no?"

Because of the mind-set he had instilled in me, I was more comfortable with his knowing critique than I would have been with praise. He was forever critical, but once I became an adult, he was also my friend.

MR. HAN EVENTUALLY left Phoenix to become director of the Washington School of Ballet. He had been there nine years—and I had been a Principal Dancer for ten years—when I was asked by The Washington Ballet, the company associated with the school, to join the board of directors. The day of my nomination I took the train from New York to Washington, DC, for my first board meeting. As I walked into the room full of men and women successful in their respective fields, I saw placards marking our places at the boardroom table, each imprinted with a name.

My card was positioned beside Kee Juan Han's.

How amazing, I thought, that we had journeyed from the dingy strip mall studio where he worked me to exhaustion late into the night to this austere boardroom where we were seated, like equals, side by side.

CHAPTER 8

I didn't consciously decide to become a professional ballet dancer. Ballet chose me. There was never a eureka moment. I simply knew that ballet was what I had to do. There are dancers who dance because they can and those who dance because they must. I was of the latter variety.

When I learned about the various companies that dominate the ballet world, I knew that American Ballet Theatre was the one I had to join. ABT dancers like Ethan Stiefel and Vladimir Malakhov graced the covers of *Dance Magazine*, and I eagerly studied their photos, absorbing every image and memorizing every quote. It is generally considered that there are two types of male dancers: Dionysian dancers like Rudolf Nureyev, who are earthy, lusty, as if rising from the soil; and Apollonian dancers like Mikhail Baryshnikov and Peter Martins, who are cool, light, airborne, originating from the sky. Both Stiefel and Malakhov were in the Apollonian mode, the style with which I connected the most. They were the sort of dancers I naturally gravitated toward.

Stiefel and Malakhov were also key parts of the exceptional cadre of male dancers who had joined ABT when Kevin McKenzie became the company's Artistic Director in 1992. Each one was unlike the others. On any given night in the theater, you could see a Dionysian dancer as Albrecht in *Giselle* and the following night a completely different interpretation of the same role performed in the Apollonian style. Kevin had created a sensation. These male dancers were dazzling and sexy, graceful and masculine. And they influenced much of the younger generation of students who aimed to be like them.

ABT was the American mecca for dance. It was also where the best dancers from around the world went to share and hone their talent and to lend their gifts to the company's unparalleled international roster.

No other company would do it for me at the time. I had no aspirations of dancing in Europe. I knew of other companies globally, of course: the flair of the Bolshoi, the refinement of Paris Opera, the precision of the Mariinsky. But I never imagined them to be attainable goals. They seemed too far away, as if in a different, unreachable world. I watched their dancers in awe and saw videos of these most storied companies dancing ballet's great works (Royal Ballet's *Swan Lake,* Paris Opera's *La Bayadère*). But I never entertained the idea of joining them. ABT and New York City were my be-all and end-all. I *had* to dance there. I *had* to become a Principal Dancer with that very company, following in the footsteps of the dancers I idolized. This was my first real taste of setting my sights on a future goal. And I would let nothing get in the way of it.

MR. HAN WAS well aware of my dream to dance with ABT and mentioned that my first way of connecting with the company should come through their Summer Intensive, a six-week training program for young dancers that often provides an inside track for admission into ABT's Studio Company and, ultimately, into ABT itself. In the winter of 1999, when I was sixteen, my parents drove me to Los Angeles to audition for it.

On the morning of the audition, I entered a studio rented out for aspiring students just like myself. Clearly, I was not alone in my ambition. Masses of kids, mostly girls, roamed the narrow hallway. All more or less the same age, we desired the same thing but knew that only a few of us would be chosen. If I had a good audition and was accepted, I would be going to New York City for the very first time to take summer classes in ABT's studios, the same studios where my idols rehearsed *Swan Lake* and *Romeo and Juliet*. How thrilling I thought, to walk through the same hallways they walked and encounter the artists I looked up to so much. But first I had to pass the audition in the sea of other kids.

I tried my best to make myself known in the turning and jumping herd. It was the epitome of a cattle call. I was desperate to be seen. I eyed the audition panel nervously. Were they noticing me amid these three hundred other young dancers? Was I good enough for them to even take note? I didn't fall or forget the exercises, but other than that I had no sense of how it went.

After the audition, we were addressed collectively by one of the women on the panel. "Thank you all for your interest in the summer program," she said. "We'll let you know."

THE WEEKEND OF the audition coincided with an ABT tour to Costa Mesa, California, where they were performing *Le Corsaire*. My parents bought me a ticket for the performance, knowing how much it would mean to me to see the company of my dreams onstage. The production was even grander and more wondrous than I had imagined. There was a star-laden cast and a massive, beautiful Corps de Ballet. Marcelo Gomes, a bright young star in the making, was debuting in the flashy virtuoso role as the slave Ali. He was incredible. The audience roared their approval. I marveled at the gorgeous, giant sets dominating the stage, including, in the dream scene, a real working fountain. I thought, *Only ABT would have a real fountain onstage!*

The performance was a harmonious marriage of prowess and refinement. I was all the more certain that I had to dance for this company. I had finally seen the quality that ABT was known for. There wasn't a dancer who didn't look in top form.

MY AUDITION AND first viewing of ABT gave me my first taste of a new sort of hunger. The hunger to work was already instilled in me, but now I felt the hunger of ambition. It would be a long time before I learned the important lesson that ambition can be an impediment to achieving the very thing one desires. But I was so eager to show the world what I had learned from Mr. Han.

Forced into an agonizing wait for the verdict on my audition, I refused to think, *I hope to get to New York City one day.*

Instead, I set aside all apprehensions and doubts.

I will *be in New York City,* I told myself, *dancing for ABT.*

A FEW ANXIOUS weeks passed before I learned that I had been accepted for ABT's Summer Intensive. In addition, I was given a full scholarship to pay for the tuition.

On the first day of classes in New York, all the students gathered on the sidewalk outside ABT's studios, waiting for the building's doors to be opened. Everyone was young and eager and, like me, convinced they were on the precipice of living their dream. The buzz and noise of New York City surrounded us. As I stood there nervously with the others, a yellow cab pulled up to the sidewalk and a tall, striking man I recognized from photographs in *Dance Magazine* came bounding out. It was Kevin McKenzie, ABT's Artistic Director. I studied him closely as he weaved his way through the claque of spellbound students.

This was the man who had invited my idols to dance at ABT. Ecstatic to be mere feet away from the director of my dream company, I thought, *There goes my future boss.*

THROUGHOUT THE SIX weeks of the intensive program, I was mesmerized by the atmosphere at "890," which, I learned, is how ABT's dancers refer to the building at 890 Broadway where they rehearse. The long, wide hallways led to half a dozen high-ceilinged studios with huge windows looking out onto lower Broadway, each room larger than the last. The sweat of the company members had stained the wooden floors. In these studios there had been countless hours of rehearsals; the mirrors had reflected the images of Baryshnikov, Makarova, Nureyev—the most renowned dancers in the world. It was like nothing I had seen before, and a far cry from the dingy allure of my strip mall studios in Phoenix.

Although ABT's spring season at the Metropolitan Opera House had ended, and most dancers had taken a summer break, on special days word would spread that Marcelo Gomes or Angel Corella was in the building. I'd run like the rest to see them. There, in the flesh, was Angel, waiting in the hallway before his morning class. All the students in the Summer Intensive would gawk wide-eyed and then attack from all sides for autographs.

Being at ABT and immersed in the cultural pulse of New York City, I knew this was where I needed to be.

THE SIX WEEKS at ABT flew by. At summer's end I was invited back for the following year, but before I eagerly returned, ambition and curiosity had prompted me to set out on what had previously seemed an unattainable course.

Although my ongoing training with Mr. Han provided the structure I required during my formative years, I now felt the need to spend one year at a major professional school. I wanted to have a year dancing in a class with boys who were as dedicated as I was, as opposed to the boys who briefly took class with Mr. Han and soon moved on. Previously, I'd had offers from several schools, but my parents were uneasy about sending me far away at such a young age. They completely trusted Mr. Han and agreed when he said that if I wanted to experience another school, the right time to do it would be for my senior year of high school.

THE PARIS OPERA'S Ballet School is the oldest school in the world for classical ballet training, as well as one of the most prestigious. I saw an informational video about the school while I was training with Mr. Han and marveled at the students' speed, clarity, and absolute command of the entire idiom of classical technique. Ninety-five percent of the school's students were French-born, making it nearly impossible for an international applicant to get in, especially at the advanced age—in ballet terms—of sixteen. I was too American, too old; I thought I didn't stand a chance. Nevertheless, I sent an audition video, filming it with Mr. Han in the studio. In it, I appeared lanky and adolescent, unaware whether anything I executed was good or bad but diligently working through the steps my teacher set for me. At the beginning of the video, I stared into the camera and attempted to introduce myself in French, a language completely foreign to me at the time.

"Bonjour. Je m'appelle David Hallberg. J'ai seize ans. Je danse depuis quatre ans a l'école de danse de Ballet Arizona. Voici ma vidéo. Merci."

TWO WEEKS LATER, I got a thin letter in the mail with the elegant Paris Opera logo on the top corner. I stood there in my kitchen, frozen. In the United States a thin envelope from a school you've applied to usually meant a one-page letter saying, "Thanks but no thanks." So I assumed the school wasn't interested. *Oh well,* I thought, *it wasn't meant to be.*

In any case, the letter was in French, so I nervously called my friend Brittany's mother, who spoke it fluently, and begged her to translate. I attempted to read it aloud to her over the phone, massacring words I had never seen with their funny accents above the letters.

"It seems you've gotten in," she said.

"What?"

"Yes. From what I understand, it says they are happy to accept you in the school but there are things they saw in the video that you need to work on. Your jump and your strength."

The next few moments were a blur of excitement and disbelief as I screamed to my parents that I was accepted at this storied school I'd thought I had no chance of getting into. We had decided before the video went off to Paris that if, by some crazy chance, I was accepted, I would go. With that having been agreed upon, I was definitely moving to Paris. The farthest I had ever traveled was to Florida. I could hardly believe my stroke of luck. And luck is what I thought it was: it didn't occur to me that I was good enough to be accepted on merit.

Like many who have never left the nest, my naiveté was immense. Before I left, I bought a year's worth of shampoo and deodorant to take with me because I didn't think I could buy those necessities in France.

I thought I was moving to Mars, and so did most of my friends. Paris could have been another planet completely. But, nervous and wide-eyed, I charged forward and prepared to move to a country that I knew nothing about.

TWO MONTHS BEFORE I would go to Paris, I returned to New York for another six weeks of ABT's Summer Intensive. My surroundings felt more comfortable and familiar, and I was much calmer than I had been throughout the previous summer. For the performance at the end of the term, I was given two leading roles. One was the opening movement and first variation from George Balanchine's *Theme and Variations*. When we learned it en masse, everyone seemed to know the ballet by heart. I not only didn't know the steps, I had no idea who Balanchine was. I was definitely in need of an on-the-job education.

Kevin McKenzie came to the final performance. The students were all saying that he would want to speak to some of us after the show. I was one of those asked to stick around and wait for him. Kevin had been a leading ABT dancer. He had retired from performing nine years before, but still had the bearing of a danseur noble, and was tall with a great shock of dark hair.

He was complimentary about the show and asked if I did indeed have plans to go to the Paris Opera Ballet School the following month. I told him I would be leaving for Paris in mid-August.

"If you plan on coming back to ABT after the year in Paris is over," he said, "I can have a contract for you. And if it doesn't work out in Paris, you're welcome to come here for the remainder of the year."

Those were the words I so desperately wanted to hear. And they came from the person I wanted to hear them from.

I tried to conceal my utter elation. All I could say was "Thank you."

I walked away, dazed and beaming.

It seemed everything was falling into place. But the year ahead would test my entire concept of what it means to live up to my commitment and persevere.

CHAPTER 9

My idea that I would arrive at Paris Opera Ballet School with my big American smile and spiky blond hair and instantly befriend my classmates was shattered in the first week.

From the very first day in Paris to the very last I was known not as "l'Américain," the American, but as "l'Amérique." Literally meaning "the America," which rendered me a cliché of the brash American rather than an individual. It was in that year that I became acquainted with the cutting art of condescension.

The director of the school was Claude Bessy. She had been a gorgeous and highly renowned ballerina whose dancing was very sensual, earthy and natural and entirely different from the manner of her fearsome and stringent directorship. The first day of class, as we were doing center exercises, she came in quietly through the studio door. The teacher announced her arrival and we all bowed (proper etiquette at any ballet school). But the atmosphere had changed instantly. The boys, shifty-eyed, continued in fear. *Why be afraid of the director?* I thought. I wondered if I should go up and introduce myself. After all, I was the new student in the room, the one she'd accepted but didn't know. But something told me to just attempt to blend in with the class. She stood there, saying nothing, expressionless, while we tried to concentrate on the exercises. Only minutes passed before she went to the door to leave.

But as she walked out, she said in French, for everyone to hear, "I didn't recognize l'Amérique. He looks like a porcupine."

The other boys snickered and I looked around, confused. I inched up to one who spoke a little English and asked him what she'd said. "Uh, she said you look like . . . what's the little animal that is very sharp? Like needles?"

"A porcupine?"

"Yes! A porcupine." He looked at me with contempt.

That remark, with its gratuitous insult about my hair, and the chuckles that ensued, set the stage for the way I would be treated throughout the year by almost everyone.

ALL YEAR LONG, the other students either ignored me or saw me as a nuisance. As far as most were concerned, it was a privilege for me to be training there. Nothing more. I did consider it a privilege to study at one of the best ballet schools in the world. But I didn't understand why I was treated that way.

From the start it was evident that the other boys didn't want me in their class. I was placed in the graduating class, where the focus for the entire year is a coveted contract with the Paris Opera Ballet. By just being in the studio with them, I was seen as a roadblock to the goal they all desperately wanted to attain. I never had any ambition of joining the company, but even if I had, it was made abundantly clear by the boys that I had no chance. They peered in my direction at times, observed how I danced, but didn't encourage any sense of camaraderie. I wasn't like them, they reminded me. I was an outsider. There was never any regard for what I could do. I came to the studio with no ego, no attempt to become the star student. I came to learn. Which was just as well, since there was no way I could prove that I had the same amount of talent as the French students.

* * *

THE HARDER I tried to make friends, to please the crowd, the more I was pushed away. I swam upstream the whole year with the current of the detractors against me.

At first, I had looked around for acceptance. I wanted my classmates to be my friends. I begged for them to like me, and by doing so gave them the power to reject me, which they happily did. It had been so easy to make friends back at ASA, where (just like at Paris Opera) we shared the commonality of dance. But here, in this foreign territory where cultural differences were rife, I couldn't crack the barrier between me and them. They excluded me from group gatherings and outings. I had no one to connect with, no one to talk to. I felt their disdain on a daily basis. I had gone from the taunting of public school to a paradisiacal student life at ASA, then, in Paris, back to being bullied, but in a completely different way. All I had to rely on was myself and my sheer will to get through the year.

One student in particular was a ringleader. Sophie was the cool girl in the school, with a mane of blond hair and a nonchalant sense of style only the French can possess. As our level finished partnering class one day, and we were on our way to the cafeteria for the afternoon gateaux, Sophie and I were side by side as we headed down the six-flight spiraling wooden stairway. Suddenly, I slipped down a couple of stairs, grabbing on to the handrail before I fell on my butt. She looked at me and laughed a coy, sarcastic giggle, as if to say, *Isn't it obvious you don't belong here, you dumb American?*

On another occasion, I walked down the corridor of dorm rooms, heading to my own room at the end of the hallway. I passed two twelve-year-old boys who made fun of my walk. Their imitation suggested a girl walking down a street perched on high heels. My blood boiled as stinging memories of being bullied in seventh grade came rushing back. I made a feeble attempt at putting them in their place, cornering them against the wall. They couldn't have cared less what this American outsider might do to them. I would be the one blamed for anything that transpired, so I just hurried away, knowing that even a hint of violence would send me right back to Phoenix. There was nothing I could do but ignore them.

EACH DAY AT lunchtime, I would wait in front of the closed doors to the cafeteria with the other kids. Through the small window I would see the cooks making final preparations and the attendant standing by the table closest to the door, sorting the daily mail. I eagerly anticipated the mail delivery. Mom would send packages every other week filled with Jif peanut butter, Kool-Aid packets, *Rolling Stone* magazine, photos. Each time I opened a package I realized how much I missed home. Mom and Dad, my car, my brother, my freedom, my friends, my peanut butter. Paradoxically, it had taken a leap away from the nest to bring me closer to my family and the beauty of home.

The cheapest way to send care packages was in the large red-and-gray envelope the U.S. Postal Service provided for a fixed price. I would eagerly peer through the door's small window to see if one was among the pile of mail. In that lonely environment, when I spotted a red-and-gray envelope, it meant that day would be better than others.

One day, I made the mistake of opening a coveted package at the lunch table alongside some other students. They peered over at me with a mixture of disgust and mild interest. As discreetly as I could, I looked through the contents and found the yearly brochure of the School of Ballet Arizona. I was on the cover doing a grand jeté, a midair split.

"*Fait voir?*" A kid in my class smirked at me. He put his hand out, gesturing for me to pass it to him. I handed it over reluctantly. He took one look at it, squinting as if to examine it more closely.

"*Mais, Daveeeeed,*" he said. "Your leg in the back. It is not turned out. Bowlegs, *non?*"

Giggles around the table. Another shot to put l'Amérique in his place.

I said nothing, but after that, I made sure to always open my treasured packages in private, where I could savor these reminders of the comforts I'd known in Arizona and taken for granted.

ONE THING THAT placed me on an emotional par with the other students was the fear we all felt when Madame Bessy was in the studio. She had no problem expressing her opinions of various students in front of the class or, for that matter, the entire school, telling some to gain weight or muscle, wear different support under their uniforms, or put on less makeup. She maintained a tight leash on the teachers and students alike.

It wasn't a pleasant environment, but as harsh and terrifying as Bessy could be, she produced the best students, who in turn became the greatest French stars: Sylvie Guillem, Patrick Dupond, Manuel Legris, and countless others.

As each daily class progressed into jumps, the students moved at a lightning pace, displaying the precision and clarity they had honed for years. Normally when the tempo accelerates the body tenses up. But the French students remained light, at ease whatever the tempo. This was the result of the majority of students beginning their training at the school by the age of eight. I was fascinated by the way their lower bodies blurred with speed while their upper bodies exuded refinement and calm. It was the French style. No huge jumps, no big tricks or multiple pirouettes. The training turned out dancers every bit as elegant, tasteful, and sleek as the quintessential French style and demeanor.

*   *   *

A COUPLE OF times a year, the entire school joined with the Paris Opera's dancers to take part in the Grand Défilé, a majestic event enacted on the stage of their home theater, the opulent Palais Garnier. The Défilé is the signature march of the Paris Opera Ballet. It consists of a stately progression that proceeds from the back of the stage toward the audience, beginning with the smallest girl in the school and finishing with "*les Étoiles*" (literally, "the Stars") of the Paris Opera.

The Défilé is French pride and style at their most conspicuous and lavish, and is meant to exemplify the grandeur and ongoing relevance of this historic institution that was founded in the seventeenth century by King Louis XIV.

I had been at the school for eleven months when all the other students began to mysteriously disappear in the afternoons. During the free time before dinner, we usually did our homework or milled about the grounds, but suddenly there was not a soul to be seen. On the third day I searched the building and finally made my way down to the lower-level theater, where the school held rehearsals. The entire student body was on the stage rehearsing the Grand Défilé, receiving their marching orders from Claude Bessy. They formed the most precise soldierly lines. Of the 180 pupils, I was the only one not invited to walk the stage of the opera house, because I wasn't French.

WHEN THE DAY came for everyone to head onto buses to the Palais Garnier and perform the Défilé, I was left to entertain myself on the school grounds. Once again, as I had been so often before, I was the outsider. The one who wasn't like the rest because I was simply myself.

The condescending form of bullying I encountered in Paris

was different from the bullying I'd experienced before. I wasn't being taunted. I was being discounted, which felt just as painful. I swallowed whatever pride I still had and got on with it. And yet, I would have recurring nightmares, seeing myself in them as smaller than the other students, belittled by the group, unable to connect with them in any way. It was a traumatic experience that haunted my dreams for years to come.

BY THE TIME the year came to a close, I was fluent in French and able to throw barbs back in the other students' direction. They still laughed at me as they had all year, but by then, I didn't care. I had changed. The absence of friends had forced me to look inward instead of outward, to search for fulfillment and happiness within myself. I would sit in my dorm room alone for hours, reading and writing. I fell in love with opera and would see at least one, sometimes two operas or ballets at Palais Garnier or the Bastille Opera House each weekend. I immersed myself in my budding interests, educating myself about art. It was in Paris that I saw works by renowned modern choreographers for the first time, some of which I would dance in the future. As I roamed through the streets, visited museums, viewed performances, or practiced in the studios alone, I taught myself that solitude is a form of contentment. The eagerness to be accepted had faded. I didn't even feel the need to try. I stopped attempting to give to people who had no interest in me. I learned how to give to myself. My sense of worth came not from the acceptance of others, but from a self-acceptance I had not experienced before. It was liberating. I was who I wanted to be. I had come as an outsider and I left as an outsider. But I was no longer the smiley golden retriever, begging to be liked. I had gone to Paris to learn what made the French such great dancers. And I had. My goals were clearer to me than ever before: Work hard. Pave my own path.

From discomfort comes strength; from hardship comes perspective. I left France thankful that I had stuck out that solitary year, but even more thankful that it was over.

Someday, I thought, *I will return there, dance there, and prove my worth to them all.*

CHAPTER 10

I was determined to return to ABT, this time as a member of the Corps de Ballet. During my difficult year in Paris I had been comforted by the fact that Kevin McKenzie had said he would welcome me back and give me a contract. Naturally, given the power of my dearly held dreams and growing ambition, I assumed he meant a contract to be a Corps de Ballet dancer, which would mean I'd be joining the company.

But when the school year in Paris was coming to a close, I received a letter saying they had saved a place for me in the Studio Company, which functions as a training ground for young dancers and, for those who do well, as a conduit to becoming a member of ABT's corps. Its alumni include some of the finest dancers at ABT and other world-class companies.

Unquestionably, it was an honor to be one of the twelve dancers chosen for the Studio Company, to be given the opportunity to develop under the watch of Kevin and the Studio Company's Director, John Meehan. But it was not the honor I had in mind.

The Studio Company? I thought, brimming with premature, youthful pride. My heart was set on joining the main company and nothing else. I wrote back, friendly but naively self-assured, saying that I greatly appreciated being chosen for the Studio Company but that I was also looking at other options with different companies. The truth was, I had no intention of dancing anywhere else, but the Studio Company invitation threw me off. I was oblivious to how much time and effort it would take to become worthy of a position in the company. I naively compared myself to dancers like Paloma Herrera, who became a Principal when she was nineteen years old, and Angel Corella, who was promoted to Principal at the age of twenty-one. Both shot up the ranks, creating a sensation when they first danced *Don Quixote* together. They were the "new, young things." I wanted to be just that as well.

But I agreed to join the Studio Company because the truth was, as Kevin clearly saw, I hadn't developed enough to be a member of the Corps de Ballet and was nowhere near the level I would require to become the Principal Dancer of my dreams. I had to face the fact that there were so many things I lacked. Basic skills like stamina and finesse. I needed to build muscle and have the time to fill out physically. Upper-body strength was crucial for me so that I could execute the required partnering. I needed to learn how to access emotion from my natural instincts; I needed to be onstage and gain experience in stagecraft. The list was long and the Studio Company internship could help me with all these things, readying me to make the crucial move from being a student to becoming a professional. It certainly wouldn't happen overnight. It would take a full year of transition at the very least.

THE DIRECTOR OF the Studio Company, Australian-born John Meehan, had been a refined, dashing Principal dancer with ABT, best known for his partnering of Margot Fonteyn in the ballet *The Merry Widow*. He had a paternal, nurturing presence and an intuitive sense when it came to helping young dancers. He could sense my hunger to push myself and my impatience to progress.

"What you want will happen in time," he told me, "but for

now you should focus less on getting into the company and rising through the ranks and more on the work at hand."

I couldn't see the work at hand. My only focus was at the top of the mountain I so desperately wanted to climb. I didn't ask myself the questions I needed to answer: What choices as a dancer do I want to make? What kind of artist do I want to become? What work is most important to me? What are my strengths? More important, what are my weaknesses? My relentless drive wasn't an asset in this situation. Sure, I was working as hard as I could, but *how* I was working was much more important. My ambition was a distraction that kept me from progressing as effectively as I otherwise could.

OVER THE COURSE of my year in Studio Company, John and the teaching staff somehow managed to get through to this young, blindly hungry rookie whose unshakable goal was to become a Principal Dancer in American Ballet Theatre. Thanks to their expertise, I became stronger and more polished. They took the time that was needed to allow me to develop properly. They saw no point in rushing into anything, but instead continued to lay the foundation down. I needed that year of transition. I needed John harping on me about my impatience, insisting I focus on the small but crucial details. But often, my naiveté and rigid ambition were stronger than my patience.

Toward the end of our year with Studio Company, each of us would meet individually with Kevin and John and be told, after all that work, whether he or she would be taken into the company as an apprentice. There were only a few contracts, and twelve eager dancers dreaming of transitioning to ABT, so this event was as anticipated as it was dreaded. Some of the dancers walked out of Kevin's office looking elated. But others exited in tears. A talented boy from Japan who had a weightless, soaring jump didn't land a contract. We all tried comforting him. But nothing we said could alter the reality that he would have to dance somewhere else. Kevin and John were fair and caring directors, and I imagined these all-or-nothing meetings must be one of the hardest aspects of their jobs.

When it was my turn to walk into the office, I took a seat beside John, facing Kevin, who was sitting behind his desk. "I'd like to offer you an apprenticeship with the company," he said matter-of-factly, "for the Met season."

The Met season is the highlight of the year for ABT's dancers, during which, for eight weeks, they perform the world's greatest ballets at the Metropolitan Opera House. This was the offer I had always dreamed of hearing. I nearly laughed out loud from a mixture of relief and euphoria. I was mindful that Kevin wasn't making a huge fuss over me or my talent. He was direct and to the point. No need for unnecessary praise or promises about my future with the company. He simply offered me the next step. It was not a full corps contract but an apprenticeship. A trial to see how I acclimated, how I adapted, how I played with others. But I was in. And I felt ready, after a year's worth of guidance from John.

As it turned out, after building strength, polishing technique, and learning choreography, the "playing with others" aspect of the equation would pose the most significant challenge.

I WAS FINALLY promoted to the Corps de Ballet one year later, bringing me a bit closer to my all-consuming goal of becoming a Principal Dancer. My mind-set was all about the work. I had a task to accomplish. Laughing and chatting with other dancers in rehearsals or when passing by in the hallways wasn't going to get me there. I didn't argue or fight with my colleagues; I just wouldn't engage. My head was in the sand.

But ABT is a big family; the dancers joked with each other in the studio and dressing rooms. When the joke was at my expense, I didn't bother to take it in. It was all work and no play for me.

Every year, at the end of the Met season, an annual roast is held during which the peccadillos of certain dancers and staff are ridiculed in front of the entire company and administration. No one is exempt, not even Kevin. Everyone is forewarned that it's all meant to be fun and is just a way of letting off steam at the end of a grueling season. Awards are passed out, including one for "Quote of the Year." To my mortification, the winner of the Quote of the Year was a certain dancer who'd said to another, "Do you ever get the feeling we are becoming less and less worthy of David Hallberg's time?"

I was blindsided. It never occurred to me that my exclusionary behavior was offensive or even noticed. Now I recognized that my drive had gotten in the way of basic human interaction. That was a personal turning point. Work hard, but also relax; say hello to others in the hallway; and notice your fellow dancers.

ALTHOUGH I SETTLED into company life through the course of the Met season, it took time to get over the thrill of taking class beside my idols on a daily basis. Eventually I got used to dancing next to Vladimir Malakhov and Ethan Stiefel, but I never stopped watching them. Rehearsals. Shows. Bows. Pre-performance stage prep. Everything. Inspiration was only a studio away, or literally dancing in front of me during a performance. Even if I wasn't on the stage on a given evening, I would watch, transfixed, from the wings, just as I had when witnessing ballet for the first time in the wings at Ballet Arizona. Ethan was in the prime of his career. I could see him furthering and refining himself as an artist in every performance while simultaneously displaying his impeccable technique. On those occasions when I was at an ABT social function with him, I took care to play it cool, calm, collected. Ethan is laid-back, with no pretensions. The last thing he would have wanted around him was a colleague blubbering on over his dancing . . . a gushing fan disguised as a company member.

AFTER MORNING CLASS one day, four months after I'd joined the company, I headed out of the stuffy studio drenched in sweat. A colleague approached me, saying, "Congratulations, Mr. Hallberg."

"For what?" I asked.

"Haven't you seen the new casting? It's on the board."

Suddenly, I was living out that stereotypical Big Break moment that has cropped up in countless dance movies: the young dancer hurriedly makes his or her way through a maze of corridors to the casting board, where other dancers are gazing at the white sheet of paper that lists the next ballets to be rehearsed and danced, and the names of the dancers who will perform them.

The list read:

Symphony in C
1st Movement: Herrera/Stiefel. Dvorovenko/Hallberg

There it was. The proof. The payoff. The chance. I had been cast, while a member of the Corps de Ballet, in one of Balanchine's greatest ballets, to dance the same role that Ethan Stiefel would be performing on other nights. I stared at the list for a few more seconds, almost as if I didn't know my name or suspected there was some other Hallberg in the company. The ball had been thrown to me. And now I needed to catch it.

Later in the day, walking down the corridor, I ran into Irina Dvorovenko, whom I would partner in the ballet. She was one of the reigning ballerinas of ABT and someone I loved to watch.

She looked at me with her vixen stare, a tutu thrown over her shoulder.

"So we will dance *Symphony in C* together," she said in her deep Ukrainian accent. More of a statement than a question.

"Yes, we will." I smiled back nervously.

"Well, don't be worried. I will break you in and teach you."

As rehearsals began, she was a woman of her word. She broke me in by gifting me with what amounted to a private tutorial on partnering. I had little skill to speak of, but she wasn't daunted. She knew what she needed from a partner and how I should provide it.

"Hold me here, down by the hip."

"Don't stop me too early. Let me go into the movement more."

"Push my hips more forward so I am not hanging back on my leg."

I was green and eager. I soaked up everything she said. Some experienced ballerinas don't want to be bothered teaching newbies how to hold them, lift them, carry them. But Irina was generous. Never condescending. I was lucky to be under her wing for this critical turning point. It was the start of my education on how to partner a ballerina. My inexperience shone like a lighthouse through clouds. I couldn't hide or fake my way through the technicalities of maneuvering her. I had to show my cards, and above all . . . learn.

I DEBUTED THE ballet with Irina at the Kennedy Center in Washington, DC. Petrified, I waited in the wings, down stage left, in my makeup and costume. I watched her make her entrance while I fidgeted nervously with my tights, constantly adjusting what didn't need adjusting. The head of the costume department once told me that male dancers get holes in the thighs of their tights because we constantly pull them up. True evidence of pre-performance nerves. As I tugged at my tights offstage, onstage Irina looked secure, confident, sharp. She had an ability to converse silently with the audience, flirting with them as she danced. Meanwhile, my nerves were telling me, *I can't do this. I'll mess up my one chance. I shouldn't be out onstage in a big role yet. I'm not ready. I'm a fake. I can't live up to this moment.*

Inevitably, the point of no return fast approached. I listened to the music leading up to my entrance. Each note brought me closer to the very moment I had always dreamed of and now dreaded.

Eight counts of eight.

Four counts of eight.

The music sounding my entrance thrust me forward. There was no more time for apprehension. I propelled myself onto the stage. I moved. I danced. I did what I had trained for years to do. The doubt, the fear, the anxiety dissipated as I was caught up in the music, the moment, the lights. Adrenaline coursed through me, the adrenaline that is such a crucial component of what defines a ballet dancer.

THOUGH IRINA GAVE me a wonderful, much-needed tutorial (bless her patience), I had a long way to go. I still didn't have the strength to properly lift a ballerina; I didn't know the right, courtly way to touch her. The relationship between two people dancing together, creating an aura of romance for the audience, is at the heart of ballet. Ideally, the two dancers have a chemistry that allows them to meld into one, connect with each other both emotionally and physically while displaying that rapport to the audience as well. But as I would discover, it doesn't always work out that way. Some pairings don't result in that rapport, as hard as both dancers might work individually. They aren't able to blur the lines between what the male supports and what the ballerina exudes. When they dance together they remain individuals.

A BODY OF WORK

I HAD BEEN in the Corps de Ballet just six months when I was paired with Michele, who was an ABT Soloist when I joined the company. Even at a young age—she was twenty-two when we began working together—she had a solid technique. She worked deliberately on her craft and you could see that work in her intense focus on and off the stage. She was always in control of her dancing. Her dancing didn't control her. That simple authority is a formidable trait, as so many dancers have problems controlling the outcome when they push for technically difficult steps or phrases (myself being one of them). Most dancers just hope for the best. But Michele showed precisely what she planned to show when she was in rehearsal or in performance.

We hardly knew each other when we began working together, but the minute we stepped into the studio it was all business and work. She was my superior, having been in the company four years longer than I had. I was very much aware of her experience compared to mine. She had a way of keeping a distance from colleagues, while I, on the other hand, having cast aside my isolation, had reverted to the person I was during my early days in Paris: a golden retriever, smiling, hoping for everyone's acceptance. I was twenty years old then. Though I had not stopped growing I was six foot one with long, thin, sticklike limbs. Michele was five foot eight, which meant that when she rose up on pointe, she was as tall as I. The longer and taller the ballerina, the more there is for the partner to control.

We had been chosen to represent ABT in competition for the Erik Bruhn Prize, a prestigious event held in Toronto every three years. Bruhn had been one of the greatest and most acclaimed male dancers of the twentieth century. A handsome Dane with chiseled features, his nobility and grace made him the perfect danseur noble. The competition he founded was open to the companies around the world with which he was most closely af-filiated. The awardees are intended to possess, in Bruhn's words, "such technical ability, artistic achievement and dedication as I endeavored to bring to dance."

All contestants are selected by their Artistic Directors, who are allowed to submit just one woman and one man. There is a small cash prize for the winners, but even being selected is an honor that marks you as someone with serious potential within your company.

Both of the taxing pieces Kevin chose for us to dance—"Grand Pas Classique," and the *Manon* bedroom pas de deux—require very complex partnering. "Grand Pas" requires the execution of pure technique, no story line but straightforward ballet at its most deliberate. The *Manon* bedroom pas de deux is a scene from the full-length ballet *Manon* by Sir Kenneth MacMillan. During the pas, Manon and Des Grieux dance alone, engaging in intricate and riveting partnering. It is an unusually intimate scene during which the audience act as voyeurs to the couple's sultry mutual passion. It also has the longest kiss in the ballet repertoire, which is nothing like the adolescent kiss in the balcony scene in *Romeo and Juliet*. This was to be arousing, passionate, charged.

I had a lot to prepare. It was a major opportunity to learn and absorb these two works and I was in over my head. Profes-sionals danced these ballets, especially *Manon*, in the prime of their careers. I wasn't even at the legal drinking age. The biggest challenge was getting a handle on how to partner Michele in a way that would allow her to trust me.

KEVIN PERSONALLY PREPARED us for the competition. During his own dancing career, partnering had come naturally to him. He'd partnered many major ballerinas, most notably Martine van Hamel and Natalia Makarova. He had the ability of all great partners: to instinctively anticipate his ballerina's needs even before she's aware of them.

Kevin is tall, slender. Someone I could easily relate to in terms of physical proportions. When he became ABT's director he established himself as a true creature of the studio whose dedication to the process of dance and to working with dancers remains paramount. He is astute and tireless and, years after his own retirement, still able to demonstrate virtuosic steps and intricate partnering.

It was a rare opportunity to have a few months to prepare two major pas de deux with Kevin, as his time was packed with rehearsing other dancers among other directorial duties. I was determined to gain as much as I possibly could from the experience.

AS REHEARSALS INCHED along (and by inched, I mean that every inch of the steps was spelled out to Michele and me), the atmosphere progressively got more and more tense. Kevin, with unwavering patience, explained every nuance of how to partner Michele. Where to hold her. How to maneuver her body into the most advantageous positions. It didn't come easily to me. I didn't sense where she needed to be and, as her patience began to wear thin, more and more I felt a mixture of nerves and fear. Nerves at setting Michele off. Fear of messing up. I had little patience for myself, even. Mentally I was frustrated that I couldn't fulfill my duties. As an example, I didn't know how to "put her on her leg," as dancers call it. This requires the man to set up his ballerina so that she is comfortably on balance while standing on pointe. Every woman is different in regard to where she wants to be and where she feels most comfortable. It takes a good deal of technique and finesse (not just sheer strength), and most important, it takes instinct and confidence, of which I had none. I understood why Michele felt like a guinea pig.

Knowing that I wasn't putting her at ease stressed me out. In ballet, the woman is meant to be lithe and feminine while the man is strong and chivalrous. A male partner has a responsibility to make the woman he's partnering feel taken care of. When you are failing at this responsibility, it chips away at your confidence.

Every day we would work on my shortcomings as a partner, and every day Michele made clear how uncomfortable she was. Since I was in the junior position by a number of years, I felt I had no right to stand up for myself or give my opinion. I knew how inadequate my partnering skills were. She began dominating the situation and made her displeasure apparent. I was humil-iated and equally upset by her attitude and my shortcomings. Kevin would always demonstrate what I needed to do. Everything seemed to work just fine when he was partnering her. She looked and felt at ease. It was a rare occurrence when things worked with me.

THE CLIMAX OF "Grand Pas Classique" contains a series of virtuosic balances for the woman. It's the male partner's respon-sibility to place her so she remains steady and on pointe. At the same time that she balances, the male lets go and does a dou-ble tour en l'air. After each balance and each double tour they both drop to one knee. This is repeated three times. If it's timed correctly it's a great effect. But if the timing is off, the sequence loses its impact and falls flat. Every day in rehearsal, we would start with the intention of achieving perfection. Things would be going relatively well (in my opinion). But we'd get to that first balance and Michele would stop. I never had her in the exact right place to balance. So we'd do it again and again and again. When it would work, I was relieved to move on.

"A little better," she would always say, not completely satisfied.

I lost patience internally but never externally. I understood that the main objective was to make her comfortable. So I listened to Kevin's corrections and learned how to partner her better. I was always ready to make improvements. But like clockwork, on a daily basis, we would stop at the same spot. Over and over. Balance after balance.

THE MANON BEDROOM pas de deux was an even greater challenge for me and my rookie partnering skills. The piece contains a series of very tricky off-balance arabesques and promenades that requires an even higher level of natural instinct than "Grand Pas Classique." It was as new to her as it was to me, so we both started from nothing and worked together on the steps. In addition to its technical demands, *Manon* also calls for intense emotional interpretation. Toward the beginning of the pas, the man and woman slowly walk toward each other. When they reach center stage, he takes her in his arms and kisses her. The kiss is meant to be sensually charged, replete with yearning lust. Neither Michele nor I had ever had a kiss like that onstage.

There is a major difference between stage kisses and making out in real life. In our own separate lives, we had both certainly experienced passionate kissing, but we were hesitant about kissing with such fervor a person we were having troubles with professionally, and to do so, no less, in the studio, in front of our Artistic Director. When we rehearsed, it became a part that we always "marked"—which means we merely suggested the kiss—rather than doing it full-out.

Finally, one day, Kevin told us to come to the center of the room and kiss—his abrupt way of breaking the ice. We walked toward each other and I gave her a peck like a first kiss in third grade. No passion, just awkwardness. "Now kiss her a little longer and a little more like you mean it," he said.

The next attempt continued as business, nothing like the way you would want to kiss someone with whom you were passionately in love. The third kiss was a little more believable but still just as awkward. I couldn't believe I was getting a lesson in kissing, a step-by-step introduction. Kissing 101. We carried on like that for a couple of minutes in the silence of the studio with Kevin coaching us, slowly integrating more passion into our attempts. But thankfully Kevin's method worked. Eventually, after weeks of laboriously ironing out the details of the intricate partnering, we were kissing as easily as we were turning and jumping. The kiss was just as technical as doing an arabesque.

THE NIGHT OF the Bruhn competition I could see in Michele's eyes a total focus and determination to succeed and win. To my relief, the partnering went surprisingly well. Michele's dancing (and the dreaded balances on pointe) stunned the audience. It was the best I had ever seen her dance. She absolutely rose to the challenge of the evening.

Though they perform as a couple in the competition, the man and woman are judged separately. After everyone had danced, we all stood onstage for the announcement of the awardees. Michele won. I lost to Friedemann Vogel, a German dancer from the Stuttgart Ballet. I congratulated both of them, but I was more upset than I let on. My loss combined with Michele's victory would give her even more of an upper hand when we rehearsed at ABT for other ballets. I knew this would create an even deeper divide between us.

CHAPTER 11

I had been in ABT's Corps de Ballet for two years when I was given my first leading role in a full-length ballet. It was one of the most iconic roles in the repertoire: Prince Siegfried in *Swan Lake*. He is a complex and in some ways a mysterious character that I would dance and question for my entire career.

I didn't make the decision as to when I was ready to dance Siegfried. No matter how hard a dancer works or strives to be great, our casting is in the hands of the Artistic Director whose company we dance for and whose job it is to assign the opportunities all dancers crave.

WHEN KEVIN DEEMED me ready to slowly prepare *Swan Lake*, I knew it was a huge opportunity as well as a huge responsibility. I was honored to be chosen to dance this role at the age of twenty-two, a role that had been performed by Nureyev and Bruhn and Baryshnikov, the brilliant dancers I'd revered as a kid, whose performances set the standard against which all others are measured.

EVERY DANCER GROWS up knowing *Swan Lake*. I had watched videos of it danced by companies around the world, and knew the haunting Tchaikovsky score note by note. The music spoke to me even when I was a boy in high school. I would listen to the third act, turning it up full blast in the car when I drove myself to school. I hadn't yet learned what the steps were, so my imagination improvised. Mr. Han's car broke down once and I had to drive him from the studio to his home (a nervous five-minute trip). As he got into the passenger seat of my beat-up ten-year-old Toyota Corolla, the male variation from the Black Swan pas de deux came blasting through the speakers. I had been in a state of euphoria as I drove to class earlier and had forgotten to turn it down. I was mortified that he caught me in my *Swan Lake* stupor, but pleased that now he knew how deeply I responded to such incredible music. What a kiss-ass I was—humiliated yet happy I got caught.

I feel a reverence for this ballet; it's like a sacred text to equally sacred music. But what I love most about it, and find so moving, is its history: Its first performances, at the Bolshoi Theatre in 1877, were choreographed by a gentleman of insufficient talent. Though the ballet remained in the repertory for six of the next seven years, it was a great disappointment to Tchaikovsky. After hearing Léo Delibes's score for the ballet *Sylvia*, he wrote to his patron, "*Swan Lake* is poor stuff when compared to *Sylvia.*"

Then came its stunning resurrection in 1895, two years after Tchaikovsky died, never to know that his *Swan Lake* was to become the most beloved and famous ballet ever created. Often, the "most famous" of anything is viewed by insiders as merely commercial, but *Swan Lake* has garnered the utmost respect and status within the dance world, where it is universally hailed as a masterpiece. The Principal roles are taken on with pride, care, and passion to meet its demands. Odette, the white swan that the prince falls in love with, is considered the ultimate role for a ballerina. It is also the hardest. I have seen all the ballerinas with whom I have danced *Swan Lake* in a frenzy of nerves before the curtain goes up. Dancing its difficult roles is as rewarding as it is challenging.

Now I was going to dance those steps to that music and become a part of its history. I felt ready for the challenge, trusting that Kevin wouldn't have given it to me if he felt I wasn't up to it. But I needed every bit of physical and mental strength I could muster. That is why, with the pressure of the past and the demands of the present, doubt seeped in and dominated my psyche.

MY DEBUT WAS scheduled as a double debut; I would be partnering Michele, who had never performed *Swan Lake*'s taxing female double role of Odette-Odile.

Our show was a children's matinee in Chicago. Though we would be taught the entire ballet in rehearsal, at the matinee we'd be dancing a shorter version designed to hold the kids' attention. Nevertheless, this matinee was my first chance to portray a character whose task it was to lead the ballet through four acts, from the very beginning to that final suicidal jump off the cliff that sends him to his death with his swan queen.

I immersed myself for months with my coach, Guillaume Graffin, a former ABT Principal and, prior to that, a protégé of Rudolf Nureyev during the historically significant years when Nureyev was the director of the Paris Opera Ballet. Guillaume is a deeply insightful artist, and was an exceptionally refined and romantic dancer. Fluent in many languages, he has thorough knowledge of dance, music, literature, art, and philosophy. He is one of the few truly analytical artists in the world of ballet. All of that suffused his coaching and allowed him to offer many insightful shadings of Siegfried's character.

The great classical roles like Siegfried have been passed down since the nineteenth century from one dancer to the next. Generation to generation. There is a beauty in that tradition. An artist who has danced Siegfried, as Guillaume did, will teach it to someone like me through words, ideas, and physical demonstrations.

He also learned the role from someone who danced it; this chain extends all the way back to Pavel Gerdt, who, in 1895, was the very first to perform the Petipa/Ivanov version that every *Swan Lake* since has been based on.

Ballet is essentially movement and expression. To create a complete character you need someone who can explain all the nuances and shadings that they themselves have worked out. That's why it's so important to have the right coach passing this information on to you.

When I was a student, Mr. Han told me what to do: how to stand, where to look, what to emote, when to emote, when to catch my breath, where to place my finger. When students become professionals in a ballet company, we have the same sort of dependence on our coaches. A good coach leads you in the right direction technically and artistically. But there are also coaches who don't have the dancer's best interests at heart. Coaches are always former dancers, some of whom had huge careers but sadly never get over the glory of being onstage and the feeling of being a star. In the studio, such a coach can be more interested in nurturing his or her own ego than in nurturing the dancer, and will deliver belittling corrections and critiques geared primarily toward bringing the dancer down while building the coach up. Dancers are vulnerable in the studio as they present what is at that moment their best work. Some coaches take advantage of that and chip away at a dancer's confidence.

Guillaume's sole concern was the dancer. I was lucky to have him in my first years with ABT. He guided me through the first important and formative steps of my professional career. He thought only of the work. He pushed me just as Mr. Han had, accepting no excuses but elevating me closer to my ideal potential. He didn't have patience for lazy or relentlessly insecure dancers. He could be very short-tempered at times. Blowouts would ensue if a dancer had an attitude. Some couldn't handle his bluntness.

He thrived on a good fight because he wasn't afraid of the truth. He expected those who worked with him to not fear it either. He gave me what I have craved and needed throughout my career: brutal truth, even when it hurt.

I would rather a coach tell me that my show was horrible than just give air kisses and insincere congratulations. When a dancer cannot hear the truth, he or she ceases to grow as an artist.

ALWAYS, WHEN DISCOVERING a new work of such complexity, the process is arduous and long but begins with simply learning the steps.

There are many different versions of the great classical ballets. I would be dancing Kevin's new reworking of the classic, strongly based on the 1895 work created by Marius Petipa, Premier Ballet Master of Russia's Imperial Theatre, and by his assistant, Lev Ivanov, who choreographed *Swan Lake*'s second and fourth acts, known as the White Acts because they feature the swans.

It is so vital to approach each move in the right way: slowly, with sufficient time to absorb the myriad technicalities. This can and should take months. If it's hurried, bad habits seep in and quality suffers. The steps look hollow and lack meaning, the performance lacks texture. The more deeply dancers work on debut roles, the stronger are the roots that ground them. You build on those roots throughout your entire career, enhancing your performance—or so one hopes—each time you dance that ballet.

Once you have learned the steps, absorbing them one by one in the mind and body, there comes the far more difficult and time-consuming process of developing them, finding the flow of a work, the nuances, the refinement. Through the rehearsal process, you work on achieving a performance level and summoning the necessary degree of stamina, which differs from one ballet to the next. Guillaume taught me when to push hard and when to save energy. He told me that if I gave 100 percent the whole time, I would run out of steam by the end of the first act and wouldn't have energy to finish the four-act ballet. I had to pace myself, establish the character at the start and build from there. The audience should see an arc in the interpretation, not the same shading during all four acts.

I am often asked how I remember all the steps in a ballet like *Swan Lake*. But remembering is the simplest aspect, largely because dancers have kinesthetic memory; when we see a series of movements we can immediately replicate them. The challenge lies in the way you dance the steps and put them together. What do you personally do with those classic movements? How do you make a ballet danced for centuries your own? The answers to these questions will determine whether yours is a character with depth or a hollow, vapid interpretation. They are questions I continued to ask for years.

SOME DANCERS WALK into their first rehearsals with an idea of how they want to interpret a role. For example, they take some aspects they like from dancers they've observed or they have ideas about how they want to dance a certain variation. I admire people who have that conviction, but I have never been one of them. I enter with nothing. When I began to work privately with Guillaume, I was too young and too naive to comprehend the feelings of Siegfried. The ballet revolves around his search for love. He yearns for true feeling, honest emotion. He doesn't know what that is, exactly; he simply knows that he feels a certain emptiness. His first true feeling comes to him when he sees a vision of perfection in the form of a beautiful swan at a lake in the woods. He throws caution away and experiences deep and impassioned love.

These are difficult emotions to convey, especially through mime and dance, and in rehearsals, my portrayal was only surface and frantic nervous energy. I just wanted to get through each scene, dance well, not screw up, and somehow make my partner happy (which of course I was struggling with). I needed to learn how to use my body to express emotion, how to gesture in mime in a way that made sense to the audience and appeared natural. It was a struggle to control myself physically, and sometimes the last thing on my mind was finding the depth and nuance of my character. The steps and partnering were difficult enough.

I WOULD ASK Guillaume repeatedly about certain steps or nuances. Anything that could be improved. He would give me a number of choices and I would then decide what I thought was right for me. He never told me that there was only one way to do it. At times he told me to leave it alone; that it was good enough and I could move on. I learned that I could trust what he told me. He had a sharp, clear eye and always meant what he said.

One of the key stylistic nuances he taught me is that a ballet set in the Middle Ages requires particular manners and a particular carriage of the body. You can't act as we do today. The connection between partners can't look too familiar. It must retain the formality of an era when class distinctions and modesty between the sexes were of paramount importance. Certain gestures can look too casual or too feminine. The roles of man and woman are not merely traditional but also archaic. This isn't to say that these ballets are not modern. The gestures may be of a certain era, but the human emotions are timeless. Love. Loss. Betrayal. The responsibility is then ours to portray those emotions honestly.

It is through that honesty that audiences can connect with a ballet set in a completely different time.

*　　*　　*

AS GUILLAUME TAUGHT me the role, he explained who Siegfried is. I had assumed that Siegfried was a two-dimensional prince, the balletic version of a Disney character. But Guillaume revealed the complex undercurrents of Siegfried's psyche. He had probed them when he danced the Prince, and required that I do the same. He asked, for example, what I thought the Prince's Queen Mother represented. I answered feebly that she is a mother figure who tells Siegfried that, at his upcoming birthday celebration, he needs to choose a bride. But Guillaume took me deeper into Siegfried, explaining that the Queen represents responsibility, and Siegfried subconsciously despises her because she embodies the life that he hates: a life of privilege, money, opportunity, ease. Responsibility but no real substance. The Prince wants more, Guillaume explained. He wants to feel alive and experience things that have nothing to do with privilege or a caste system. He craves a raw, unabashed love. And here is the Queen Mother, reminding him of his dreary and loathsome duties as Prince. She wants him to be exactly what he was born to be. He wants the complete opposite: to be a free soul. As he begins to realize the demanding pressures he was born to, he becomes ever so slightly aware of his hatred for his mother. And so, on the eve of his birthday, when his mother reminds him that he must choose a royal bride the next day, he flees. He runs away to the lake, away from responsibility. This is the kind of psychological explanation I would get from Guillaume. Not only about the Queen Mother, but also about the adherence to long-established rules that the Prince's tutor symbolizes, about the frivolity of his closest friends. And, above all, about Siegfried's yearning for the swan who embodies the promise of true love.

For Guillaume each step had meaning. Even the smallest gesture was a mirror into Siegfried's soul. He gave me the intellectual nourishment I needed to plumb the depths of Siegfried's character, not just for that abridged performance but so that I could continue to find new meaning as I matured in years to come.

MICHELE AND I worked on the *Swan Lake* partnering in the studio with Kevin. The patience and generosity that make for a good partnership were rare between us though I felt I tried to provide them. Nothing was ever verbalized. We didn't fight. It was simply clear to me how uncomfortable she was.

Increasingly, I began to dread my time in the studio with her. I was constantly walking on eggshells and repeatedly being told that my best attempts at partnering weren't working. I was absolutely deferential to her requests. The more she dominated, the more I stood down.

She barely spoke to me before and after rehearsals, just a quick hello before we started. We never joked or chatted. We were awkward around each other. I didn't know what to say or do.

Even after we had been rehearsing for months, each time I saw our names together on the rehearsal schedule my heart would drop and beat faster. As time passed, I felt like she regarded me less as her partner and more as an annoyance she had to tolerate. There were other men in the company, more experienced as partners, whom I knew she preferred. When I would see her dance with them, she was a different person. She smiled. Laughed. Joked. Looked comfortable in their hands. Between us, there was unbearable tension.

I went to Guillaume for guidance. I was at a loss as to how to handle her or myself. He had seen the woeful dynamics of our relationship firsthand and told me, "You must stand up for yourself. That's the only way you'll be able to move forward and balance the partnership out."

I knew he was right. But somehow I didn't have the courage. Both Michele and I avoided confrontation at all costs. And so our partnership staggered along, with the same imbalance.

*   *   *

IN BALLET, THE divide between artistry and technique can be a chasm. Artistry connotes the dramatic and emotional values you bring to a role; technique is concerned with the quality and level of your dancing.

What makes classical ballet so challenging is that you must dance the steps precisely as they are meant to be danced. The steps can be altered by the choreographer, or even by the person staging the ballet. Or you can have input when a new ballet is being created. But with an existing work, the steps are rarely changed by the dancer.

You become a part of the history by adhering to this entrenched custom. If a step doesn't look right on you, if you can't do it well, your only choice is to work on it.

At the beginning of my career, I perceived certain ballet traditions as a form of rigidity. There is a box, and you are expected to soar to great heights within that box. The first box I questioned was *Swan Lake*. I was driven to dance it well, but found no intense personal feeling in what I danced. I was who people told me to be and, more significantly, who I thought I should be. From my first foray into Siegfried, and for years to come, I would walk, act, and dance around the stage with an unnatural aplomb. It was my attempt at doing it "the way it had always been done."

I tried too hard to conjure the feelings of a prince. I forced my emotions. Guillaume continually encouraged me to relax and be myself.

"You don't have to act the Prince. You already look like the Prince. So just stand there. Feel the weight of stillness and what that can mean. Do nothing. Just be."

I didn't believe him. I felt like I had to be doing something. Whether I was moving my arms, shifting side to side, even cocking my head a certain way. What I didn't understand was that the dancers who had excelled as Siegfried had found the character through simple and basic emotional honesty. Erik Bruhn, Rudolf Nureyev, and Anthony Dowell each filtered the Prince through their own unique personality. In fact, Guillaume was right: I just had to be. But I lost my true self in my perception of the rigidity of history and what I thought my place in it should be. Physically I executed. I didn't embody. It's the difference between doing the steps and being the steps—a crucial distinction that separates the good artists from the transformative ones.

I BARELY REMEMBER that first *Swan Lake* performance. The show was a blur of nerves and doubt. Beyond the point of no return, once the overture started, I charged full steam ahead and tried my best not to mess up, miss a lift, or fall. Although adrenaline propelled me forward, I wasn't completely present in the moment. I went through the actions and movements that I had rehearsed so thoroughly with Guillaume, Kevin, and Michele as if on autopilot. I tried to shine, but the sheer shock of it all overrode any natural feelings of deep character or connection. Nor did I have the confidence to take risks. I just didn't want to fail. I gave up the idea of trying to soar in the moment. All I cared about was getting through it.

The performance seemed to fly by in an instant. Nothing catastrophic happened. And most important, no missed lifts with Michele. As we took our final bows I felt shell-shocked from what had just happened. I think she felt the same.

Any lead couple dancing Principal roles follows an elaborate, traditional protocol for bows. Although the show is over, the bows are just as choreographed as the performance. The male dancer presents his ballerina, moving her forward and then taking a few steps back, ceding to her the closest proximity to the audience. After she slowly bows, you come together again, then separate and bow to each other, essentially thanking each other for the performance. During our bows for *Swan Lake,* that mutual acknowledgment, which is meant to be heartfelt and gracious, wasn't particularly genuine. I knew I hadn't lived up to expectations, not my own or Michele's. Though I hadn't missed any lifts I had struggled with some of them; they looked strained and laborious. The partnering as a whole lacked finesse. I certainly had tried my best, but I knew it wasn't good enough.

After the curtain came down, Kevin and Guillaume walked onto the stage. I have always been able to tell when Kevin truly enjoyed the show and when he thought it was just adequate. Although I had conquered my first full-length ballet, it was lacking in the polish that would come with years of dancing it. So while there was the celebration of having gotten my first *Swan* under my belt, it was evident to us all, without anything needing to be said, that I had a lot of work ahead of me. Especially when it came to partnering.

"You have to start somewhere," I kept assuring myself.

CHAPTER 12

Despite our mutual antipathy, Michele and I went on to dance many more ballets together: Petipa's *Raymonda*, George Balanchine's *Ballo della Regina*. It was rarely enjoyable and she continued to make clear to me how uncomfortable she was. It was consistently humiliating. I could, at times, understand her frustration, considering that before I danced with her I'd had no concept of leading the woman in a pas de deux and taking control of the partnership. I would watch her dance with stronger, more experienced men and try to learn from them. What was so hard for me to absorb seemed to come so easily to them.

In time, I danced more and more with other women in the company, and although I still needed to improve, I had a different rapport with them. It flowed. We would banter back and forth. They seemed to accept my shortcomings and were happy to dance with me. Above all, they treated me with equal respect.

My inexperience as a partner was handled most patiently by Julie Kent, an American ballerina and an artist of extreme integrity and delicacy, who influenced a generation of dancers around the world.

Julie was in the prime of her career, and a ballerina at her peak would normally insist on a male partner who had the experience to match hers. But when Robert Hill wanted me to dance the role of Dorian, in his ballet based on the Oscar Wilde novel *The Picture of Dorian Gray,* he proposed to Julie that I partner her for the premiere. Surprisingly, she agreed. When we began, I was in a stress-induced sweat knowing I was dancing with such a legend. Robert was a former ABT dancer with great partnering skills, who would toss women around with no great effort. As he created the pas with Julie and me, I tried to keep my head above water. The partnering was at a level I had never attempted before. But Julie never faltered or lost her calm, gently letting me know precisely what she needed from me.

"Hold my hips, not my waist."

"Put me more over my supporting leg, and less hanging off it."

She always began her requests with "David, could you please . . ." or "I'd love it if you could . . ."

I was the same partner with Julie as I was with Michele, trying my absolute best to accommodate and be forthright about my shortcomings. I wasn't an ideal fit for Julie at that time in my career, but her response to my lack of experience was entirely nurturing and constructive. Dancing with her wasn't only an honor; it was a joy.

Another ballerina I began partnering early on was Gillian Murphy, a young dancer of brilliant ease and clarity whose technical prowess had begun to awe both audiences and other dancers. When I entered the company, Gillian had just become ABT's newest Principal, and in a year's time, we were making numerous debuts together. She was my first ballerina in Balanchine's *Theme and Variations.* I was her first Romeo. Alexei Ratmansky created his *Nutcracker* on us. Together we discovered the constrictive world of *Pillar of Fire.*

In countless rehearsals and performances, I watched Gillian from the wings or in the studio and marveled at the unforced nature of her talent. She took everything in stride, never crumpling in a pool of tears the way some dancers did but laughing things off if they didn't work. She was always the first to make fun of herself. After performances, sweat-stained and wiping off what remained of our makeup, we would debrief in one of our dressing rooms, still feeling the adrenaline buzz. Because we were so deeply rooted as friends, when things went wrong I never blamed her and she never blamed me, and we were able to laugh about what didn't work as well as we had hoped. We adored and respected each other, and the simple, natural rapport between us was something that I didn't feel with anyone else. There was a balance between the two of us. An ease.

But no matter how much I tried and no matter how much I improved, I never had any rapport with Michele. We certainly kept trying our best to make things work, given that we had to dance together. A couple of years into our partnership we met one day to air our grievances. At last we were finally being honest. She said that at times she felt I worried only about myself. I told her yes, of course I worried about myself—we were both young and ambitious and eager to make our mark. But I was, and had always been, more worried about pleasing her and making her feel comfortable. I explained that I needed her to treat me with more respect and to give me just a little room for error. I was absorbing how best to partner her and this took time and patience.

We both agreed to try to alter our approaches when working together. There was no right or wrong. Not one person better than the other. We would both work on smoothing out the rough edges. And for a time it worked. We would try to verbalize our issues in the studio the moment they arose, being extremely careful about how to best articulate the problem. But dancing together remained a constant struggle because, ultimately, nothing we said changed anything. We simply couldn't meet on the same level. Once again, I was on one side of the studio and she was on the other.

*   *   *

GEORGE BALANCHINE'S *Theme and Variations* is among the most challenging of his many difficult creations. What you accomplish technically in four acts of other ballets, you do in the thirty minutes of *Theme*. I learned the first movement at the ABT Summer Intensive when I was sixteen years old. It gave me a small glimpse of what was to come. To dance the lead role in its entirety is another beast altogether. *Theme* is a rite of passage at ABT. I've heard it said that Mikhail Baryshnikov deemed it harder than any full-length ballet.

Theme's virtuosic steps demand perfect execution, with an ease of style but at whiplash speed; even the slightest error of timing or balance is obvious to the audience. Both the man and the woman begin with incredibly rigorous variations (the term used to denote a solo). The second male variation is the true test: a consecutive series of seven double tours en l'air, each followed by a single (or at times double) pirouette, until the end of the solo. When executed perfectly, it is the type of sequence that causes the audience to roar with approval. If you're even slightly off, you end up popping around the stage like a kernel of corn in hot oil. This was always the most stress-inducing part for me. I imagined the worst and rarely met the required lofty standard. As I jumped around in the middle section, with the music building to that series of tours, I waged an internal war between confidence and doubt.

It's nothing, just do it.

No! It's impossible. I'll never be able to do it.

Use your plié.

Go easy.

Don't pop the pirouette. Use it as a preparation.

At times I gritted through it, just making it by the skin of my teeth. After the solos, in the pas de deux, both lead dancers slowly descend into fatigue. I was glad to have danced my first *Theme* with Gillian. She made this epic test of a ballet seem a bit easier.

FOUR YEARS INTO our partnership, Michele and I were rehearsing *Theme* for ABT's spring season at the Metropolitan Opera House. By that point, we had danced it together many times, but we still approached the ballet with the intensity and focus of dancers who had never done it before. The entire company packed into Studio 1 for a final run-through, a rehearsal where, even if certain steps didn't work, we pushed on, simulating a live performance. With the eyes of all your colleagues on you, up close in the studio, these run-throughs can be more stressful than the actual performance.

We started the ballet like any other run-through, a mixture of nerves and confidence. I danced my variation. She danced hers. I danced my second variation. She followed. Audibly puffing, we finally met in the pas de deux. Just after the start, Michele began fidgeting when I would partner her, as if she was extremely uncomfortable. When a ballerina on pointe is off her leg and wants her partner to put her back on her plumb line, she shakes her hips as if to adjust back on pointe on her own. It's a universally understood nonverbal signal that speaks volumes to the partner. She's saying, *I'm not on my leg, dammit. And I'm going to prove it.*

It's a rude and inconsiderate gesture. I would have much preferred her to simply say, "Could you get me farther back on my leg?"

Michele shook her hips a number of times. She then stopped dancing altogether, merely walking through some of the steps as the music continued and I stood behind her trying to press on. She was blatantly demonstrating to the company how uncomfortable she was dancing with me. The pas de deux runs five minutes, and for those entire five minutes the company looked on in shock. You could feel the tension in the room. Here was the perfect picture of

111

our partnership for all to see. Passive-aggressive behavior devolving into a complete lack of any decent working relationship. We continued with the pas, dancing some steps but walking around marking for most of it. My blood boiled. The pressure cooker was bursting. I could feel it. I was silently enraged, humiliated, bewildered. When we finished the pas, no one applauded as they ordinarily would. The room was embarrassingly silent. The company joined us in the finale and we finished the ballet but something had clicked for me. I had hit my breaking point. I had been patient; I had made myself a better partner through the force of will and fear; we had tried to create a more harmonious relationship. But all that amounted to was this: a display of what it truly meant to her. Our partnership could never evolve.

Afterward the ballet masters tried to skirt around the problem by giving us their corrections. There was everything to say about what had just happened but nothing to be said at the same time.

When they left the studio, Michele turned to me and said, "It was okay . . . I thought." She looked at me blankly. I could sense an apologetic tone in her voice, as if she knew she had gone too far. I stared back at her, lost in shock.

"It was not okay," I said. "It was horrible. You humiliated me."

I didn't even look to see if there were still dancers in the room, though I later realized that everyone was there, awkwardly listening in on what we were saying. In the moment, I was so enraged I didn't notice. We walked over to the side of the rehearsal studio. I addressed her in a hushed but direct tone.

"I've had it," I told her. "Years of disrespect and this fight to make things work are over. You clearly don't want to dance with me and I have tried everything I could to make you as comfortable as I can. But then you come into this rehearsal and belittle me in front of everyone."

She just stood there, wide-eyed and frozen.

I was furious. It takes a huge amount of build-up before I lose it (in this case years), but when I finally break my anger goes beyond the point of no return.

"If you don't want to dance with me, then, fine, that's perfectly all right," I continued. "I want to dance with a woman who does. You can put all the blame on me. I don't care. I will accept full responsibility. I'm finished being treated this way."

AFTER OUR CONFRONTATION, I went on with my day, knowing that Kevin would hear about it eventually. I felt no need to run into his office and explain my side of the story. I was certain about how I felt. Later in the day I had a rehearsal with him alone. He walked in and immediately said, "I know everything. You don't have to explain it."

Kevin is levelheaded in heated moments. He thinks rationally when no one else is doing so. There was no way around the fact that Michele and I had to dance together in the Met season, which would begin in a week's time. Casting had already been announced and it was too late to make any changes and switch dancers around. I understood the situation, so we got on with it. Michele and I came to terms with dancing the few works we were scheduled to perform together. Those performances and the rehearsals for them were focused, cold, efficient, impersonal. We clocked in and we clocked out. We did what we needed to do to get the shows on.

It was a terribly disappointing outcome for both of us. And now that I have much more appreciation for the ruthless role that time plays in a dancer's life, I wish we had been able to enjoy dancing together and to reap far more positive benefits from all the work we put in. I walked away feeling that I did my best. I did know, too, that a more experienced dancer would have done better. But, at the end of the day, as in any part of life, you don't vibe with everyone. And Michele and I didn't vibe.

Now, after many years, I've honed the skills to make my partners happier. It's not lost on me that, to a large extent, I have Michele to thank for that. Through my fear of her and my desperation to make her content and comfortable, I willed myself to become a good partner. It was the fear, I feel, that produced the best results. During our four years of tribulations I was forced to work harder and become more studiously attentive than I might otherwise have been. Once again, as in Paris, my greatest learning was through struggle.

CHAPTER 13

If a ballet dancer's goal is to become a Principal in the topmost rank of dancers, he or she must remain committed and patient and accept that any ascension is gradual: occasional small roles lead to frequent featured roles and then to some major ones. In other words, it takes a long while—if it ever occurs—to do what the Principals do, which is to dance leading roles all the time. One usually waits a number of years to be promoted to the next level; sometimes that promotion never comes. It happens differently for everyone. I spent three years in the Corps, all the while wanting to be a Soloist. When I was promoted to Soloist, I was obsessed with finally becoming a Principal. I was always seeking what I hadn't yet achieved.

With the goal of becoming a Principal in mind, I immersed myself in each opportunity Kevin afforded me, working tirelessly on role after role as I sought to prove to him that I was prepared to handle the responsibilities the coveted title of Principal entailed. Each role, whether standing center stage or on the side amid the group, was a part of my progression. I couldn't have danced a Principal role without first mastering the building blocks that Kevin deemed necessary. I needed every step.

*   *   *

IN 2006, TWO years after my promotion to Soloist, the company made its annual tour to Costa Mesa, California, to dance at the theater known today as the Segerstrom Center for the Arts. In this series of performances, I was making major debuts in two beautiful ballets: Sir Frederick Ashton's *Sylvia*, a very stylized ballet created originally in 1876 and reworked by Ashton in 1952 for Dame Margot Fonteyn, and George Balanchine's *Apollo*, a ballet whose title role is another of those precious rites of passage for a male dancer, and one I had dreamed of dancing for years.

Choreographed in 1928 with a score by Igor Stravinsky, it depicts the journey of the young god of music, Apollo, from boyhood to adulthood, aided by the inspiration of three muses who represent poetry, mime, and dance.

A long line of male dancers have tackled this role, most prominently Baryshnikov, Peter Martins, and Serge Lifar, on whom it was created. It's a stunning showcase for a leading male. I was taught the bulk of the role by one of Balanchine's "great Danes," Ib Andersen, who had learned it from Balanchine himself. This was a true example of the art being passed down from generations. Balanchine created it. Ib learned it from him. And twenty-three years after Balanchine's death, Ib taught it to me.

Ib explained each movement and its imagery. The first step: arms moving from down by the hips to high above the head, hands outstretched as if "pushing the weight of the world in your hands." The sous-sous: with hands crossed in an angular, birdlike way just above the head, "like an eagle spreading its wings." He told me how a series of kicks side to side is like "a soccer player kicking a ball back and forth."

There are no virtuosic steps in *Apollo*. But the entire work can be virtuosic if approached with the right style, which is to create movement with purpose and substance. I had found that to be true in all of Balanchine's ballets. It was never just ballet as technique, which is at times (in my generation of dancers) mistaken for enough. But with Balanchine's works, even if the ballet is technically virtuosic (like *Theme and Variations*), it's always choreographed so musically that it reads as movement and not just as empty steps.

In one of the most beautiful parts of the ballet, after Apollo exhausts himself by dancing alone, the three muses, each clad in a pristine white pleated dance skirt, simultaneously clap their hands, then offer their hands as a pillow for him to rest his head. He is weary and winded. Four chords sound, each one a brief moment apart giving Apollo an instant to raise his head just slightly off their hands. Chord. Head. Chord. Head. One by one. On the final chord he raises his hand in the air as if reaching to his father high above the skies. In the apotheosis, Apollo is summoned into ascension, to Parnassus, by his father, Zeus. Balanchine said that this is the point in the ballet when Apollo "hears his father calling."

There is very little to do technically, but the stillness and simplistic movement communicate in an enormous way. That is the purity of *Apollo*: so much depth behind each and every note and movement. Stravinsky and Balanchine created a masterpiece.

I had just scratched the surface with my first *Apollo*. Each time I have danced it since then I have discovered some new avenue that allows me to explore his character more deeply than before.

THE MORNING AFTER my initial performance, with the buzz of a premiere settling into deep fatigue, a meeting was scheduled for the entire company after daily class. I schlepped into a small room in the theater with the other dancers, anticipating the usual details of an upcoming tour or other administrative logistics. Kevin opened the meeting. "Well, there isn't really anything else on the agenda except that I would like you all to help me congratulate David Hallberg on becoming the newest Principal of ABT."

In an instant, the room exploded with applause. All eyes shot over to me, at the back of the studio, where I had been hunched over wearily in my postclass sweat. There were beaming smiles everywhere. I was stunned.

It is a moment one never forgets. As if it were a movie flickering before my eyes, I envisioned the years of training in Phoenix, of nurturing a dream, and the endless work and focus that had gone into achieving goal after goal. Debut after debut. And so that very moment I'd always dreamed of had arrived, in the same theater where I saw ABT perform for the first time when I was sixteen years old. I sat there, looking around the room, awestruck and speechless. I could hardly take it in. I had done it. From obsessing over other dancers who had attained Principal status—Angel, Ethan, Vladimir—it had become a reality for me. With American Ballet Theatre. One never knows how one will react when a dream is realized. My subdued reaction surprised me and was purely shock. Internally I was screaming at the top of my lungs.

Kevin came over to me and gave me a huge embrace. He had worked for this as much as I had. He had guided me, had been patient with my shortcomings and had nurtured me for years. He took his time and had given me opportunities when I was ready. He gave me room to fail, never pushing me too fast. I will always be grateful to him for his patience and watchful eye.

LATER THAT DAY I called Guillaume to tell him the news. He had left ABT the year before to be a ballet master at Dutch National Ballet. I'll never forget what he told me.

"Now is when the real work starts."

He was absolutely right.

CHAPTER 14

I t seemed to me then that there was nowhere higher to climb. My first two years of being a Principal were intoxicating. I added more classical and contemporary work to my list of roles and each one was either a new challenge or a milestone. I wanted to make my performances consistently better, find a continual flow of inspiration, and give the audience something worthwhile to watch.

Each new ballet required my full strength and attention and demanded that I maintain the highest degree of stamina and tenacity. If not, my work would suffer. Each role consisted of virtuosic steps created in the nineteenth century. I was never at ease with what they required of me. I needed intense bursts of energy for Albrecht in *Giselle*, cleanliness and regality for Prince Désiré in *The Sleeping Beauty*, and masculine weight for the warrior Solor in *La Bayadère*.

As much as I loved dancing these illustrious ballets (and as much as they challenged me), I struggled to find an individuality in these roles, just as I had when dancing Siegfried.

People had set ideas as to how I should perform each role. I heard a lot of "Do this." "Not like that." "That looks wrong." "This is right." "That's too much." "It's not enough." There was always the specter of those who had danced the role before, and usually better than yourself. You are told, "The greatest Prince

119

in *Swan Lake* was Erik Bruhn." "The greatest Solor in *La Bayadère* was Irek Mukhamedov."

There are dancers who are always evolving in the classics. Every rehearsal and performance seems as fresh as when they first danced it. I have watched in awe as they consistently plow through the same variation over and over with the same full commitment as in months or years past. I envied that drive to keep fresh what has been done before countless times.

But for me, when the reverence for such important works faded a bit and the excitement of dancing these roles dimmed, I was left to find something of meaning and value in works that existed scores of years before I did.

I never believed there is only one way to dance a role or that there is some particular way that is the gold standard. That's why art is subjective, and why certain interpretations can be so controversial without being wrong. And I was convinced that I couldn't make my mark on these roles with the weight of the past on my shoulders. I felt like I was just carrying the history of ballet forward, doing my part to maintain the traditions of the work. Like a prop doll, almost. Consistently, I found myself wondering how to break free of the chains that felt so confining.

I was primarily cast as the Prince. A prince is regal. At times disconnected. And stiff. Usually looking for a life outside his own. I had a hard time relating to this man. Who was I in these roles? I didn't feel like my true self as an artist. I felt like an interpreter. Or an imposter.

WHEN INSPIRATION FADES, an artist naturally looks for new sources of interest and stimulation. I began to explore an artistic world that existed outside of classical ballet. I ventured to small theaters in New York City like Judson Church and The Kitchen. I found a community of choreographers who created work that blurred the boundaries between modern dance, visual art, music, and theater. Their work was different from anything presented on the stages that I danced on. I had been sweating away in the ballet studio for years, deeply embedded in the beauty of that art form, when all this was happening in the same city. After a day's rehearsals I would rush off by myself to a performance that bore little or no relation to my everyday work. The doors of creative inspiration flew open and I dove headfirst into educating myself. The audience was a different crowd altogether, who rarely, I soon learned, went to see anything "uptown." "Uptown" was Lincoln Center, where I danced. "Downtown" was the community I was growing to love, appreciate, and find nourishment in. I would view these works and think about how I could incorporate this new, foreign environment into the one I directly inhabited. Was there anything in it that I could use to push my own art form further along? Because more and more I questioned the ballets I danced. Compared to this new sphere of work I viewed so enthusiastically, I found them lacking relevance for my generation. Watching the work of these choreographers turned my ideas of performance in a completely different direction.

Lar Lubovitch, a choreographer with a deep respect for ballet and modern work alike, knew of my budding interest in other forms of dance and asked me one day what was to be my first ballet for the Met season.

"Oh, just another *Swan Lake*," I told him.

He looked at me in shock and snapped back, "Don't ever undermine your art form like that. Your art form is just as important as any others. One is not better than another."

I didn't understand it then, but he was absolutely right.

I WAS NOT the only person who saw the traditional world of ballet and the world of modern, experimental dance as two entirely

121

separate spheres. On the rare occasion that anyone recognized me, they would ask in disbelief what I was doing there. Why would someone from the ballet world come to the downtown dance scene? I was shocked by this closed-mindedness. Why *wouldn't* I be there? Art is art, regardless of where it is presented. It seemed that members of each camp viewed the other with mockery. One evening, after a long day of rehearsals, deep in the creative process for Alexei Ratmansky's new *Nutcracker*, I sat in a downtown theater next to a well-respected choreographer. She asked me what I was doing now at ABT.

"*Nutcracker*," I told her.

She laughed. "Figures," she said dryly.

On the flip side, I became known at ABT as the one who goes to see "the weird stuff."

I TRIED MANY times to forge connections with choreographers who deeply inspired me, hoping for a mutually beneficial collaboration or simply a dialogue. My efforts were usually met with disinterest. One exception was Jérôme Bel, a choreographer once described as "the naughty French *philosophe* of contemporary dance." Jérôme is an original: intellectual, inquisitive, provocative, and comical. His work changed the way I thought about how dance is presented onstage.

I first heard of Jérôme after he created a piece for the Paris Opera Ballet. *Véronique Doisneau* is an eponymous solo work for the then forty-two-year-old retiring Sujet in the company (the term "Sujet" meaning a dancer who is two rankings below the highest rank of Étoile). Jérôme stripped away all that defined the Paris Opera Ballet (the hierarchy, the set and costumes, the glamour) and created a verbal narrative work about Véronique's career on the picturesque Garnier stage. Speaking directly to the audience, wearing plain rehearsal clothes, she explains (and at times dances) what it felt like to be in the company as a Sujet. Her greatest moments. The roles she always wanted to dance. The roles she hated most. All in brutal honesty. She describes what she did before and during the White Swan pas de deux in *Swan Lake*, known as the Love Duet, which is performed by the "star" dancers.

"One of the most beautiful things in classical ballet," she tells the audience, "is the scene where thirty-two female dancers of the Corps de Ballet dance together. But in this scene, there are long moments of immobility, the 'poses.' We become a human decor to highlight the 'stars.' And for us it is the most horrible thing we do. Myself for example, I want to scream or even leave the stage."

Then, to the music for the pas de deux, she shows the audience exactly what she does during one of the most revered passages in classical ballet. She stands there, moving minimally at times, throughout it. Jérôme has the audience watch the entire seven minutes of motionless poses. Her demonstration showed me a completely different way of looking at ballet. It wasn't just that ballet isn't always beautiful and weightless. This pas de deux can be seen from a different perspective by someone in the same scene. Boiled down. Shown in its rawest form. Watching this on DVD in my apartment, I was moved to tears. It broke down all barriers of what is considered performance.

AFTER WATCHING THE film, I immediately sent Jérôme an email through his website explaining how much his work moved me and forced me to reconsider my own thoughts of dance. I expected nothing back. I had a response from him within two hours.

How does a dancer from ABT know my work, he wrote, *and why are you even interested in it?*

I'm curious about other ways of presenting dance, I wrote back, *and your work has changed my perspective.*

At the end of the email I mentioned that if he ever had an interest in working with me or even discussing doing so, I would visit him in a heartbeat.

THAT INITIAL EXCHANGE began a year-and-a-half-long collaboration. I flew to meet him for the first time at the Walker Art Center in Minneapolis. He could sense my lack of fulfillment. A discontentment with the world I inhabited. Why else would I be searching outside its boundaries? We decided to work together on what would be a deconstruction of my career thus far, detailing my interests, my challenges, my critiques. We would present these issues to the audience in a narrative form, along the lines of *Véronique Doisneau*. I couldn't wait to get started and hear his ideas about the world I loved and respected—but questioned all the same.

WE WORKED DURING intermittent free moments in our individual schedules. I flew to Paris. He flew to New York. Trip by trip we ironed out the structure of the piece and eventually created a very strong body of work. We spent our days mulling over the timing and pace. I felt pushed beyond my comfort zone. Each time I rehearsed, I found more honesty as I verbalized my critique of my own place in the ballet world. I talked about dancing the same pieces over and over again, about my inability to find my true self in characters created in the nineteenth century, about my longing to be a creator rather than an interpreter.

"There isn't enough conflict," Jérôme suddenly stated one day, after a run-through in Paris of the semifinished product. I stared back at him, uncomprehending, having just poured out my rawest emotions in front of him.

He demanded to know, why was I there with him? What was it in the ballet world that I didn't like? And what was I so afraid to say?

I told him that I had said everything I felt: I'd told him about feeling uninspired, insufficiently creative, and confined. I had been totally frank with him. But I could not convince him that I wasn't holding something back.

Jérôme kept probing for more conflict, more angst.

It struck me that he wanted me to denounce this ballet world and the princes I played. I got the feeling that he regarded ballet princes—and, more to the point, those who dance them—as wooden and vapid and overpaid. It seemed that he wanted me to say something along those lines. Which I wouldn't do. I didn't believe it. Yes, I was there with him because of a certain dissatisfaction. But no, I would not denounce the art form that often gave me extreme fulfillment.

OUR PARTING THAT day was tense. We agreed to meet again the next day for lunch, but I knew, after the year and a half of work, that the collaboration had ended. I was devastated. I had had such hopes for it. It pushed me in such an intensely challenging way and made me try to find true answers to questions I continually asked myself. I still admired and respected Jérôme. But now that our connection was bruised I couldn't wait to get out of Paris (once again), to get home. My attempt at reaching farther afield had amounted to nothing. I was left hungry with no new tastes to satisfy my craving. I needed and wanted more.

But as it happened, what I required was right in front of me the entire time. I didn't need to search the world for inspiration. I just needed to practice a little patience. In the form of new partners, I would find what I needed above all: a fresh, personal, deeper sense of purpose in my art form.

CHAPTER 15

I began dancing with Natalia Osipova in 2009. Natasha, as she is known, is petite, dark, mysterious, and private. One never really knows what is going on behind those eyes. She has a unique energy. You feel it the moment you meet her. It's as if there is an idle pilot light within her just waiting for the right moment to blaze to life. I found watching her in the studio or on the stage to be equal parts inspiring and daunting: inspiring to witness the freedom of her expression and movement; daunting to know that if she could find that freedom in classical ballet, I myself had a lot of work and exploration before me.

Natasha was a gymnast as a child, but an injury ended her early hopes. She began taking ballet lessons simply as a physical outlet, though she found it boring and sometimes even amusing. "It was really funny," she once said, "to see boys in those tights."

But the more she danced, the more she enjoyed it. She was eighteen when she was given a contract at the Bolshoi Ballet, despite the harsh opinion of "purists" who insisted she wasn't Bolshoi material. She was brought into the company by Alexei Ratmansky, at the time the Bolshoi's Artistic Director.

The first time I saw her dance was at a gala in New York. She performed the *Flames of Paris* pas de deux with the wunderkind Ivan Vasiliev. Watching from the wings, I thought her style was somewhat brash and too externalized. She was reaching for steps beyond what is asked of a ballerina: more turns in the air, higher jumps, more outward energy. It seemed to me that she lacked care for the purity of the work. But there was no denying the energy coming from within her. And the audience adored her. She excited crowds to a fervor you rarely see.

At the Bolshoi, she climbed quickly up the ranks, seized the attention of the global dance world, and became an astounding dancer and an artist who had to do things in her own way. Not out of stubbornness or rebellion, but from an absolute necessity to express her honest feelings through her dancing and the roles she portrayed.

Controversy ensued when she debuted the role of Giselle at the Bolshoi Theatre. Entrenched balletomanes thought she wasn't the lithe, ethereal Giselle needed for that ballet. That she didn't have the right temperament or physical attributes and couldn't create the harmonious lines or express the fragility required for this iconic role. In other words, she wasn't like the standard set by the ballet world and especially by the Bolshoi's most revered ballerina, Galina Ulanova, the company's prima ballerina in the 1940s and '50s and its most beloved Giselle. But Natasha stood her ground, refusing to imitate her brilliant predecessor and follow (like a proper ballerina) the traditions imposed on her. It was a remarkable stance for a young dancer to take; even then, she knew who she was.

WHEN NATASHA MADE her debut in *Giselle* with American Ballet Theatre, she already had a worldwide reputation. New York balletomanes and ABT dancers had been stunned by videos of her performances, which evinced her excellent Bolshoi training. The movement of her arms came from her back, finishing with soft, unforced hands and fingers. The quality of movement wasn't academic, as some styles of dancing are. It was all about release, pure emotion originating from the core of her body and extending outward, in all directions.

Originally another dancer was scheduled to dance opposite her in the role of Albrecht. But when he fell prey to an unfortunate injury days before her premiere, Kevin asked me to step in.

I WALKED INTO the first rehearsal feeling apprehensive. I thought she would surely out-jump me (she has one of the highest, lightest jumps in ballet). I felt she would certainly overpower me.

I knew we would be mismatched. Physically and emotionally Natasha and I are opposites. She is tempestuous and passionate; I am subtle and restrained.

We looked at each other and smiled as she continued to warm up around the studio, prancing back and forth as if she were preparing for a sprint. She seemed focused, a little nervous. Natasha and I had no common language, as she spoke absolutely no English. I spoke no Russian.

Irina Kolpakova, who had been a legendary ballerina of the Kirov Ballet and then become a ballet mistress at ABT, rehearsed us with Kevin at her side. Natasha and I were both tentative and cautious. With a new partner, there is always a period of feeling each other out. We moved through the steps easily, trying to sense each other's energy. There were certainly no fireworks from the start. It felt studious.

I knew first off that I couldn't rely on the version of Albrecht that I had previously performed. It wouldn't fit with Natasha. She was too different from other ballerinas for me to give her what I had done previously. Therefore I made the decision early on to allow myself to feed off her instincts of character and movement. I couldn't dictate what I would like from her; I had to sense her inclinations and meld them with mine. But time wasn't on our side. We needed to find a certain level of rapport quickly, and, more important, we needed to work out the fundamentals of how we were going to dance together. She had nuances from the Bolshoi version she had danced and I had the ABT version for which Kevin had coached me.

Once we aligned these different versions, we could do nothing but leave the outcome to the universe. I had no expectations about the performance. No feeling that this would be the spark of something more lasting. The performance would either take off and be a memorable experience or it would go in the memory bank alongside other *Giselle* performances, and each of us would go our separate ways, dancing with other partners.

I HAD NONE of my usual preshow nerves leading up to the performance. It was pure excitement. I was a horse chomping at the bit, waiting inside the gate. Usually the familiar doubt and fear and dread would creep in a full day before, especially for an important show like this. The usual *I can't do this. I'm going to fuck this up. I can't handle the pressure. I wish it were just over and done with.*

This time, I had nothing like that roller coaster. There was pure adrenaline pumping through me. I knew the ballet well enough to feel comfortable in it. And I could sense the anticipation from all around. The dancers. The audience. The New York dance world. I could feel the energy of expectation through the closed curtain. The audience was ready, and I was ready for whatever Natasha would throw my way.

In *Giselle,* or any full-length ballet I dance, when the overture starts with the curtain down as other dancers heed the stage manager's call to places, I always stay onstage for a moment alone. It's then that I dive mentally into the performance. I close my eyes, feel the floor with my feet, the perspiration on my forehead. Once I'm calm and present, I open my eyes and view an empty stage. I look at the vast curtain. The sets. The dancers peering onstage or warming up in the wings. The stage manager in the front wing about to signal the opening of the curtain. I feel a rush of adrenaline, and the first sound of the strings propels me into the evening. Always, I remain onstage until the very last moment before the curtain rises. I draw energy from the music, the hushed audience, the story I am about to portray, the ballerina I am about to dance with.

On this occasion, the ballerina and I were on our first date. Anything was possible. The prospect was equally unnerving and arousing.

JUST BEFORE THE curtain went up, I looked apprehensively at Natasha, who was standing in the wings. She seemed preoccupied, disconnected from me as her partner. Understandably nervous. She could certainly feel the anticipation from the audience, the buildup to her debut with ABT. I wondered what would transpire once we got onto the stage together. Would we connect and create something unique, capture the moment and live up to the anticipation? Or would she be too nervous to connect to what I would give her? There was nothing I could do but wait and see.

ALBRECHT COMES ONSTAGE before Giselle. He makes a mad dash down a ramp from the back of the stage with a cloak flowing behind him as he moves to center stage. He is there to woo Giselle, and goes boldly to her house to knock on the door—the famous knocks, choreographed perfectly to the music. The applause upon my entrance was strong. When I first enter for any role that traditionally has "entrance applause," I can always feel whether the audience is primed and ready or a bit lax. That night they were at attention, eager to witness Natasha's brilliance, the applause purposefully direct. The feeling that coursed through me was that enlivening sense of being on the brink of an unknown discovery. I fed off that applause. It energized me, fueling my own anticipation of Natasha's entrance.

At the start of Act I, Albrecht's purpose is to convince the shy country girl Giselle to come outside and dance. After he knocks, he hears her coming and hurries behind the house, hiding from her. In one of the most iconic entrances for the ballerina, Giselle opens the door and steps onstage. Natasha's entrance was greeted by loud, supportive applause. She bounded in a circle, suspending herself in the air looking for whoever was knocking. As she is searching, Albrecht sneaks toward her as she literally bumps into him. The moment we locked eyes, I knew how the whole evening would unfold. Our individual energies bound together. We became a unified breath. She was completely different than in rehearsal. She was vulnerable. Fragile. Yet at the same time, she radiated, like the force of the purring engine of a race car. I felt like I could reciprocate her energy, as opposite as we were. I had no choice but to respond to her presence. All preconceived reactions and thoughts went out the window. It was electric. Even if I wanted to dance the way I always had, I couldn't. Her force was too strong.

So I chose to react. I chose to lose everything I thought I knew about Albrecht and his love for Giselle. I went on the ride with her. Ups and downs. Curves and loops. I surrendered, every bit as enthralled with her as the audience was.

THIS BEING OUR first date, I didn't know how she would react to something I gave her, and she didn't know what my response would be. Our interaction became alive and spontaneous. Even a simple gesture, like when Albrecht asks Giselle to dance with him, created a moment in which she gazed so intently at me, then responded as if this was the most exciting but intimidating proposal she'd ever received. In everything she did there was complete belief and conviction.

As the evening progressed we fed more and more off each other. She pushed me further and further into uncharted territory. Her energy was so intense and consuming that at times I felt overpowered. Like I was just trying to keep up. I had to dance at my absolute fullest to meet the challenge of dancing with her. She reached such heights technically that I had to go far beyond anywhere I'd ever been.

Her interpretation, her attack, awed the audience. She took the smallest variation or step beyond usual notions of what it could or should be, imbuing it with her personal sense of how it can be done. Her Giselle was completely unique even down to the placement of the arms.

Her movements all came from within herself. Her performance was completely true and honest. Any art is subjective: you could love it or hate it, seeing it as a breaking down of a noble heritage or a reinvention of meaningful standards for our generation. Some thought it too much, but what I found on the stage, dancing with her side by side throughout the entire evening, made me rethink how far I could push myself both artistically and technically.

I had danced with partners who had their own distinct artistry before, but in those instances I often worried that I was being dishonest in my individual approach to dancing and acting. I felt like I was wearing someone else's clothing that didn't quite fit. But dancing with Natasha was totally different. She trusted me. She emboldened me. I didn't give her what people told me to (arm here, reaction there). I just observed her. I watched her artistic choices, her ability to express a character's emotions as if she were truly living them. Those observations informed what was possible for me. For the first time, I felt like I wasn't acting. My emotions flowed abundantly and naturally. It was a revelation and an awakening. A spark had been ignited. I realized I had to be my own dancer. Natasha opened my eyes to artistic freedom achieved with integrity and purpose and commitment.

THAT NIGHT, NATASHA captivated the New York audience. The performance was also the beginning of our tender, undeniable connection. Though we are different dancers with such different temperaments, somehow we came together as one, our disparate natures blending into the proverbial whole that is greater than the sum of its parts. Following that performance with Natasha, I understood more deeply than ever before why I dance: for those transcendent moments of truth and the hope of creating them.

Once you have experienced that onstage euphoria, you hunger for it. Yet you have to accept that it is as rare as it is precious.

MONTHS LATER, I was boarding a flight to Moscow to dance another *Giselle* with Natasha, this time at the Bolshoi Theatre.

Before I left, Irina Dvorovenko, the ballerina I had partnered in *Symphony in C* a few years before, gave me some advice, telling me to just do my own thing and stay strong. The Bolshoi, she said, is a hard company to dance with as an outsider. They are extremely critical; they might eat me alive. It was a daunting warning, and it stayed with me all the way to Moscow.

I HAD PERFORMED at the Bolshoi once before, in 2004, at a gala where Michele and I danced "Grand Pas Classique." That invitation had come from Damian Woetzel, a long-standing Principal Dancer with New York City Ballet, who had put together a small troupe of American dancers to perform at the Bolshoi

Theatre for an American Gala Evening. It was my first gig with dancers from other companies whom I had always looked up to.

It had been a dream back then to be going to the historic Bolshoi Theatre. I recalled images from videos I had seen as a young boy of the theater's dancers, performing on what I would soon come to regard as that intimidatingly enormous stage.

I thought, *This is a once-in-a-lifetime moment.* I was sure I would never have the chance to dance on that stage again. So I coerced my parents into traveling to Moscow to watch the performance. They needed to experience it as much as I did.

Russia was like nothing I had imagined. By first impression, I found Moscow to be an intimidating city. Enormous ten-lane streets were edged by Soviet-era buildings, brutalist and imposing concrete bunkers that seemed to provide a harsh corrective to the fanciful edifices topped off with multicolored domes that dominate Red Square.

While other theaters in the world are at times dwarfed by their surroundings, Bolshoi soared above the rest. Even from the exterior, one got the sense of its importance and purpose. Today, this massive mecca of ballet and opera is the color of cream, with gargantuan Roman pillars on its facade. And at the top, looking down to the Kremlin and all of Moscow, is Apollo, the god of music, standing on his chariot with four horses rearing before it. My appreciation of this theater's majesty never subsided, even years later when it had become my second home.

But on my first trip there, Bolshoi Theatre had not undergone its huge renovation, and it was a far different place than it is now.

Dancers and staff passed in and out of the stage door on Petrovka Ulitsa, the fabled door number 13. Inside, a surly old babushka held court, manning the door from behind a creaky desk. She treated anyone foreign to the theater like a terrorist who potentially threatened the very structure of Moscow's cultural gem. After I proved my identity by presenting the proper

ID, she then, conveniently, saw my name written in the guest log. Surprised to find it, she nonetheless muttered something under her breath. I imagined it to be "We're watching you, young man."

Along with my American compatriots, I made my way into the well-worn maze under the stage. A soiled odor permeated the air. I recognized it immediately, having already been told about the legions of cats who live at the Bolshoi and the resultant stench of cat piss throughout. I assumed no one tried to get rid of them for they were a legend unto themselves. I never actually saw any of these cats, but I heard their screeching emanating through the walls, like the Bolshoi's Phantoms of the Opera.

We walked along corridors under the stage, then up old staircases, and found the dressing rooms. Each was ancient, comfortable, cozy, with dark wood lining the walls, a small table beneath a three-sided mirror with a few lightbulbs, and a closet. There was no modern flashy glamour like the Met Opera dressing rooms with their wall of mirrors, red carpets, showers, and chaise longues. But the Met, as prestigious as it is, didn't have the feel of history these dressing rooms had. It was enchanting. The very first Siegfried, Victor Gillert, had prepared here in 1877 for the premiere of the first production of Tchaikovsky's *Swan Lake*. Gillert may have warmed up in the same room where I stood. You couldn't ignore the weight of that history or the reverence that all of Russia had for this theater. It was their pride. Their blood.

We Americans had no idea how we would be accepted by the Bolshoi dancers. Something, though, had occasioned their interest, because it seemed like every member of the Bolshoi Ballet was hovering in the wings, giving us stone-cold looks as we danced. What can feel like judgment to outsiders is really just the Russians' way of interacting with anyone they don't know personally. We were not their friends, but they watched with complete curiosity.

Every company has different policies about people watching from the wings. ABT allows no one there except the performers. If a certain handful of dancers want to watch, they stand very far back, clearing the way for dancers to enter and exit the stage and, at times, bound into the wings at full propulsion.

Bolshoi's policy was the exact opposite. The dancers fought for the closest perch possible to the stage. They were in our way when we exited, leaping offstage and practically onto their laps. Some seemed to be inches from being exposed to the audience, just a thin black edge of a wing keeping them from view. They didn't seem fazed by any of it and made no effort to accommodate the performers.

We all thought this was rude, a way of enforcing that this was their theater and not ours. But in truth, it was their curiosity and interest that drew them, by the dozens, closer and closer to the stage. And there they stood, wide-eyed, watching.

After the show I ran into Julio Bocca, then a virtuoso Principal with ABT, who was in Moscow to dance *Don Quixote* as a guest artist with the Bolshoi. I asked if this was his first time dancing with them.

"No, no, many times before," he replied.

His answer impressed me. Being invited as a guest to this famed company was already a huge compliment, but being invited a second time provided the heartening affirmation that you had danced so well that they wanted you back. I pictured Bocca, one of the greatest dancers of his generation, being welcomed time and time again to the Bolshoi. I thought, *I'll never have that privilege of being invited to dance with this grand company.*

FIVE YEARS LATER I was en route to Moscow to dance *Giselle* with Bolshoi Theatre. I was extremely intimidated at the thought of performing there. The company was huge, the audience educated and opinionated, the city cold. The pressure to deliver was on. But this time, I had Natasha at my side. I knew I could trust our partnership on this fearsome foreign ground. When the surrounding elements were overwhelming, I could look to her for support.

The first time I took class with the company, there were about eighty of us in one small studio. I was warming up at a barre by the piano. Everyone eyed me as they walked in. I imagined them thinking, *Who is this? Hallberg who? ABT?*

As class began, the teacher came over to me, took me by the hand, and led me to the center barre, already crowded with dancers. He said something in Russian, only to be met with hushed silence. Eventually I learned that at Bolshoi, Principal Dancers and Guest Artists use the center barre and nothing else. There is a protocol you must abide by. I respect that. It is the custom of the theater. The way it has always been.

Though I had felt no sense of acceptance when I danced at the Bolshoi previously, this time it was different. I had been *invited* to dance there. With Natasha, no less.

NATASHA WASN'T AS guarded on her own turf. She wasn't as distant or withdrawn. Revisiting *Giselle* together was a blissful reunion for us. It brought back memories of that evening when New York fell in love with her and we began our partnership.

Given the connection Natasha and I had when we danced together at ABT, I had been wanting to experience again the euphoria we shared. That nonverbal connection demonstrated the founding assumption of ballet: that there is, at times, no need for words.

*　　*　　*

OUR PERFORMANCE WAS in conjunction with a festival honoring Vladimir Vasiliev, an astounding Bolshoi dancer who defined the Soviet style. The Bolshoi has two versions of *Giselle*: Vasiliev's and another by Yuri Grigorovich, who, for thirty years, beginning in 1964, was the Bolshoi's chief choreographer.

I was to dance Vasiliev's *Giselle*, a version that wasn't much different from the ABT production I had previously learned. The only major change was the ending of the ballet. Most *Giselle*s end with a solemn, chastened Albrecht, who repents his own fecklessness, which has led to Giselle's death. The final act has such tender moments of pathos as Albrecht surrenders to his guilt, to his love for Giselle, and to the terrible recognition that he will be forever without her. But once Giselle has descended to her grave, Vasiliev chose to have Albrecht dance a huge manèges around the stage in an elaborate outpouring of emotion. I struggled with an ending that showed such an externalized show of angst and love for Giselle.

Vasiliev's personal character and his persona onstage fit this ending perfectly. He embodied expression in acting. Needless to say, I was obligated to finish the ballet in the way he wanted. He critiqued each step of a work I thought I knew. He never settled for my initial interpretation, gesturing and yelling corrections, most of the time in Russian, a translator trailing behind him. At times he would correct me in a way I couldn't understand and the translator would turn to me and say, "More intensity." My *Lost in Translation* moment.

Vasiliev didn't focus on how turned out you were in a step, how many pirouettes you did, how high your cabriole was. He insisted that you bring artistic integrity to the role.

I had seen the same aesthetic priorities when I rehearsed *La Bayadère* with the Russian-trained ballerina Natalia Makarova, who had been a great star of the Kirov Ballet (now called the Mariinsky) and later ABT. She wanted my true convictions in professing Solor's love to Nikiya. She wanted ethereality in the Shades scene, when Solor has a dream in which he envisions Nikiya after her death. The steps were hard, yes, but belief in the role was paramount. Both Makarova and Vasiliev demanded that I tell the story, believe the intentions of the character I was portraying, and emotionally connect with my partner and with the audience.

One day when we were rehearsing Giselle's death scene at the end of Act I, I flailed around the studio, desperate to gain Vasiliev's approval. When I finished, on the ground, embracing the dead Giselle in my arms, he looked at me and dryly said, "Stanislavsky would have never believed you."

He confirmed what I had questioned for years and had become increasingly sure of: that movement is meaningful only when it emanates from the truth you find within your own artistic intention.

GISELLE AT BOLSHOI Theatre was a turning point for me in terms of handling the pressures that an opportunity like that can present. The stakes had been high and I had tried my best to stay in the moment and remain as calm as I possibly could. Through that performance, I finally got a taste of the appreciative Moscow audience. They know *Giselle*. They have watched it for generations and have a standard for how it should be danced. Apart from the generous way the audience responded to my dancing, I witnessed how they responded to Natasha. Strong, enthusiastic applause was given to her when she entered, when she danced her solo, and again when she entered in the second act and tore through her opening variation. For our final bows, in front of the Bolshoi curtain, Natasha led the way, moving from one side of the theater to the other, bowing to one balcony and then the next. Non-Russian dancers are at times critical of what they perceive as the overindulgence of the way Russians bow. But in Moscow there is no other way, as the applause is loud and sustained. Audiences show their appreciation by clapping long after the show has ended. It is a tradition that you find in no other country.

CHAPTER 16

M y Bolshoi debut was timed with another Russian debut in an equally storied venue: the Mariinsky Theatre of St. Petersburg.

The Mariinsky Theatre opened in 1860, replacing the original theater, which burned down, having been built in 1783 to house opera and ballet. Named for the Empress Maria Alexandrovna, wife of Tsar Alexander II, Mariinsky Theatre hosted performances of what became known as the Imperial Ballet, the company for which Marius Petipa, Premier Ballet Master of the Imperial Theatres, created the entire classical canon, including the ballets that dancers sometimes refer to as the Big Five: *Don Quixote, La Bayadère, The Sleeping Beauty, The Nutcracker,* and *Swan Lake.* The composer of the last three of those works was Pyotr Ilyich Tchaikovsky.

Later, the company was known as the Mariinsky Ballet. During the Soviet years, it was renamed the Kirov, reverting to the Mariinsky Ballet after glasnost.

The Mariinsky Theatre is where George Balanchine first performed, as a boy, in *The Sleeping Beauty,* dancing the Garland Dance and appearing as a cupid; it's where he watched that ballet from the wings, entranced by the glorious scenery and Tamara Karsavina's portrayal of Princess Aurora, and knew that he wanted a life in dance. It's where Rudolf Nureyev made his ballet debut and began imposing his own ideas on long-held traditions, and where he had his costumes altered (as Vaslav Nijinsky had done before him), requesting that his tunics be shortened to make his legs seem longer.

The Mariinsky, or the Kirov, was also the original company of ballet's most mythic and heralded dancers: Nijinsky, Anna Pavlova, Mikhail Fokine, Irina Kolpakova, Natalia Makarova, Mikhail Baryshnikov. All were trained there, as were Nureyev and Balanchine. They all left eventually to dance or coach or choreograph in the West, in the process creating and defining twentieth-century ballet. And what they took with them and built upon was the art form they had been steeped in at the Mariinsky.

ONCE THE FINAL curtain closed on my Bolshoi debut, I boarded an overnight train to St. Petersburg with Natasha, who was also going to dance at Mariinsky, and her then boyfriend and friend of mine, Ivan Vasiliev. Natasha and I were still somewhat sweaty from our show, which had ended just an hour before, and had faint traces of stage makeup on our faces. A surly conductor checked our tickets. The midnight train was old, utilitarian, showing the wear of countless trips back and forth from Moscow to St. Petersburg. The interior featured red velvet curtains with gold tassels; worn red carpet lined the narrow corridors. My sleeping cabin had a narrow bed on one side and seating on the other. The smells of gasoline and stale cigarettes permeated the air throughout the train. We were starving and in desperate need of a post-performance beer, so we made our way to the dining car.

The three of us sat down in a booth as the train left Moscow. For the next four hours, until we weren't able to keep our eyes open any longer, we ate pierogi, borscht, and *kotletki*—breaded chicken—washing it all down with cold Baltika beer. Ivan, always one to foster a good time, ordered a carafe of vodka for us to toast with. And as we chugged along into the pitch-black night, we lifted one vodka shot after another to each other, to distant friends, and to the moment. Our only verbal communication was the little English Ivan spoke, as he acted as the go-between for Natasha and myself. But we didn't need language, just the sheer joy of being together, in between debuts, on this train.

I looked out the window and thought how I would have never imagined vodka toasts with Russian friends in the middle of the night on a train heading northwest to St. Petersburg. It was blissfully satisfying.

WE ARRIVED IN St. Petersburg exhausted, after three hours of sleep in our single cabins. The air was fresh with the sun coming up on a crisp March morning. We dropped our bags at the hotel and continued on to rehearsal at the theater.

Ah, the theater! I was just as moved to lay eyes on Mariinsky Theatre as I had been when seeing the Bolshoi for the first time. Smaller in scale, the exterior is a pastel green and every bit as majestic as its counterpart in Moscow, but more subtle, less dominating. Fear, excitement, anticipation, nerves; all were mixed into my first sighting as I pulled up to the front, finally edging around the side to find the stage door.

I was guided through the long, narrow corridors by a Russian translator who had worked there almost his entire life. His was a common story among the employees of the theater: his parents had devoted their lives to Mariinsky and passed that devotion down to him. He spoke excellent English and was warm, welcoming, accommodating. Proud to show the maze of corridors to the lost American. I changed into my rehearsal wear in an old dressing room where the walls displayed photos of the legends who had dressed there as well. After, we entered a studio where dancers were rehearsing. They stared. Some seemed to recognize me. Most didn't. We tiptoed by, through the room, to a wooden door that led to another intimate, worn studio of the same size. I was nervous, wide-eyed, intimidated. Left alone to warm up, in this empty studio, I quickly forgot about last night's debut at the Bolshoi and instantly switched gears, readying myself for a rehearsal of *Sleeping Beauty* with the Mariinsky's Artistic Director, Yuri Fateyev.

I had met Yuri two years before on Martha's Vineyard at a summer program that Ethan Stiefel organized. Ethan had brought Yuri in to teach. That was when I started to understand the meaning of Russian training. Yuri's passion was his work in the studio. His classes were strong, meaty, with a heavy emphasis on pure technique. He had a special understanding of the execution of turns and jumps for men, breaking everything down to the most minute details. The way the first leg reaches across in a glissade. The placing of the hands in preparation for a pirouette. He has an eye unlike that of anyone else I've worked with.

In contrast to many Russians, he doesn't have a curt facade. He is open and accepting, with a huge, giving heart and a broad smile. It is the beauty and rigor of ballet that he loves; he appreciates dedicated and humble workers. Dancers with potential and no pretense. His world is ballet, and he offers it to whomever he works with, giving selflessly.

YURI WAS ALSO a man of his word. He had taken notice of me in Martha's Vineyard, and then invited me to perform the Prince in *Sleeping Beauty* at the Mariinsky. That invitation shocked me. Early in my career, I watched a video of someone guesting at Mariinsky, all the while thinking that I'd never have the opportunity to dance at such a historic company, just as I had upon hearing about Julio Bocca's guesting at the Bolshoi. Yet there I

146

was, warming up in an empty studio at the Mariinsky. With our first rehearsal just forty-five minutes away, I took out my camera and photographed my mirrored image. Bundled up in my warmers. Humbled by the surroundings. I was still recovering physically and emotionally from the evening before on the Bolshoi stage. But there was no time to rest, to think. I told myself, *You are already warm; just move the body and break a sweat. You are ready for this.*

I went over my steps in the ballet, which I had learned from studying a DVD. I watched the clock nearing the time of rehearsal. Finally the door opened. Yuri entered. A warm hello, in English. A big smile. Energetic, committed. It was time to start.

AT THAT STAGE of my career, although I was progressing as an artist, it was crucial that I have the incisive eye of a good coach watching and guiding me during those long hours in the studio. Many things had changed over the years I had danced professionally, but the need for a great coach was the one thing that never would. I had found that coach when I worked with Guillaume Graffin, but after he moved on, I hadn't found anyone to replace him. Having the right coach was so vital to me that I went to Amsterdam to work with Guillaume when I was rehearsing my first Albrecht at ABT. But I'm not like some artists who shut themselves off to everyone but one coach, thinking there is no one else who can offer assistance. I think that attitude blocks you from growth. Everyone I have ever worked with has helped me in one way or another. I am grateful to them all. But there are some who hit a special chord. They understand me and push me beyond all limits I've set for myself.

Finding a coach in the United States is different than in Russia, where there are many possibilities to choose from and you pick your coach at a young age. In America there are usually only one or two coaches to choose from in any given company, and you are generally not given a choice of which you'll work with. Hopefully you connect artistically with one of them, but if not, you have to find a way to forge a relationship and try to make it work.

But I have always believed that I was more difficult to coach than others, partially because of my late start in ballet at the age of thirteen. I didn't learn at a young age the foundations of the big male jumps, for example. While others, who started young, had that technique rooted within them, I simply tried to propel myself into the air and hope for the best. I needed more than the usual amount of time in the studio. I needed to be shoved over the edge, beyond my comfort zone, to where I was free-falling and had nothing but unexplored territory below. This was when I grew the most.

I'D GOTTEN THE feeling, in the brief time I worked with Yuri in Martha's Vineyard, that he knew my capabilities as a dancer. He was the coach I had been looking for. We had a natural rapport, making it easy for him to translate corrections and equally easy for me to understand what he wanted. There was no language barrier, since he speaks English fluently. But often, as I had found with Natasha, there was no need for words.

At the Mariinsky, we spent hours in the studio, repeating step after step. He pushed me to a level far beyond what I had experienced. I fed off the energy this mode of work engendered. I sweated and sweated and sweated, soaking my way through numerous rehearsal shirts, providing visual proof that I was working hard. And as we worked, just the two of us in a studio in the depths of the theater, I was given the artistic sustenance I had craved. I prepared a single role for two entire weeks, hours at a time during the day. Every nuance was analyzed. Picked apart. The result was large strides of progress, based on new ideas and techniques I couldn't have realized without him. I knew I responded well to someone pushing me hard. And Yuri was just that person, telling me in all honesty what needed work, what had improved, and how I hadn't reached the full potential of something as minute as a reach of the toe, a turn of the head, a hand gesture. It was all about the details with him. I couldn't see those details myself. Yuri was a coach who could spot even the most subtle movement.

It was never about quantity with him: the number of turns, the height of the jump. It was about the quality of every step (which would lead to a higher jump or more turns). He would demand. Question. Repeat. Refine. I saw Mr. Han in him, only twelve years later.

Yuri emphasized French style with Russian training, refinement, warmth, port de bras (the carriage of the arms). I would start a variation with the presentation of one arm; my first movement before a big solo. He would stop me immediately. It wasn't good enough.

Use the fingers, he'd say. Finish the movement with the palm of your hand presented toward the audience, inviting them in.

We would repeat a section four or five times, just for one movement of the arm.

It could be better, he often said.

We spent a full hour on a forty-five-second variation. This was something I wasn't used to. Elsewhere, there was always barely enough time to devote a full hour to an entire ballet. I had been taught to be efficient in rehearsal, to get through two or three variations in thirty minutes. With Yuri, the attention to detail lavished on one series of jumps was eye-opening.

Another thing he saw was the deficiency in my execution of a manèges, that virtuosic series of leaps around the perimeter of the whole stage. Just like Mr. Han, Yuri drilled me, correction after correction, circle after circle. A manèges is a difficult but impressive step. If you make the slightest mistake, the entire audience will know. You need to turn, skimming the air as you split your legs, then land softly and repeat the same step as you continue to encircle the stage. This had never been my forte. I lacked the instant coordination to execute that low, airborne split perfectly, without strain. I would throw my legs, always dipping my body to one side and taking too much time to get to the final position.

Yuri told me to throw my advancing leg right in front of me as fast as I could, so I would hit the position instantly. Sometimes that would correct the problem, but at times that approach wouldn't achieve the result we were looking for. Then he would tell me to use my arms to help get me aloft, jetting the front arm out quicker than the legs. He told me to open my back leg when I jumped to create the illusion of lengthening the whole position in the air. Yuri was weeding through all the mess that clouded the purity of the positions. That mess was another result of my late start.

AS YURI AND I worked on my role in *Sleeping Beauty*, he showed me shadings and colors that I never knew the ballet possessed. I had danced Prince Désiré many times before and always felt a dryness, a one-dimensional quality in this character who kisses a princess into wakefulness and finds his true love. I was almost bored with it, distanced from a role for which others said I was a natural. I had been told, since I was very young, that I had a "noble air," and that was something that Yuri emphasized to me, making my understanding more complete and sure. Yet emotionally, I still had difficulty connecting with those noble characters. In pushing me to my physical limits, Yuri turned my one-dimensional Prince into a three-dimensional character. The style and refinement I had never found when dancing *Sleeping Beauty*, I found through Yuri. He humanized and validated the role of the Prince for me. He gave it depth and true meaning. He showed me that Prince Désiré is a character who has been blessed with all the material things in life. Privilege. Power. Wealth. Everyone at his beck and call. But what he lacks is a true existence. A reason to live. And honest love. Something is amiss, and he can't pinpoint what it is until he finds love in the form of a sleeping princess. I knew these feelings we spoke of, that feeling of not recognizing true love until it hits you right in the face and, from that moment on, you can't live without it. At last, I could understand the Prince.

Yuri's coaching was a revelatory experience that changed me as a dancer. I needed to work with him more.

The night of the performance approached, and with it the ensuing nerves. I had just one evening to prove myself. Something I grew to crave even as I dreaded it was the pressure of an upcoming show, especially when the stakes were so high that you knew you *had* to dance at your best. Sure, I loved being onstage, but that was never the sole focus of my dancing. My primary interest was the preparation, the buildup and that exhilarating, inescapable pressure. This was certainly the case when I debuted at Mariinsky Theatre partnering Alina Somova. There were the audience's expectations to grapple with, as well as my own, and my determination to show Yuri that the time he had so generously given me had not been wasted. In the end, Yuri seemed satisfied with the work we put in because he saw it pay off during the performance.

CHAPTER 17

American Ballet Theatre performs for audiences around the world. Each country and audience is distinct. Some, like the Americans, love the excitement of beautifully executed technique, whereas the French savor refinement and purity of line. Some, like the Cubans, are loud and boisterous, showing their appreciation with piercing bravos, while the Japanese are silent vocally but fervent clappers. Wherever we went, we could look out at ecstatic audiences during curtain calls and see how profoundly this wordless art speaks to people of diverse ethnicities and cultures.

When I went with the company to Japan I quickly learned that the Japanese audience has an abiding passion for dance and especially its individual "stars." Fans would meet us at our hotel to welcome us. They stood in the lobby for hours in the mornings just to get a picture and an autograph. And hundreds would wait at the stage door after a performance to show their appreciation. It was like no other post-performance stage door scene I have yet experienced. During my first tour to Tokyo, we opened with *Le Corsaire*; Ethan Stiefel performed the lead role. I was in the Corps de Ballet at the time, dancing as one of Ethan's pirate sidekicks. After the show, I approached the stage door and saw at least five hundred clamoring fans in roped-off areas at both sides of the exit. As I tried to move through them I was mobbed. I felt like I was in a head-on collision. They were mad for an autograph. Mad for a picture. Mad for anything.

But as I signed their programs, something didn't feel right. And I eventually became aware of *what* I was actually signing. They all kept pointing with their pens to Ethan's picture. It made total sense then. They weren't going crazy for me, the pirate at the back of the stage. They were going crazy for the lead pirate, who at times looked like my doppelgänger. Blond hair. Blue eyes. All signs pointed to me being him. I panicked, refusing to sign his picture. I sheepishly tried to sign the opposite blank page instead, pointing to his image and saying "It's not me," to no success. I'll never forget the look of disappointment on their faces.

Why wouldn't Ethan sign his picture? they thought.

It was a moment when a common language would have instantly fixed the mix-up.

ON A RETURN trip to Tokyo years later, I convinced my family (as I had for Moscow) to come and witness Japan and its culture. I was a Principal Dancer by that point, and the crowds were asking me to sign my own picture. I had warned my parents about the fans in Tokyo.

They are like no others, I had explained.

My dad has always been very supportive of anyone who waits for an autograph and instilled in me, at a young age, that each of them deserves a moment of my time, a picture, a signature. As a crowd waited at the stage door in Tokyo, he made it very clear that I "must sign any and all autographs." Which meant hundreds. As I walked out to meet my parents and the mob of fans, I saw my dad eyeing me, watching, waiting for me to sign everyone's program. He wouldn't settle for less. Therefore I wouldn't settle for less. Supporters of ballet, or of any art form for that matter, are what keeps it alive. If you cannot connect with them, not only on the stage but after the show, then you are turning away from the very people who make it possible for you to express your passion. My dad's attitude is something I have carried throughout my career. *The reason you are there is because of them,* I always hear him saying.

CUBA IS ANOTHER country where ballet has a huge and fervent following. When ABT went to Havana in 2010 for the first time in fifty years, it seemed as though the whole country was waiting to see us perform. After baseball, ballet is the thing Cubans love most. As one would expect from a Latin country, this makes for highly audible audiences that cheer endlessly and whose loud shouts of "Bravo!" throughout the show are pronounced with a rolled *r* that makes them seem all the more emphatic.

The Cuban passion for ballet was made abundantly clear to me as I hopped in a taxi to head to the theater before a performance. The driver, eager to practice his English, asked the normal questions of where I was from and what I was doing in Havana.

"I'm here performing with American Ballet Theatre," I told him.

"Oh, my friend!" he said. "It is such an honor to have a ballet dancer in my taxi. Welcome to Cuba. I will watch you tomorrow night on the television. Your performance will be live across the country."

He asked if I knew Alicia Alonso, the most celebrated Cuban ballerina ever, who danced with ABT in the 1940s. I told him that ABT had been invited to take part in the twenty-second International Ballet Festival of Havana and to honor Alonso's ninetieth birthday. I was thrilled to be dancing Balanchine's *Theme and Variations* for the celebration because Alonso was the ballerina on whom Balanchine had created the leading role in 1947.

ON OUR FREE day after our arrival, class was scheduled at the National Ballet of Cuba for whoever wanted to take it. I knew the atmosphere of the studios would be something I couldn't miss. Something uniquely Cuban. This company had made its global mark on the ballet world, training its own style of dancer, and the studios I entered, housed in a large Spanish colonial–style building in the heart of Havana, were where Cuban ballet was born. They were completely run-down, but much like the feeling of Bolshoi Theatre, they showed their proud and significant history. Wood was still used as the flooring in the studios, instead of the more standard Marley. A large, decaying staircase dominated the middle of the building. Out-of-tune pianos echoed in the hallways. There were no water fountains anywhere. It had a rich, wonderfully unique texture.

The building buzzed with dancers and fans milling about. Many came to observe class, with a large group of onlookers filling the doorways of the studios and sitting in the balconies perched above the room. The tropical climate kept my body warm and sweating from the first exercise. I stood at the barre close to a large open window, mentally recalling countless pictures I'd seen of this same room. "Studio Azul," with its light blue walls, had huge stained-glass windows open to the street, lessening the stuffiness caused when fifty dancers crammed into it.

A Cuban class is unique. It doesn't start with the usual pliés followed by tendus. It starts with tendus and then pliés. The exercises are deliberate, strong, purposeful. There isn't the finesse of a Paris Opera barre, with its elegant clarity. Class in Cuba is about strength and power. This is a huge part of what I relish as a touring dancer: the different styles, the altered approach to steps we perform universally, just done a different way.

The meditation of barre, this daily series that we execute throughout our entire careers, can take many forms depending on where you are. I first experienced a wave of change when I trained in Paris. There, barre was fast, clear, and clean, and completely different from Mr. Han's methodic work. A Russian barre usually lasts only half the time of the French but includes the same number of exercises, if not more. Whatever the culture or country, barre exercises reflect a particular style of preparing a dancer for the center work and eventually a performance. It is paramount to their identity. To experience these diverse methods of training is to enrich your own technique and texture. The more you open yourself up to taking a class at the National Ballet of Cuba or at ABT in New York or at Bolshoi Theatre in Moscow, the more choice you have in expressing how you feel as an artist. We all speak the same language. There is no right or wrong style.

MY FINAL TRIP in 2010 was a first-time visit to Australia, where I was scheduled to dance *The Nutcracker* with The Australian Ballet. I had eagerly accepted an invitation from the Artistic Director, David McAllister, to join the company as a Guest Artist. I felt a strong attraction to the Aussies. Somehow, I connected to them.

Boarding the Sydney-bound flight, I imagined the next twenty-four hours of my journey to a country that I knew nothing about. I didn't know the audiences, the people, the culture. It was more geographically remote than anywhere I had ever traveled. I had been dancing professionally for nearly a decade, and hadn't been this excited about a destination in a while. After years of dancing throughout the world, from one-evening galas to a week's-long guesting, I had become accustomed to the cities and countries I visited. But Australia was a faraway land yet to be discovered.

I slept deeply on my evening flight, and woke just as the sun was peeking over the horizon as we approached Australia's shores. I had landed in too many cities around the world to remember what each looked like when seen from so high above, but I'll never forget the sight that unfolded when skimming the sky over Sydney. The harbor is its own unique wonder, bustling with boats, houses, and bridges connecting it all. But just at the tip of the land is the magnificent Sydney Opera House. It is unmistakable from the ground, but from the air it looks like a shore-bound shark, fins arching straight up toward the sky. More often than not you see a landmark in a photo before you actually lay eyes on it. Some thrill in their splendor when seen in person, while others disappoint. The Sydney Opera House and its surroundings, first viewed from fifteen thousand feet in the air, trumped all photos I had seen. Here was Australia! The fins of the Opera House spiked out like embracing arms, welcoming me, inviting me to experience the country's culture. Then the beautiful image vanished as quickly as it appeared as we landed and I headed off to board a connecting flight to Melbourne, where I would be dancing.

I had no idea at the time that this was the country I would seek out in a few years when I was brought to the depths of loss and needed to be restored to physical and emotional life.

MANY DANCERS THROUGHOUT the world view Guest Artists with resentment. Guests fly in (usually without enough time to properly rehearse), perform, and then immediately leave, heading on to another company to do the same. Their presence often means that a full-time, hardworking company member is deprived of a leading role.

This is hard on the dancers in any company, though it is, at times, unavoidable since audiences love to witness something new, and the addition of a foreign dancer tends to boost both ticket sales and excitement. That success, in turn, can create a culture of recurring Guest Artists stealing the limelight without having to do the work company members have put in. But if there are just one or two guests in an entire season, as there often are at Australian Ballet, it can inspire the company's dancers and alter the way they view their work and performance. It can be more of an educational tool than an annoyance or a burden.

WHEN YOU ARE guesting, you find that every company treats you differently. Some are warm. Others don't seem to care that you are there, remaining friendly but never penetrable. You can work for four or five hours during the day, then, as you finish up, you have no one to eat with, talk to, go out with. Being a guest artist makes for an isolated existence.

The true Aussie spirit is kind, open, generous. There was a warm welcome for me on my first workday at Australian Ballet, with everyone on staff piling into the vast studio 8 to join in. It seemed like every dancer and member of the administration introduced themselves over the course of the first week.

Still, on day one I was far more nervous than I let on. Internally, I was buzzing, wanting to make a good first impression. When I was younger, I would treat the first ballet class with the entire company as a proving ground, dancing full-out, knowing that all eyes were peering my way. By this stage in my career, I had realized that it's best to pace myself. To let things settle. Feel the atmosphere. Calm the anxiety. Don't blow it out all in one class.

The first few days I tell myself, *Take deep breaths. Ground yourself and your mind. Never show off. You have nothing to prove . . . yet. Nerves, when not in conjunction with a performance, are wasted. You will deliver your best later, knowing that everyone is expecting something greater than the reality of what you can do.*

Greater than the reality. A thought that rankles when paranoia gets the best of me. Expectation is a double-edged sword. On one side, you can start to believe you'll meet all expectations, which leads to ego, which can lead to ruin. On the other side, there's nothing more dispiriting than failing to deliver what the audience expects of you. I have seen the disappointment on people's faces when I haven't performed as they imagined I would. It can paralyze me, make me cower. In other words, managing my own and other people's expectations makes for a tricky game no matter how I play it.

AFTER THREE WEEKS of rehearsal for *The Nutcracker*, it was time for a dress rehearsal in the theater. Each theater has its own aura. State Theatre at the Arts Centre Melbourne had a feeling of lush grandeur. Although Sydney Opera House is an icon, the interior houses a minuscule stage and concrete bunker–like lobbies and dressing rooms. State Theatre in Melbourne is the nation's best, its treasure. Cloaked with a red curtain with gold leaf threading, it looks appropriately grand.

On the day of the dress rehearsal, the pianist and ballet mistress waited onstage. I was in my pink costume. *Pink? Why bright pink?* I wondered.

Along with becoming acquainted with the stage and the lights, I was also making last-minute adjustments to the costume. If a costume doesn't fit perfectly, it makes everything more difficult, from lifts to jumps to breathing.

My partner warmed up as well, testing out steps. Kirsty Martin was a radiant ballerina with brown hair and almond-shaped brown eyes. She too was in costume. A huge tutu, for such a small ballerina.

Two minutes after we began dancing, Kirsty slipped. We stopped, both of us surprised by how slick the floor was. We started again, this time more tentative and shaky. Again, Kirsty slipped. This was not going the way we imagined. We started for a third time. In a simple glissade to arabesque, Kirsty rose up on pointe. She hit an angle on the outside of the tip of her shoe. Her ankle twisted. She shrieked in shock. In pain, she fell to the floor and grabbed her foot.

"Oh no. Oh no!" I could hear the despair in her voice.

She sat there, welling up in tears, holding her foot tight, in panic, crying, I could do nothing but stand beside her, speechless, in my pink costume. The last three weeks of hard work, during which we had incrementally built a fine rapport, flashed through my mind. I wanted to help her in whatever way I could, so I quickly ran to find the physical therapist, whose office was outside the theater, across the street, at the company's studios. She raced back with me to attend to Kirsty, who was now lying on the State Theatre stage, her foot clearly sprained, swollen right where she twisted it.

I threw her on my back and carried her to the studios. It made for a ridiculous sight we would laugh about later: me in that bright pink costume and gray tights piggybacking her with her sprained foot and big pink tutu.

THANKFULLY IT WAS a minor sprain. The mind is our most powerful tool in moments like those, a truth I would get to know all too well during my lowest moments of injury. There is a fork in the road. One way leads to a downward spiral. You succumb to the accident and let it envelop you, making it that much harder to climb back up the ladder to where you were before.

The other path is the one Kirsty chose: to will yourself to push on and achieve what you've worked for and planned. It requires fighting the odds. Calming the mind. Pushing forward. She was back in action in four days.

THE USUAL NERVES kicked in twenty-four hours before my premiere with The Australian Ballet. Continual support from all dancers in the company, including opening-night flowers, cards, and "chookas"—a word for good luck in Aussie—reassured me that I belonged. I was part of their clan. Their ballet clique. But even so, there came the worry. The doubts. The pressure. Inwardly, I recited my usual mantra: *Don't fuck this up.*

After my first entrance, I caught sight of the other dancers in the wings watching me. Interested. Suddenly I was calm. The buildup beforehand is when the doubt really attacks, coming on in waves through my entire body. But once I'm onstage, there is no return, no time to question. I have to present. The Australian dancers' generosity inspired me to share, to give back, to connect with them, to learn from them. And so we all went on the ride together. And we brought the audience with us.

DURING THE BOWS, I felt a sense of unity with the entire company. Not like a Guest Artist, dropping in and taking a role, but a part of the company's bigger picture, a cog in a wheel that would roll on grandly without me, but which I was integral to for the moment. Then, it was over. The applause and congratulations subsided. I showered. Shed the costume. Left the theater. And I went out to eat. Alone.

A BODY OF WORK

AFTER FOUR WEEKS with The Australian Ballet, my friendships there were deeper than those I usually established when guesting. Still, a dancer's life is filled with contradictions. There are the worldly destinations, new cultures, and different companies, all of them fascinating, inspiring, and challenging. But then there's that pervasive solitude. The return to being by yourself. To passing time. Going from one city to the next, sometimes for many weeks in succession.

I have learned what to do with my hours of idleness. I love discovering a new museum, restaurant, café. I like to get lost in the streets and tune in to the specific beat of a city, balancing those wanderings with my routine.

Overall, I had become a pro at travel. I didn't let living out of a suitcase bother me. I packed minimally and grew accustomed to new cities quickly. To hotel rooms and their sterile cleanliness. The essential sameness of every ballet studio and its stale, sweaty smell. The espresso that tastes the same in every part of the world. Ultimately, my surroundings didn't matter. I was in a city to do a job, and being alone was part of the nonnegotiable price paid for my calling. The only thing that really mattered was what happened in between those solitary moments, when I was rehearsing or performing.

AS I WRITE this, I am alone in Melbourne once again, this time to remedy the injury that has plagued me for too long. I can't perform. I won't have the sold-out house. The gifts and "chookas." The stress and the thrill of dancing. The doubts about my own ability to rise to the occasion.

I am experiencing a different sort of loneliness here: the kind that comes with deep depression. Because this is a different moment of doubt. Not one that lasts a few hours and ends in applause. This is more dire. Desperate, even. The question now is, Will the time I devote here result in my being able to dance again? Or will I have to accept that I've reached the end of a fulfilling, dearly loved career?

Just as if I were here for a series of performances with Australian Ballet, I arrived alone and will leave alone. But what happens this time, in between those solitary moments, will determine my future as a dancer.

CHAPTER 18

I went to Washington, DC, in February 2011 because the Mariinsky was performing there. I was eager to take class with the company and to work with Yuri again. There is a unique air about the Russians. After all, the classical ballets were created in Russia. You can understand why they believe ballet belongs to them. That ballet everywhere else pales in significance. So it is not the most comfortable situation to be an American, the sole foreigner, in a room full of Russians taking morning class. I had not forgotten what happened at school in Paris. How I was shunned for the whole year. I was determined not to make the same mistake twice. Never again would I beg for the approval of my colleagues.

But in class the dancers surprised me. To get as much as a nod and a half smile is to get a lot from a Russian you do not know. In that sense, they were friendly. Obviously, they were not going to throw me a welcome party. Nor did they introduce themselves, which at ABT is standard. But it seemed that if I worked hard and well I could earn their respect.

Yuri and I rehearsed *Swan Lake,* which I would be dancing with the company in St. Petersburg the following month. During the four days we worked together, I was once again pushed into realms previously unknown to me. A coach like Yuri is found once in a career, if ever. I learned that he has the highest regard for dancers who can push themselves, as opposed to those—like myself—who work best when someone else is cracking the whip. So I cracked my own whip in his presence, spurring myself on at every moment and without being told to go higher and faster, to dance more cleanly and precisely.

The result was that he, in turn, took me even further. As always, I responded well to that incisive person in front of me, studying me, critiquing me, picking at me, motivating me. Yuri had become a major part of my career, unlocking a depth of understanding about how to execute steps and translate character using my entire being. He shed new light on roles I still struggled with.

I was convinced that if I was ever to reach my full potential, I needed Yuri in the rehearsal room.

IN NEW YORK, another Russian had an equally strong impact on me. I had first worked with Alexei Ratmansky when he joined American Ballet Theatre as Artist in Residence in 2009. Over the years, I have been in the studio with many great creators. But none as quietly demanding as Alexei. His work has made him ballet's most sought-after choreographer.

Bringing him to the company was a coup for ABT and affirmation of Kevin's ability to bring in a choreographer capable of amassing a significant body of new work for the company. It was not long before his initial contract, set to expire in 2014, was extended to 2023. His strong commitment to ABT sparked a significant wave of inspiration among the dancers of the company.

Born in 1968, and trained at the Bolshoi Ballet Academy, Alexei spent his dancing career in a number of companies around the world, each one adhering to a particular training system and style. These diverse experiences outside of Russia allowed him to absorb many different methodologies of classical dance, which he augmented with an encyclopedic knowledge of its history and the utmost respect for its traditions. After his initial foray into choreography, he returned to the Bolshoi Ballet in 2004 to become its Artistic Director. He stayed five years, creating new works, invigorating the company with fresh energy, and building the roster with dancers he found to be the future of Russian ballet. He specifically nurtured two young dancers, who rose quickly within the ranks, thrilling audiences with their risk taking and raw power onstage: Natalia Osipova and Ivan Vasiliev.

Alexei's first and most passionate calling was to create. He felt the inner pull to get steps out of his mind and onto dancers. So he left the pressures and responsibilities of being a director and became a free agent, creating numerous works on every major dance company throughout the world. His arrangement with ABT allowed him to continue to work with other companies, a liberty he sought when he left Bolshoi. It was a win-win situation for Alexei, and his arrival instigated a journey of discovering new ways of interpreting movement together.

Alexei has achieved an interesting balance between upholding traditions of classical ballet, utilizing them as essential tools to his creative process, while also pushing dancers beyond the standard limitations of the art, the usual ideas of what dance or movement should look like. When creating in the studio, Alexei begins with an idea, a series of movements. He explains them to us, demonstrating some of them himself, and then observes how we do them. He sees what is possible, what can successfully translate from his imagination to actual dancing. But also what cannot. He has very specific ideas about what something should look like. He is curious to know how the movement feels for the dancers and how it can evolve beyond a dry execution of steps. We are the blank canvas, using nothing but our abilities and our bodies to translate his ideas. He wants dancers with no ego, no affectation, no air about themselves. Because he exemplifies that humility and simplicity himself. It's all about the work. The process. The evolution. The idea.

What we dancers bring to Alexei is our own approach to dancing. Everyone has an individual movement style. Some are more refined, some more passionate and carnal. He uses those assets to push everyone beyond the way they think they can move. He sees more in the dancers than the dancers see in themselves.

Working with him is an intense experience. During rehearsals, he starts us off with an eight-count of steps. We study it, attempt it, and almost immediately the onslaught of corrections starts. Some choreographers allow a grace period, letting us test out the movement and get it into our bodies before it is analyzed. Alexei gives us no such grace period. You can see the intricacies of the step rolling through his mind, almost faster than he can explain the concept. Certainly faster than we can pick up each and every nuance he corrects. We desperately try to keep up. Every move is scrutinized, questioned. He bombards us with a constant flow of new shadings. Soon I am in information overload, thinking of this small change, that small correction of the head or arm. Desperately trying to remember everything he said.

In creating ballets like *On the Dnieper* and *Seven Sonatas* and, later, his *Shostakovich Trilogy*, he utilized my natural gifts—my height, my lightness, my lyricism—but altered my sense of weight distribution and added more heft to a sometimes fey movement quality. Without explicitly saying, "Make it heavier," he corrected the movement with that in mind, in the process making me more Dionysian and less Apollonian.

Working alone with Alexei in the studio is a meditative, quiet, determined process. The work is the absolute focal point. It's not about Alexei choreographing and it's not about me dancing. Instead, the axis is this third, overarching entity: the movement. We're subsumed in the creative process, and when we communicate

168

it's as if we're conversing with the movement and not with each other. He gives me steps. I work them out with my body. Then begins a heightened level of correspondence between the two of us, searching for the perfect way a step will translate from him to me.

The time devoted to texturing the steps is paramount. Even revisiting a Ratmansky ballet I've danced before, I couldn't simply have two or three rehearsals to brush up on the work. He always sees it anew, excited by the opportunity to make his preexisting ballet better, with deeper meaning and purpose. He will break me down to build me back up, solely focused on the role I'm portraying or the steps I'm dancing. Putting them under a microscope, dissecting them, then stepping back to see them whole once more. He is quick to notice missing details. The work is arduous but rewarding. He's not one to quickly praise. But when he does give a compliment, you know he means it. Ballet after ballet, we built an honest professional rapport based on mutual respect and investment in the work at hand.

MY CREATIVE PROCESS with Alexei was food for the malnourished. He cast me in his creations, molding them to my body and artistic inclinations, and encouraged me to make them my own. Nothing compares to dancing work that is tailored specifically to you. This is why dancers from George Balanchine's era at New York City Ballet attest to it being the golden age of creation. There was nothing like Mr. B. creating something with you specifically in mind, I would hear over and over. I understood that when works were created on me.

IN 2011, ABT was set to premiere *The Bright Stream*, a comic ballet Alexei had resurrected for the Bolshoi Ballet, complete with a cycling dog, dancing farmers, and a male dancer performing on pointe and in drag. Sadly, both despite and because of the comedic nature of the ballet, it had a tragic and tortured history. The original version of *The Bright Stream* was created in 1935, and was the work of three of Russia's most gifted, ingenious talents: Fyodor Lopukhov, its choreographer and librettist; his co-librettist Adrian Piotrovsky; and the brilliant composer Dmitri Shostakovich (also Alexei's favorite). Theirs was a saucy ballet at a time when Russian ballets had little sauce, especially if they dealt with—or seemed to mock—the noble Russian peasant, a subject about which the nation's tyrannical ruler, Joseph Stalin, was deadly serious. As a result of their perceived disrespect, Lopukhov fell out of favor and his creative career was effectively ended. Piotrovsky was sent to the gulag and was not seen again. As for Shostakovich, he never wrote another ballet score. His life after *The Bright Stream*, he said, was "gray and dull and it makes me sad to think about it."

In the wake of the vitriolic reception the ballet received in Moscow, the original choreography was never notated. Alexei resurrected it by working from what he called Lopukhov's "brilliantly detailed" libretto. Given all that went before it, his staging of *The Bright Stream* was a political statement as well as a major artistic achievement. It clearly spoke to Alexei's drive to resurrect works that were seemingly lost.

The role I was to dance in *The Bright Stream* was the Ballet Dancer. Sent to the farm from Moscow to dance for the peasants, my character and several others decide to play a trick on an old couple in the town. The choreography requires the Ballet Dancer to put on a long white tutu of the type worn by women in Romantic-era ballets such as *Les Sylphides*. A Romantic tutu consists of a three-quarter-length bell-shaped skirt made of tulle. My outfit included a tightly fitted bodice, tulle shoulder bands, a coronet of flowers and pointe shoes.

It was the tutu that gave me pause. The prospect of donning it, of dancing in it onstage in front of thousands of people, brought back a flood of scarring childhood memories, of all those youthful tormentors calling me a girl. The wounds were still there. True, I was no longer the outcast I once had been. I had found my world and was accepted by my colleagues; I fit into my community. But somehow, putting on a dress seemed to invalidate it all. I remembered the perfume being poured on me at school. I felt painfully vulnerable once again.

I was by no means going to pull out of the ballet. So I needed to assure myself that Alexei wasn't making me look effeminate. I knew it was time to set aside my childhood insecurities and focus on the artistic gain of collaborating once again with him. Tutu or no tutu, I was working with a man who inspired me creatively. And this trumped the memory of every bully from the past.

During the rehearsal period, I had strengthened my feet enough to be able to stand on pointe, something male dancers never train to do. Standing on the tips of my toes, which were crammed into the pointe shoe's narrow wooden box, was a completely new way of supporting my entire body. The flexibility in my feet was a blessing and a curse. Although the bend of my foot creates a harmonious line of the leg, it proved potentially dangerous when dancing on pointe. I could easily go over on the shoe and sprain a ligament in the ankle. But the right amount of incremental daily training allowed me to properly execute the choreography. Thankfully, given the ballet's jocular nature, I didn't need to look as lithe as a real ballerina. I could use my lack of comfort in my tutu and pointe shoes to comedic advantage.

Still, I was apprehensive about the way the audience would react. My first entrance in drag was a fast run from one side of the stage to the other in a typical sylphlike pose, fingers and arms outstretched, leading the body forward. On opening night, I waited in the wings, and when my musical cue came, I bolted onstage and dashed noisily across it. As I ran, I waited to hear the response from the packed theater. They gasped in shock, stunned to see me in a costume worn only—until that moment—by my female partners. Then the audience roared with laughter. Alexei had taught me to simply present the movement and never sell it for laughs. The timing and simplicity of the gestures he'd given me were my saving grace. My childhood memories dissipated. This was about something bigger than that.

CHAPTER 19

The Bright Stream turned out to be a demarcation point. I had been dancing as a Principal with ABT for five years. The work was a continual and rewarding challenge. Though very early on in my career I had felt the need to look beyond my immediate surroundings for inspiration, after the Jérôme Bel collaboration failed, my focus on ABT had become absolute. The consistent opportunities to work with artists like Osipova and Ratmansky, among many others, gave me ongoing nourishment and responsibility that kept me from becoming bored or complacent. The pace was at times more difficult and more intense than I could handle, but this strengthened me. There were always new horizons to conquer, with new partners and new styles of movement and interpretation. There was barely a moment to come up for air. I felt supported and nurtured by everyone around me. I trusted the decisions of the artistic staff as to when I was ready to tackle a role or deemed a good enough partner to dance with a specific ballerina. When the time came for a new role I just took it on, did my best, and moved forward, learning from the lows and rejoicing in those moments and performances when everything flowed and I was able, at times, to satisfy even myself.

In those years, I had found a life that fit, including friends and the pleasures of a successful career. But that life was not what I really wanted. Or at least not *all* I wanted. I needed to keep testing myself, to do what frightened me, to dare, to find new ventures, to overcome my fears and reservations, to expand my work, my life, myself.

Once again, I began craving something new and uncharted. The unknown. The risky. A new artistic focal point. Something I had, perhaps, never yet dreamed of nor experienced. A new purpose of discovery that would shake me, once again, to the core of my being. Just like my move to Paris had done. Just like ABT had done. My mind began to burn at the idea. I have always had that longing for *more. More* to dance. *More* to read. *More* to listen to. And above all: *more* to discover artistically. The potential of dance has always seemed limitless. But what is not without limits is the time in which to do it.

NATURALLY I BEGAN having fewer debuts in the full-length classics, as there are only a limited number of them in the ABT repertoire. But instead of diving further into my character development and finding richer interpretations, I started to lose the drive that propelled me into the big ballets in the first place.

I would go to class every day, which always motivated me. But in rehearsal for a role I had already danced, I'd constantly look at the clock. I spent more time scheduling after-work activities than I spent thinking about my own artistic contribution to the work I was given. At times I ached to be anywhere but the rehearsal studio. I would rather have been out exploring the city, or at home, or having a coffee with some friends.

I hated that about myself.

And I knew that the problem wasn't anything happening, or not happening, at ABT. The problem was me and the restlessness I couldn't help but feel and couldn't contain.

*　　*　　*

WHEN REHEARSALS BEGAN for the 2011 Met season, I struggled to find the deep-seated motivation I knew I had in me but which was somehow maddeningly inaccessible. I felt embarrassed by the idea that I wasn't pushing myself to better my own dancing. I had tasted the fruits of that labor and benefited from its focus, but now I had lost the hunger that I relied on to drive me. It wasn't that the challenges posed by the classical ballets, technically and artistically, ever waned. What waned was my interest in digging ever deeper for meaning, for reinvention, for a richer texture of the work that I already knew.

Natalia Makarova came to rehearse her production of *La Bayadère* just as the season opened at the Met. She is the legendary former ballerina who danced with the Kirov and then made a home with ABT after her defection. Like Natalia Osipova, she is known to her colleagues as Natasha. Small and delicate, with a swanlike neck, she is tough and exacting in the studio, never shying away from voicing her opinion. After a dress rehearsal in which I danced the lead role of Solor, she came to me as the stage crew busily changed sets and lights around us. She looked deeply into my eyes.

"What happened?" she asked.

"What do you mean?"

"There is no life in your interpretation. No true belief. It was so much better the last time you did it. Are you not inspired? You need to find more meaning before tomorrow's performance."

I stood there speechless, still sweating in my costume and towering over her petite frame. Physically I dominated her, but her blunt honesty whittled me to the size of a child. She spoke the truth. And I had to hear it. My lack of inspiration showed, and I was caught in the act. I knew something needed to change. I had coasted too long, looking for others to inspire me without looking within myself. No one was going to motivate me but me.

CHAPTER 20

A merican Ballet Theatre was to perform at Bolshoi Theatre in March of 2011. It was a major event for ABT, for we were returning to Moscow after a twenty-year absence. We chose a very strong collection of repertoire. *Theme and Variations* showcased the dancers in a fresh, original Balanchine light and was a staple we toured the world over, given that it was essentially "ours" (having been created for the company in 1947). It was danced to the final movement of Tchaikovsky's Suite No. 3 for Orchestra, which seemed an appropriate musical offering to the theater that had debuted Tchaikovsky's *Swan Lake*.

The link between Bolshoi Theatre and ABT was Alexei Ratmansky, who had become ABT's Artist in Residence shortly after he vacated his post as Bolshoi's Artistic Director. We would also present works he created specifically for ABT to the Moscow audience, which was very familiar with Ratmansky's canon of ballets for the Bolshoi. They knew and respected him, referring to him as "our own."

MY FIRST EVENING in Moscow, jet-lagged and semideliri-ous, I raced to Bolshoi Theatre to see Alexei's restaging of *Flames of Paris*. I settled into my seat and watched Natasha Osipova and

Ivan Vasiliev lead the company in this two-act ballet about the French Revolution. I had seen them dance it once before; this time was different. The evening changed my entire outlook. I was stunned by what I saw on the stage. It was a new Bolshoi. The company danced with vibrant life. The flair and fire Bolshoi was so well known for had been reignited. Gone were the dust, the overacting, the archaic gestures for which the company was sometimes criticized. That show redefined everything I thought of the Bolshoi and, beyond that, about the purpose of ballet and how much vitality still abides within this art form. I sometimes think, *What if I hadn't gone to see* Flames *the night I arrived in Moscow and walked away inspired? What if I hadn't been so impressed by a new generation of Bolshoi dancers?*

One of the few people I vaguely knew there, other than Natasha and Ivan, was Sergei Filin, previously a Premier Dancer with the Bolshoi Ballet who had just been made the company's Artistic Director.

His ascension to the directorship had taken place a mere two weeks before my arrival. Sergei, at forty-one, had a buoyant, boyish energy. A romantic dancer, gifted with strength and good looks, he developed a great rapport with his Moscow audiences. Equally, he had the respect of his dancers and a knowledge of the ins and outs of the famously complex institution that is the Bolshoi.

Before his Bolshoi appointment, Sergei had directed the Stanislavsky Theatre, inviting me to dance there at times, though scheduling issues kept me away. Soon after I arrived in Moscow, his assistant approached me and asked if I had time to meet him for lunch.

"There is something he would love to discuss with you," she said cryptically.

We set a time to meet and my mind raced at the prospect of what he could possibly want to say to me. Would he want me to dance at the Bolshoi with Natasha for one or two shows? *Swan*

Lake perhaps, or *Giselle*? It seemed fitting that, in his first weeks at the helm of Bolshoi, he would ask certain dancers to perform with the company. And so I dreamed, even if the reason for the meeting wasn't that at all, of dancing again with this company for a few performances. A hopeful wish.

THE AFTERNOON OF opening night was my dress rehearsal for *Theme and Variations. Theme* (as ABT calls it) is a ballet that will always let you know, in no subtle way, what shape you are in. It demands everything from you, never getting easier no matter how many times you have danced it. The male lead has a solo that finishes with a daunting seven double tours en l'air in a row. It engenders barely controllable stress. The music builds to a climax, phrase by phrase, until you prepare in the center of the stage for the double tours. Every time I dance this moment, I coax myself away from doubt and toward the optimism of executing the final phrase cleanly and confidently. You are naked onstage. There is no character to hide behind and no scenery. Just you, and your technique.

I danced the dress rehearsal as if it were a performance, acclimating myself to the raked stage and knowing, from previous experience, that its slanting surface is a major factor to contend with. It affects balance, the placement of the body, and the alignment of the spine, legs, and feet, and requires a subtle but imperative adjustment if you aren't accustomed to dancing on one like it.

Under normal circumstances, if I were to dance *Theme* for opening night, I would save my energy during the afternoon dress rehearsal. But since I was slated, for the evening performance, to dance Ratmansky's *Seven Sonatas,* a lyrical but less technically taxing ballet, I took the opportunity to dance *Theme* full-out in a coveted stage rehearsal. Everyone wants to have a full dress rehearsal of a ballet they're soon going to perform. And dancing on the Bolshoi stage, with ABT, in a ballet as stress-inducing as *Theme*, I knew I was lucky to have the chance to rehearse the work. And so I blasted it out, not saving any ounce of energy, knowing I would have enough time to rest before *Seven Sonatas.*

That evening, thirty minutes before the show, as performance nerves began to rise backstage, I was lying on the physical therapy table getting checked up for some tiny ailments. Necessary ministrations, but nothing serious. Kevin's assistant, Tina Escoda, came into the physio room looking concerned. She darted toward me. Immediately my heart, attuned to moments like this, rose to my throat.

"We need you to do *Theme* tonight."

"I'm sorry?"

"The dancer who's set to do it has a stomach virus. There is no other option."

I couldn't demur or argue. I had to adjust immediately: *Theme* was the opening ballet, starting in thirty minutes.

THERE IS A switch that turns on in any dancer. That switch has a name: adrenaline. When it pumps at full throttle a dancer propels himself forward, never looking anywhere but to the mission at hand. One minute before I saw Tina, I was just beginning to get into show mode. Adrenaline wasn't yet pumping. I was looking forward to enjoying Alexei's *Seven Sonatas*, and dancing a work that was created on me. A minute later, I was shot into action.

There was no time to question or doubt. No time to bemoan the fact that I had danced full-out in rehearsal and potentially wasted some much-needed stamina. Luckily, Gillian Murphy was the opening night ballerina, and I'd danced *Theme* with her many times before. I rushed into gear, throwing some makeup on my face, slipping into my still-sweaty costume from the dress rehearsal that afternoon, and bolting onstage to join the cast. I needed no warm-up; I didn't need to review any steps with Gillian. Adrenaline took care of everything.

AS IT TURNED out, I had released all my nerves in rehearsal. The stress of the situation had the effect of calming me down and forcing me to be completely in the moment. Onstage I found, to my amazement, that rather than being exhausted, I had the perfect balance of mental and physical ease. It felt like one of the most solid attempts of *Theme* that I'd ever danced. Not that it was flawless. There were moments in the pas de deux where our lack of rehearsal was evident. I also couldn't turn cleanly for the life of me, though more often than not my pirouettes worked in the studio (a continual frustration that has plagued my entire career). But that night, amid the pressure of producing at the last minute, I refused to obsess over those details. Yes, if they had worked, the overall show would have been marginally better, for myself personally and hopefully for the audience. But I had to allow myself a certain perspective, a sense of the whole picture. Gillian is always exemplary in that regard, and for once, I was able to let those details go. Too often, they have left me questioning too much, doubting too much. They have driven me mad.

THE FOLLOWING DAY I eagerly waited for Sergei while standing by the elevators of the vast Bolshoi Theatre administration building. Employees of the Bolshoi milled about; I knew not a single person. Dancers mixed with opera singers mixed with administrative staff, their foreign language echoing through the atrium. Then Sergei, followed by his assistant, came bounding out of the elevator with an intoxicating energy, as if he were swallowing up all that life brought his way.

"Hello, David!" he exclaimed. "You were so good last night. Very, very good."

Sergei had a way of saying "very" over and over again. If something was "very good," but he wanted to describe it more passionately, it turned into "very, very, very good." It was a relief to hear him speak a little English, since my Russian was nonexistent. Even with his limited knowledge of my language, every word was uttered with passion and purpose. We walked across the street to a sushi restaurant (*Sushi in Moscow?* I thought) and installed ourselves in a "very, very" large half-circle booth. The restaurant attendants seemed to know who he was; I assumed this was not only because of his days dancing on the Bolshoi stage but also because of his new post as Artistic Director. Muscovites are up to date on the latest news of Bolshoi Theatre, as it's reported on by the major Russian news channels, making someone like Sergei a recognizable public figure.

I mindlessly ordered some sushi, the kind of business lunch order one makes when there are more important things at issue. The smell of smoke from the other diners hung thickly in the air. At that time Russians could still enjoy a cigarette while they ate, and most did. We continued with our small talk for a while, but when the elephant in the room finally had to be acknowledged, Sergei switched to Russian and his assistant translated.

"Now, David, I have two offers to make for you."

A pause for translation.

"The first one is something that doesn't interest me so much, but you are to choose whether it interests you."

Translation again.

I leaned in, my eyes fixed on him, impatient at the pauses between when he spoke and when I could actually understand what he said.

"The first one would be that you could come to Bolshoi and be a Guest Artist. You could dance some of the classics of your choice. Come in, perform, and that would be it.

"The second offer I have is that you join Bolshoi Ballet as a full-time company member. You become the first American Premier Dancer in its history. But most importantly, you will become a member of Bolshoi Ballet. This is what I personally want to see you do. I see you in the company and I want to make a place for you here."

Sergei stared straight at me as his words were converted to English.

I was dumbfounded. Shocked to hear an offer I never expected or sought out. From childhood, this was never on my near or distant radar. Moscow, the Bolshoi, Russia, a huge move like this. A life-changing offer made between courses of unagi and toro.

"This is your choice to make, of course," Sergei continued. "I believe in your dancing and I want to give you some of the best opportunities I can. This is something that I want to offer you because of my belief.

"I have gotten all the approval I need to make this offer," he went on. "I have approval from the general manager at Bolshoi Theatre, and I have all the approval from the government. Everyone knows I am offering this to you and everyone is behind me. We all support you joining Bolshoi Theatre and all that needs to happen now is that you say yes."

I could see that he was certain of everything he told me. I could see it in his eyes and in the way he presented the offer. I immediately knew this was not something he would go back on. He was determined to make this happen.

"I don't want you to be in a golden cage—I want you to be free," he said. "But I do want you to make a commitment to the Bolshoi. I'm very serious about this."

"Wow," I managed to stammer out. "First . . . thank you. I'm stunned that you would offer this to me. But you know I'm very happy at ABT. I love the company and it's my home. It's where I was brought up. I couldn't leave that company altogether."

"I am not asking you to leave ABT," Sergei said. "I am just offering that you come dance with Bolshoi and divide your time between Bolshoi and ABT."

"What would I do if I came? Where would I live? Who would help me acclimate to the city and the company?"

"We will help you in everything. We will help you get your work papers, visas, and an apartment close to Bolshoi Theatre."

He had a clear answer to each of my questions.

A sudden sense of dread came over me. I thought, *This will never work out.* To dance for the Bolshoi would inevitably mean ending my work with Yuri at the Mariinsky. Clearly I couldn't do both. How could I set aside the deep connection Yuri and I had established or turn away from his inspiring belief in my potential?

I looked at Sergei with apprehension. "I have worked with Yuri for a while now," I told him. "I have looked for a coach like Yuri for years. We have a very strong understanding of each other and of the work we do in the studio."

"I know Yuri very, very well. He is an amazing coach, I know this. And I do not want any conflict between him and me. This is your decision to make. I am simply offering you what I came to offer today."

I tried to take in all that he'd said. My career and life had just opened up in an unimaginable way. It was as if everything had changed: the direction, the focus, the pressure, the importance, the scope. I was exhilarated. We left the lunch in a celebratory mood. Sergei told me to take my time and think about it. It was a huge step, and he knew I would have to closely consider it.

As we made our goodbyes, he smiled and said, "I'm sure you will have a good show tonight."

*   *   *

AFTER LEAVING SERGEI, I felt the need to discuss his overwhelming offer with someone who could help me sort it out. Alexei Ratmansky was in Moscow working on a new ballet for the Bolshoi and was the first person I confided in. After hunting him down in the theater, I asked him to meet me for a coffee the following morning.

Then I went back to the hotel, rested, returned to the theater, and danced *Seven Sonatas*, my last ballet of the tour. Sergei was right about the performance. His offer had given me an unbelievable sense of elation. I thought, *This is the change I was craving. This is what I was searching for: the risk that scares me.*

WHEN I MET with Alexei the following morning I told him everything that Sergei had offered. Because Alexei had been Artistic Director of the Bolshoi and knew what it was like to be a Bolshoi dancer, his advice held considerable weight with me.

"You must take this," he said. "This is historical for everyone involved and you must take this opportunity. This is huge. It is a great moment for the company and for you."

His answer stunned me.

Alexei had affirmed what I had sensed: it truly was a life-altering offer. Opportunities like this seldom presented themselves. I thanked him for his time and honesty and he went back to Bolshoi to finish creating his work. That day I boarded a train to St. Petersburg, my mind racing between two great companies, one in the city I was leaving and the other in the city I was traveling to.

"Mine was a true American childhood, at least for a while." *From left to right:* Dad, me, Mom, and Brian. Phoenix, age nine. (*Courtesy of the author*)

"All of that was changed one evening by a mysterious man gliding across our TV screen. His name was Fred Astaire." First dance recital, age eleven. (*Courtesy of the author*)

"Classical ballet was like my black hole, a gravitational force pulling me in deeper and deeper." *The Sleeping Beauty*, age fifteen. (*Courtesy of the author*)

"'*Mais, Daveeeeed.* Your leg in the back. It is not turned out. Bowlegs, *non?*'" The brochure criticized by a Parisian classmate, age seventeen. (*Courtesy of the author*)

The Summer Intensive Program at Arizona Ballet School offers four weeks of quality training by the School's excellent faculty and international guest teachers. Arizona Ballet School is centrally located in Phoenix. Students are trained in three spacious studios with full mirrors and all classes are accompanied by professional pianists. Class sizes are kept small for more individual attention. A performance will conclude the summer program for students who have completed the last three or all four weeks in Level Three and above. The others will have their final presentations on the last week of the program at the School.

"Mr. Han would stand five feet from me and pick me apart. I absorbed all of his criticism. . . . I had total trust in what he asked of me." A rare moment of teacher/ pupil camaraderie, age fifteen. (*Courtesy of the author*)

"My Sunday *New York Times* routine with breakfast at my local diner where everybody knew my name." NYC. (*Photograph by Henry Leutwyler*)

"If we think we don't need class and the daily focus it provides, our work slips and that slippage is eventually visible on the stage. The audience can tell." Daily class. (© *Christopher Anderson/Magnum Photos*)

"That is the purity of *Apollo*: so much depth behind each and every note and movement. Stravinsky and Balanchine created a masterpiece." (*Photograph by Rosalie O'Connor for American Ballet Theatre.* Apollo *Choreography by George Balanchine © The George Balanchine Trust*)

"*Theme* . . . is a ballet that will always let you know, in no subtle way, what shape you are in. It demands everything from you." *Theme and Variations*, age twenty. (*Photograph by Rosalie O'Connor for American Ballet Theatre.* Theme and Variations *Choreography by George Balanchine © The George Balanchine Trust*)

"He is a complex and in some ways a mysterious character that I would dance and question for my entire career." Prince Siegfried, Bolshoi. (*Photograph © Stephanie Berger, courtesy of Bolshoi Theatre*)

"This young, blindly hungry rookie whose unshakable goal was to become a Principal Dancer in American Ballet Theatre." "Grand Pas Classique," ABT. (*Photograph by Rosalie O'Connor for American Ballet Theatre*)

"I fantasized about the moment when I could feel at home on the Bolshoi stage, when the audience would get to know me and there would be a rapport between us." Evgenia Obraztsova. (*Photograph by Batyr Annadurdyev, courtesy of Bolshoi Theatre*)

Paloma Herrera aided me through many a debut with a work ethic matched by few. (*Courtesy of the author*)

Amber Scott was ethereal and earthbound, exemplifying Aussie warmth. (*Photograph by Kate Longley*)

"Once you have experienced that onstage euphoria, you hunger for it. Yet you have to accept that it is as rare as it is precious." My partnership with Natalia Osipova. (*Photograph by Rosalie O'Connor for American Ballet Theatre*)

"Then, in a flash, the house lights were brought to full strength and the interior of Bolshoi Theatre was revealed in all its glory." Onstage selfie, Bolshoi Theatre. (*Courtesy of the author*)

"The nourishment from Sasha, his eye for tiny detail and his honest feedback, pushed me beyond my preconceived limitations. And as consistent routine bore the fruits of that labor, I could see my dancing becoming broader, bigger, more open." (*Courtesy of the author*)

"Yet apart from the grayness and bitter cold of Russian winters, there is a romantic side to those long months as well. . . . I found the beauty of Moscow as I walked through the streets in the black of night, bundled up as I went home from a dinner or a performance. You could almost hear the silence through the frigid air." (*Courtesy of the author*)

"What would be one of the most important and high-pressure performances of our careers. . . . One way led to failure, buckling under the pressure that was so palpable to me. The other way, to conquering that pressure and using it to my advantage." The eve of *The Sleeping Beauty* premiere, Bolshoi Theatre. (*ITAR-TASS Photo Agency/Alamy Stock Photo*)

"In my dressing room alone, with my makeup and hair readied by Lena and the music of the Prologue reverberating through the closed door, I felt as though I were in a pressure cooker. It was unbearable." *The Sleeping Beauty* premiere. (*Photograph by Alan Andacht*)

"We then continued the bows, coming out until the theater held only small groups who wouldn't go home until they had shown their appreciation a final time." Bows at Bolshoi Theatre. (*Photograph by Alan Andacht*)

" 'My congratulations,' " said Medvedev in English. " 'I hear you don't speak much Russian.' '*Tolka chut-chut*,' I replied. *Only a little.*" Russian president Dmitri Medvedev (center) and Kazakhstani president Nursultan Nazarbayev. (*AP Photo/RIA Novosti, Dmitry Astakhov, Presidential Press Service*)

"Audiences show their appreciation by clapping long after the show has ended. It is a tradition that you find in no other country." Bolshoi Theatre. (*Courtesy of Bolshoi Theatre*)

"I couldn't fit my feet into anything but large supportive Nikes, which I had to use even as dress shoes. . . . I even wore those Nikes at the White House when meeting President Obama." (*Courtesy of the author*)

"Anticipation mounted around me as the two New York performances of *Swan Lake* loomed. . . . But through all the attention and anticipation, I was distracted. I felt a mounting unease about the pain that would not subside." Bolshoi tour, NYC. (*Courtesy of the author*)

"After the performances were over, Henry captured Svetlana and I hugging onstage. There is such relief in my face, a happiness that I made it through without major mishap. Though internally, I knew I was broken." Last performance, Bolshoi tour. (*Photograph by Henry Leutwyler*)

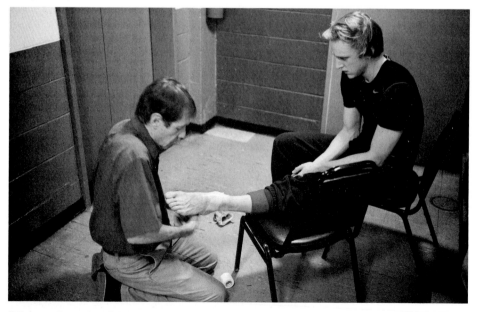

"I felt a twist and pull in my left ankle. I knew something had happened." Backstage with Peter Marshall, ABT. (*Photograph by Henry Leutwyler*)

"The moment my foot was revealed from under the cast, it was bulbous and red. Like a balloon that never lost its helium." (*Courtesy of the author*)

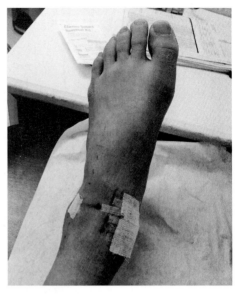

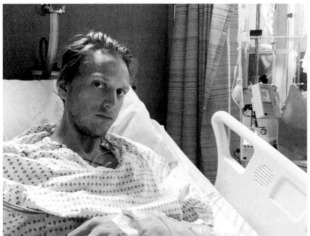

"The worst-case scenario had become real. Eleven months after my first surgery, I needed another." Post-op, second surgery. (*Courtesy of the author*)

" 'Goodbye, New York. There's some stuff I have to take care of once and for all.' " (*Courtesy of the author*)

"And so my education started. I'm baffled as to why I hadn't already known what Paula was teaching me about my instrument." Paula Baird Colt. (*Photograph by Lynette Wills*)

"Megan looked at me in disbelief. She laughed, having witnessed the obsessive dissection I put myself under." Megan Connelly. (*Photograph by Lynette Wills*)

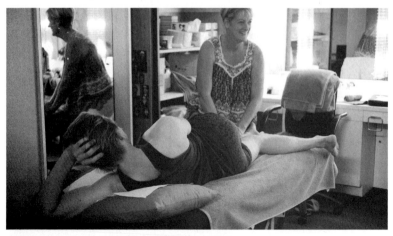

" 'But more importantly, what will give you peace of mind? What can we do to convince you that you are doing this? That this is actually working?' " Dr. Sue Mayes. (*Photograph by Kate Longley*)

" 'Today is the first day I'm dancing on a stage in over two years.' " With Brooke Lockett, State Theatre stage, Melbourne. (*Courtesy of the author*)

"I was finally ready to leave Melbourne. Ready to return to New York. Ready to explore again." Fourteen months later, leaving Melbourne. (*Courtesy of the author*)

"I clasped my hands together, closed my eyes, and bowed my head. There was nothing else for me to do but feel thankful for every bit of my past experience." The rebirth after two and a half years. (*Photograph by Kent G. Becker*)

CHAPTER 21

It felt strange to arrive at the Mariinsky this time, to meet Yuri again. I sensed his excitement and warmth at having me back. I was there to dance *Swan Lake*'s Prince Siegfried, and to do so effectively, I had to put Sergei's offer out of my mind.

I realized on that trip that every theater has a unique scent, something that sets each one apart. The Mariinsky smelled of aged wood and generations of sweat and makeup. I felt I could literally smell its iconic past: Nureyev's debuts, Petipa's creations, Tchaikovsky's music. It was all around me. I loved the fact that the theater was so old that it used to have traditional wood floors in the studios that needed to be moistened before each class. In those days, the lowliest dancer had the task of circling the studio, tin watering can in hand, sprinkling the floor as you would a garden.

When I walked in the stage-door entrance, it was like walking into history. I passed through wooden doors that must have been there since the theater was built in 1860. I thought about the artists who had touched those door handles: Prokofiev, Pavlova, Nijinsky, Balanchine as a young boy in the Imperial Ballet School, and, years later, when he returned to this theater in 1962 as the illustrious cofounder, Artistic Director, and chief choreographer of New York City Ballet.

Ascending the stairs to the dressing rooms, the side closest to the stage door was the men's side; the women's side was on stage right. My first time in the theater, I had been waiting for a ballerina on the women's side and was promptly questioned by the women's dresser as to what I was doing there. Her cool Russian stare let me know that my sitting in that side was not proper.

The dressing rooms were reached through a set of swinging doors whose paint was worn and showed through to the bare wood beneath, an emblem of the infinite cycle of performances: opera after ballet after opera, singers warming up their voices in these dressing rooms, dancers spending their careers and lives in this one theater. And as the theater fell deeper and deeper into disrepair, it became more and more alluring, its inhabitants consumed in their daily artistic routines.

The three Principal dressing rooms were bare, with feeble lights, wooden makeup tables, cloudy mirrors, and three chairs, two made of cheap metal, one of dark wood. No photographs. No warmth. If you looked at it objectively, the place was falling apart. Xander Parish, an elegant British Principal in the company, recalled having arrived at the theater for the first time and being shocked at how astonishingly worn it was. Granted, his previous theater was the newly refurbished Covent Garden in London, where no expense was spared in a complete overhaul. But the Mariinsky is such a significant and lauded historic house that, in my view, there is no other way it should appear.

WHEN I FIRST danced on the theater's raked stage, it hadn't intimidated me as much as I feared it would. Raked stages, common to older theaters throughout the world, including the Bolshoi, are raised at the rear of the stage and tilt downward toward the audience. During my initial rehearsal on that stage, I stood in the middle of it looking out at the theater. I marveled at the golden, gleaming Tsar's box, centered at the rear of the orchestra and separated from all other seats. Bedecked in statuary, topped off by a golden crown, it remains a fitting reminder of the generations of tsars and tsarinas who established the Imperial Ballet, then personally funded it, their love of ballet and their largesse ensuring that an art that had always been French would become irretrievably Russian.

Most impressive to me were the side boxes placed over the orchestra pit, dividing the theater and the stage. They make for some interesting connections during the performance when you can run to the front of the stage and catch the eyes of an onlooker only three feet from you, both of you behaving as if this fugitive moment of contact has not occurred.

As legendary as it is, the theater felt remarkably intimate. Even when I was at the top of the stage, gazing at the whole scene and into the house, I still felt that the audience was part of the action. I sensed that the audience and performer were one while I danced.

I PLUNGED DEEP into rehearsals with Yuri once again. True, I was there dancing yet another prince role, my Mariinsky debut a year earlier having been Prince Désiré in *The Sleeping Beauty*. But whether it was the environment or Yuri's ability to push me beyond my boundaries, we stripped *Swan Lake* bare and then rebuilt it.

It was a two-week crash course. He hurled information in my direction faster than I could absorb it. With Yuri's dynamic coaching

I became immersed in Siegfried. Over and over we would review the variations, the preparations, the toes, the fingers, the head, the accents. Every movement and gesture was corrected. I felt, once again, like the pupil responding to Mr. Han's commands. Repeating one step endlessly until it was deemed good enough that I could move on to the next.

I had to trust that the deeper I dove into work with Yuri, the greater the end result would be. As the performance neared, there was nothing to do but trust that the work I had put in, the devotion and commitment of the past two weeks, would pay off onstage when I needed it to.

I HAD A new partner, Ekaterina Kondaurova, a tall, sensual Russian. It was also a new production of *Swan Lake* for me, with new passages to learn. Many well-known ballet figures attended the performance; among them was Sergei Filin.

There are dancers who thrive when the pressure is at its highest, dancing better than they have in any previous rehearsal, stunning the audience with their risks. I was never one of those dancers. I respond to methodical and repetitive work, which develops over the course of a slow process. I knew this more than ever before after my *Swan Lake* with Mariinsky. I felt reincarnated onstage, with new shadings and attack. It was as if it were the first time I had ever danced that familiar role with which I had become bored and disillusioned. It reminded me that I needed to find that spark wherever I danced.

I had left each coaching session with Yuri exhausted, unable to do another step. He had worked me to my core, wringing out each and every nuance. Our intense work in the studio meant even more to me than being on the stage. I was a creature of the studio. Was this the last time I would work with Yuri? We had a unique rapport that I cherished. It was harrowing to think of letting go of what I had so desperately searched for in a coach and finally found.

Yet I couldn't escape the fact that Sergei's offer had come at such a fitting moment in my career. Maybe it really was that much-desired "risk" that I craved.

CHAPTER 22

When I returned to New York, the only people who knew about Sergei's offer were Alexei; my manager, Peter Diggins; and a very few people in my inner circle. I needed it to remain intensely private so I could make as clear a decision as possible, on my own terms and not clouded by everyone else's opinions. Were I to make the move, I would be walking away from everything familiar: my friends, the city, the English language, my apartment, the foods I like having in the fridge, my own bed. I wouldn't have my Sunday *New York Times* routine with breakfast at my local diner where everybody knew my name.

On the other hand, it would be a move that was big, that was bold. Among other things it would give me something I deeply wanted: many more opportunities to dance with Natasha.

I SPENT WEEKS mulling it all over. There was one half measure available to me: I could go to Bolshoi as a Guest Artist. But I knew all too well what guesting entails. As a Guest Artist, you come into the company, work with the dancers for a finite period of time, perform, and the next day you leave. No matter how much you dance there, you never have the chance to become part of that company's culture. The dancers may welcome you warmly, but you remain an outsider. Guesting had almost always left me craving more substance from the experiences.

Joining the Bolshoi would allow me to make a real commitment, as I had with ABT at the beginning of my career. I would integrate myself into the Bolshoi culture. I would put in the time it takes to become a part of it. I'd be looking from the inside out and not the other way around. A commitment like that seemed more fulfilling in the long run.

I NEEDED TO share the news with Kevin. I was apprehensive when I sat across from him in his office overlooking Nineteenth Street. I needed his honest advice about the offer. I always needed that from him, the harshest truth, even if it stung.

He listened. Then he responded in his usual calm and rational way. His reaction was incredibly generous. He could easily have been annoyed or angered that I was even contemplating this proposal, which would inevitably affect the amount of time I could spend with ABT. But he didn't try to persuade me one way or the other, he just asked questions and told me to not think emotionally.

"Think realistically," he said. "You have to listen to yourself and decide what is going to bring the most fulfillment."

I left his office feeling no more resolved in either direction but fortified by the reassuring sense that Kevin would be in my corner no matter what.

I DREADED TELLING Yuri about the Bolshoi offer. I kept putting off calling him in St. Petersburg, fearful of how he would feel and what he would say. When I finally steeled myself to place the call, it killed me that he sounded so happy to hear from me. Pacing my apartment, I told him what Sergei had proposed and that I was seriously considering it. He listened quietly. When I finished talking, his first statement was "You are not a Bolshoi-style dancer. You have the Mariinsky style."

He asked whether this meant I would be a guest with the Bolshoi or a full-time company member. When I hesitatingly said I would be the latter, he said what I already knew: it just wouldn't be possible for me to dance with both.

The disappointment in his voice was unmistakable. That was what troubled me the most. I knew my life and career were shifting. But I did not know which way to go. I cherished my relationship with Yuri. The prospect of disappointing him, or of turning down Sergei, paralyzed me.

THE NEXT WEEKS were a haze of stress, anxiety, insomnia, tears, elation, exhilaration. I had wanted something to shake me to the very core of my being. And I had gotten it. I would start the day with the thought of conquering a world of which I knew nothing, and finish the day in complete fear of it. And then there was my litany of what-ifs: *What if the offer never fully solidifies? What if I imagine it to be something it is not? What if all the dancers see me as this usurping outsider? What if I never make friends? What if I risk nothing, stay in New York, and regret my decision?* But above all others: What if all my talk of wanting a risk was fraudulent and, deep down, what I really wanted was the life I had created in New York City over the years that encompassed familiar places and customs and happiness with friends?

As the weeks stretched on, I came no closer to a decision. My friends noticed a change in me. I was closed off and distant. Some confronted me, noting that I wasn't smiling or engaging with anyone. I was adamant that few people know about my pending decision, which made it even harder to properly communicate with friends.

The offer Sergei had made was an honor. Not a stress. But the prospect of changing my entire life was the ultimate stressor.

Each day I would bounce from one decision to the other: Go to Moscow. Stay home.

IT IS OFTEN said that artists must make sacrifices for their calling. The word "sacrifice" implies that we give up something important to possibly gain something else. In literal terms, yes, that's what happens. Once I began dancing I gave up the possibility of a normal childhood and life. I hadn't seen my family with any regularity since I was seventeen, missing Christmases, Thanksgivings, birthdays, family reunions. When I was training late into the night for four years before that, I would miss family dinner every weekday evening and instead eat a microwavable dinner on the hallway floor at Ballet Arizona. But I never regarded any of this as sacrifice because there was no other choice. I *had* to dance. To follow that path. To see where it would lead. My curiosity and fascination with the art form took precedence over everything else. In that sense, what some would regard as sacrifice is, in my own private lexicon, a combination of duty and destiny. Which eventually turned into a responsibility.

What, I wondered, is my responsibility to this art form? Talent is an unearned gift; but talent is also an obligation. One thing I truly did believe was that I was morally bound to use whatever talents I had been given.

As the days and weeks passed, one question kept reverberating in my mind: *If this is the challenge you say you so need and want, then what is the hesitation?*

I HAD CERTAINLY taken risks before. The risk that every dancer takes, in every performance, is to go onstage with thousands of people watching and execute ballet's taxing steps. But then there are the dancers who go even further, who dance with a commitment and abandon that allows them to enter another realm where the risks are so heightened that the outcome can only be dazzling success or degrading failure. Those are the dancers I look to for inspiration, as I have always wanted to be that kind of artist. Not the one who steps off the stage—as I sometimes have—just happy nothing was messed up or that he didn't fall. The Bolshoi provided an opportunity to take a risk on an enormous platform.

In fact, I would not be the first American or foreigner to dance with the company. Michael Shannon, an American dancer, had spent years with the Bolshoi as a Soloist when the country was restructuring itself after the fall of the Soviet Union. The world was not as global then, and living in Russia would have been an even bigger risk for him than it would be for me.

In interviews I had often said that art is risk taking and it's the duty of the artist to chart unknown territory. I always knew that this wasn't something I could just pontificate about. If I really believed it, I needed to act on it.

I realized this one afternoon as I explained to a friend that my fear was deterring me from making a decision one way or the other.

"You know why you are becoming so emotional about it all, don't you?" he said.

"Why?"

"Because you know the answer and it scares you. You know what you need to do."

At that moment I recognized exactly what I "needed to do." Not because it didn't scare me to death but because it did.

The decision to join the Bolshoi had been made. I wanted no regrets. I didn't know who I would become. Whether it would be the best move for me in the long run. Or how it would end. And yet I knew, through my fear, that this was what I was craving and searching for. Finally, I was able to step into the unknown. And live up to the responsibility that I believed I owed the art.

MY MANAGER AND I were on the phone with Sergei the very next day at nine a.m., placing a call from the press lounge at the Metropolitan Opera House. The mood was ecstatic on both sides.

"Welcome to Bolshoi Theatre!" Sergei said.

But I hadn't simply committed to a ballet company. The commitment was to change all aspects of my life in order to better my work. I would bring my knowledge of dancing, my years of being a professional at ABT. But I would also discover a style I knew nothing about, a style that wasn't my training. Yuri was right: I had no "Bolshoi" in my dancing. Others in the ballet world, as I later learned, also thought I was more Mariinsky or Paris Opera; a more refined style with less fireworks. And that was precisely why it thrilled me to join the company. I planned to absorb their technique like a sponge, soaking in nuances of style that I hadn't been exposed to previously.

I would observe everything around me. Russian life and culture, the ballet world in Moscow, the people, the language. I fantasized about the moment when I could feel at home on the Bolshoi stage, when the audience would get to know me and there would be a rapport between us, much like the rapport I now shared, developed over years, with New York audiences.

The one thing that was hard to live with was that I had disappointed Yuri. Yet I was certain that I had chosen the right path. I believed in living my artistic life to its absolute fullest. I was doing it. I was answering the call.

CHAPTER 23

The news was officially announced in Moscow and New York on September 22, 2011. A tidal wave of media came hurtling my way. I had no idea that people would care so much. The widespread curiosity about the move was astonishing. I was bombarded with requests. First, a mention in the arts blog of the *New York Times*. Then the whole story, first on the *Times* home page and the next day on the front page of the print edition. *This is front page news?* I asked myself. I was stunned seeing my image, jumping through the air, on the front page of the paper delivered to my door each morning.

The article in the *New York Times*, written by the paper's dance critic Alastair Macaulay and Daniel J. Wakin, viewed my move through a historical prism. It began, "Exactly 50 years after Rudolf Nureyev grabbed the world's attention as the first major Soviet dancer to defect to the West, another symbolic journey is taking place—this time in reverse."

The other major defections from Russia had been those of Natalia Makarova in 1970 and Baryshnikov four years later. But since the end of the Cold War, many Russian dancers had performed in the West; Natalia Osipova, Nina Ananiashvili, and Vladimir Malakhov were among those who had done so as ABT Principals. It had been different in the nineteenth century, when Russian ballet was coming into its own and routinely imported the finest dancers from Italy and France, not least among them the Frenchman Marius Petipa, who would become known as "the father of classical ballet."

But over the course of the last hundred years, Russia had rarely engaged Western dancers. It was said they didn't need them, that the exquisite training in Russia produced all the dancers they required. That made sense to me.

Boundaries or no, I was still an American dancer joining a Russian company. Some would find much to criticize in that fact. American ballet doesn't always receive the recognition it deserves. Some believe it's devoid of history and refinement. While it's true we lack the historical roots of other balletic lineages, America still produces world-class ballet dancers, and has done so for decades. In the interviews I gave, I spoke about the responsibility I felt as a representative of American ballet. I told the *Times,* "I have to do it justice."

MY FINAL PERFORMANCES before my move to Moscow were in California, dancing in a presentation called *Kings of the Dance.* I geared myself up to bid a momentary farewell to American audiences. My parents came to the shows. They were never short of support for what I felt I needed to do, and moving to Moscow was no exception. Naturally it scared them a little. But so had my move to Paris.

I knew what awaited me in a few days' time on the other side of the world. I would dive into the work. Force myself to acclimate quickly to a style and city unknown to me. I would simply work, more focused than ever before. The pressure waited for me. The angst and indecision were gone. My nerves were beginning to feel like steel. Impenetrable.

So I was hoping to enjoy these last few days in sunny California, dancing in a performance with colleagues with whom I loved sharing the stage. Marcelo Gomes from ABT. Guillaume Côté from National Ballet of Canada. Denis Matvienko from Mariinsky. And my new colleague from Bolshoi Theatre, Ivan Vasiliev. It would be my last experience of a pleasurable, relaxed atmosphere in repertoire that didn't hold to the rigid traditions of classical ballet.

NATALIA MAKAROVA ATTENDED the opening night at the Segerstrom Center for the Arts in Orange County. As I had discovered when she'd critiqued my dismal rehearsal of *La Bayadère,* she was always prepared to offer an unvarnished opinion.

When I was told she had made a special trip from her home in the Napa Valley to see the *Kings* show, it immediately brought me to attention. I did not feel ready for Natasha. I had just gotten off a flight, and prior to it had packed up and closed my apartment in anticipation of the looming Moscow move. I was not in shape to dance in front of someone as knowing and eerily exacting as Natasha.

The ballerina Paloma Herrera had a great way of describing a show that was nothing to write home about. When asked, "How did it go?" she would simply say, "It went." And that night, thanks to jet lag and lack of sleep, my show "went." Natasha came backstage afterward and basked in the worshipful attention bestowed upon her by all of the dancers.

I was eager to have a moment alone with her. Ever since the decision and subsequent announcement of my move to the Bolshoi, I had blocked out most opinions. But the viewpoint I had been most curious about was that of a Russian dancer who had defected to the West. I wanted to know how she felt about my moving to the land she left years ago. Would she regard it as a mistake?

She invoked nerves in me whenever we met up, in the studio

or out of it. She affectionately pinched my ribs as we all sauntered offstage together, en route to our dressing rooms. "I'm so tired of reading about you in the Russian newspapers," she said.

I laughed nervously.

I told her that I had reservations about the Russian press because what I said could get lost in translation and give the wrong message. But she assured me that all was relatively positive; my decision coming across as rational and well thought-out.

Later, when we were seated next to each other at dinner, she noted that she had been twenty-nine when she defected. I was at the perfect age, she said, to make a move like this. She too had been in the prime of her career when, as I was about to do, she'd launched into something about which she knew so little.

"But I never regretted it," she said to me. "It was the greatest move of my life. I see many parallels between my situation and yours. You are at that moment in your career when you are young enough but you know what you are doing. And this is a risk you will never regret.

"Don't try to be like the Bolshoi. Show the Bolshoi who you are. You have nothing to prove. Show them something different."

I took her words to heart. She could relate to what I was about to experience. And she said the words that I longed to hear: "You will never regret it."

THE PERFORMANCES IN California finished and the time to leave for Moscow had finally arrived. I dreaded that moment when I would hug my parents and say goodbye. But dread was laced with eagerness to hone in on what was offered to me.

After the last performance I headed with my parents over to the Westin Hotel for our final supper. We could all feel the looming hour of parting, but we soldiered on, emotions held for the time. We followed the routine we'd set for whenever they would come see me dance in California, at the same theater where I first watched ABT as a Summer Intensive hopeful. Our farewells were always exchanged in this hotel lobby. We ate the same lobby bar food; I always had a martini to start, a beer to finish. The same waitress served us each time, chatting about the same things. There was nostalgia in the air. And melancholy.

Finally, we headed out of the hotel, followed by a television crew from *CBS News Sunday Morning* that was filming my final moments in the United States for a segment to be aired in a couple of weeks' time. My bags were at my side, the taxi idling, and I turned to my parents for one final hug. That last moment. Mom was in tears. We held each other tightly. My voice cracked as I said the word "goodbye." All caught on camera.

I climbed in the back of my taxi alone, exactly the way I'd imagined it many times over.

A few hours later, I walked onto the plane and took the plunge, fully aware that most of my American friends were convinced that I must be fucking crazy.

CHAPTER 24

Moscow Domodedovo Airport was a melting pot of Russian culture. There were immigrants, many of Mongolian descent, coming to the city for jobs. It seemed as though they had been there for days. They were sprawled about in every corner of the terminal, on the benches and floors, their belongings in plastic sacks held together by duct tape. Then there were the Russians who live in the suburbs of Moscow. They pushed their way through everything: lines, baggage claim, passport control. It was an intimidating sight. Passport control in Japan and other countries that pride themselves on organization and order welcomed foreigners. Russia just got on with it. This characteristic impatience seemed to harken back to the Soviet years, when endless lines were common and citizens had to wait in them to get basics like food and clothing. It must have felt like survival of the fittest.

Getting a cart for my luggage at baggage claim was a minor battle. People waited impatiently for the carts to be collected by an attendant and restocked, and when they appeared chaos broke out. Many people had told me that once I arrived in Russia I needed to assert myself, be strong, and stand up for myself. Politeness and social grace would come in handy at times (as I would learn from my generous colleagues inside the walls of Bolshoi Theatre), but they are never useful at Domodedovo. So I pushed, just like everyone else, for a metal cart to carry my luggage.

Outside, in the pickup area, hordes of cars were bundled in a tangle, some parked, some slowly idling, some fighting their way out of the cluster. I did not blend in. I had the Russian blond hair, blue eyes, and maybe the cheekbones, but I did not have a Russian character. I dressed differently. I looked like a foreigner, lost and confused, immediately taken for such by one taxi driver after another who asked if I needed a ride. Luckily, the Bolshoi had sent a car, and after wending my way through the disarray of the waiting vehicles I found the driver, who tossed my luggage into the trunk and sped away.

As we approached the city center, with the Kremlin on the left, riding down Ulitsa Okhotnyy Ryad, Bolshoi Theatre came into view, just as majestic as before but more meaningful now.

I HAD PREVIOUSLY learned that finding an apartment in the center of Moscow would be a logistical nightmare. Leases, brokers, safety concerns; I was rightly persuaded away from my scheme of dwelling in a sprawling Soviet-style apartment, which I pictured as cold, stark, minimal; a reflection of the life I would lead in Russia. Instead, during the six-year renovation of the theater, Bolshoi had built apartments directly behind the theater for visiting artists to live in. I was graciously offered one of them. As beautiful as they were, I was initially dismayed. These apartments were literally one hundred feet from the stage door, and steps from the rehearsal studios. The windows looked onto the back of Bolshoi Theatre and the glass footbridge connecting it to the administrative building. I could see the dancers arriving at the stage door, passing through the walkway, going to and from their daily rehearsal schedule. Work would be too close to home here.

But when I weighed all my options, this seemed the best bet. Sergei was again showing his commitment to my comfort, and for that I was extremely grateful. After all, the apartment would serve to remind me of why I came to Moscow: to work. I would have no distractions during my ten-second commute to the stage door. I imagined going to the theater at any hour during the day, sneaking in at night to rehearse privately when I wanted, or heading back home in the middle of a rehearsal day for lunch or a nap. It was an ideal scenario for the focus I craved.

After a brief stay at the Hotel Metropol, I was told my apartment was ready for me to move in. I dragged my luggage across Ulitsa Teatralnyy to my new abode. Everything around me was ornate but impersonal. I walked through the furnished one-bedroom apartment. It smelled of fresh paint. The furniture was brand-new, mismatched. A pale green leather couch. Pale yellow textured wallpaper. A faux wood armoire. Layered royal-blue crushed velvet curtains with gold tassels covered the deep double-paned windows to keep the Moscow winters out. A gold chandelier with large glass bulbs and matching sconces lit the room. In the bedroom, cream-colored crushed velvet curtains with gold tassels. Nothing else but a bed and a single overhead light. I was accustomed to my apartment in NYC, where my most coveted possessions were my books. My entire living room and entrance hall were stacked with books I had obsessively collected since I was fifteen. Nothing made me more comfortable than being surrounded by them. There were no books in my Moscow apartment.

I stood in the middle of my new living room. The only noise was my footsteps on the wood floor. I was beginning to understand what it means to uproot your entire life. There were no friends to call, no common language to speak, no schedule or objective but to work. I felt lonely and vulnerable. The sun was setting outside on a frosty October evening. Everything seemed new and crisp and empty.

*   *   *

A MONTH BEFORE I stood alone in my new apartment, I had gone to Moscow to close the contract with Bolshoi. One morning, during that trip, I'd joined the entire roster of 207 dancers in a rehearsal studio for a company meeting. I stood in the back with my translator, the rest of the dancers leaning against the barres or sitting on the floor in groups. By then the announcement had been made that I was joining the company. Some dancers knew me. Most didn't. Many sent inquisitive glances in my direction. They whispered among themselves. I couldn't speak to anyone except my translator, so introducing myself was out of the question. The meeting was about company logistics for the start of the season, and it was important that I knew the information being announced. Listening to the company manager leading the meeting, I stood blushing in the back as my translator whispered to me.

When the meeting adjourned, dancers began filing out of the studio. I nervously looked around, meeting the eyes of strangers who would soon become my colleagues. One of them, whom I had been eagerly but nervously waiting to meet, came up to me and introduced herself.

Svetlana Zakharova, known worldwide as one of the greatest ballerinas of her generation, was to be one of my regular partners. She was petite, with high cheekbones, hair pulled back covering her ears, wrapped in rehearsal clothing in all different shades of pink. We shook hands, peered at each other timidly, then smiled and kissed on the cheek.

I first saw Svetlana dance when I was nineteen and she came to ABT as a Guest Artist. I had just gotten into the company, and was dancing small parts in the Corps de Ballet. That night, as she danced Nikiya in *La Bayadère*, I stood watching her from the side of the stage. Her polished Russian training was enhanced by her long, thin legs and perfect proportions that comprise the ideal physique for a ballerina. She was unique, ethereal. It was clear to me why she was becoming a global sensation. She knew nothing of me then. But I certainly knew of her, the beautiful ballerina invited to dance with ABT.

Now, ten years later, the ballerina I had admired so much from a distance had agreed to let me partner her in *Sleeping Beauty* on the occasion of the opening of the newly renovated theater. And so we met for the first time. Our exchange of words was succinct but friendly. There would be time to get to know each other later. But even then we knew that the performance would soon be upon us and we would have to be in it together.

CHAPTER 25

In coming to Bolshoi, I was prepared to absorb a new style of dancing, but I hadn't anticipated such a conflict between what I previously knew and what I was being taught. It was truly a different approach to classical technique. During the first week of jumping, my lower calves screamed at me, *Uncle! Uncle!* I limped around between rehearsals, sore from this new approach and probably just teetering on the verge of a calf pull (which is notoriously one of the hardest injuries to heal). But inevitably, as rehearsals would gain momentum, adrenaline kicked in and the pain and soreness became subsumed in the pursuit of more important things.

I was to dance *Giselle* with Natasha and then *Sleeping Beauty* with Svetlana. But Svetlana was also dancing *Giselle*, with a different partner, and we would not start rehearsing *Beauty* until we finished our respective performances, a mere three weeks before our debut together. This was the way it was done and had always been. I was reminded of what I learned at Mariinsky: one ballet at a time, one gem of the repertoire at a time. Another adjustment for me, from which I would benefit immensely. The emphasis placed on one ballet (rather than five at a time) meant that it could be absorbed completely and fully in every nuance and aspect. My stress level was high nevertheless. I continued to work on my solos, but our "mere" three weeks alarmed me, as it meant Svetlana and I had little time to establish the requisite rapport and trust prior to what would be one of the most important and high-pressure performances of our careers.

FROM THE START, the culture of Bolshoi Theatre intrigued me. It was a lifestyle, a commitment one makes at a young age to one theater and one style. Not just a job but a way of living. This was not something I had experienced at ABT, where the company rehearsed at our own studios but performed at theaters elsewhere, rented out for the length of a particular run. Bolshoi dancers have a theater to call their own. They typically spend from ten a.m. to eleven p.m. in the theater six days a week, going from morning class all the way to the end of a performance late at night. The canteen, dressing rooms, studios, and stage are all under one roof, giving them pride of place.

Every morning I entered the theater through the "administration entrance." No less than eight stone-faced security guards protect this one entrance of Bolshoi Theatre. If you don't have an ID or are not on a clearance list, you cannot talk your way in. No exceptions. Climbing the three flights of stairs to my dressing room, I would pass some of the corps girls sitting in the stairwell in between floors, dressed in their pre-class warm-up clothes, chatting and smoking. As I walked by the cloud of smoke hovering over them, we would acknowledge each other in a typically Russian way: a brief moment of eye contact and a quick, terse, almost imperceptible nod. Very subtle. No smiles; closed tense lips. I adapted to this form of greeting quickly. At times I would hear a *zdrastye*, a quick form of "hello," but only within the camaraderie of Bolshoi walls. Never outside among strangers.

To walk from my dressing room to my morning class (one of eight morning classes offered daily), I traversed a long wooden balcony overlooking the studio, descending a staircase at the end to reach the ground floor. Dancers already in the studio below could watch whoever walked the length of the balcony. I kept my head down, feeling self-conscious. I was determined not to be overly friendly or desperate to quickly connect with new faces; I had made that mistake in Paris. Nor did I want to be unfriendly to my new colleagues. I knew they were trying to figure me out, from a distance. I never felt rudeness or a sense of unwelcome, just stares. I warmed up silently, doing my stretches and exercises, then took my place at the barre, in my designated "premier" spot. Dancers would banter and laugh at someone's joke. I understood nothing.

In line at the canteen one day I was waiting to get a snack before my rehearsal. There were dancers in all parts of the cafeteria, seated at nearby tables, standing behind me, talking, gossiping, laughing, and I could sense them watching me as I placed my order. *Will he speak Russian? Does he need help?* Embarrassed, I grabbed a ready-made cheese sandwich and asked for a bottle of water. I botched my feeble attempt at saying "water" (a simple "*vada*" in Russian) and was met with the cashier's quizzical look. She responded with a strong "*Shto?*" ("What?") I resorted to English. One of the dancers behind me chimed in and told the woman what I was asking for. I thanked her, poorly hiding my embarrassment, then quickly paid and left. I couldn't even order water without everyone in the cafeteria looking to see what nonsense would come out of my mouth.

Still, I was more assured than I had been at the Paris Opera School, and not so anxious to have people accept me. I had my craft to rely on. I kept my head down and just worked. I was ready to take any experience for what it was and try to grow from it, appreciating the easier times and enduring the harder ones.

*   *   *

I BEGAN TO learn the routines of my new company. Simple daily things like where to go to put my feet up during a break. The fastest route from one end of the building to the next. Which studio was better to rehearse in. My name wasn't written in English on the vast, finely detailed daily rehearsal schedule. To decipher it I looked for the *X*. The Cyrillic character equivalent of *H* is an *X*; and there were few dancers whose names started with it. I would scan the tangle of Russian last names and ballets being rehearsed, searching for that *X*. Холберг was me. After honing in on my name, I could then see how each ballet was written as well. Захарова; Холберг; Жизель: "Zakharova; Hallberg; Giselle," or Холберг; Спящая красавица "Hallberg; *Sleeping Beauty*." I didn't miss one rehearsal, thanks to my thorough search for the *X*.

THE BOLSHOI HAS a long-standing tradition of dancer/coach mentorship. In most Russian companies, the coaches are former ballerinas or premier dancers who performed with that company. A coach can choose a dancer to nurture from a young age, or when a dancer starts to perform more solo roles, he can ask a coach to work with him. The relationship then builds, and when bigger roles come along, the bond between dancer and coach is already formed. The well is deep by then. There is a trust built over years.

These relationships become very meaningful. The coach develops you, combats your weaknesses while strengthening your individuality. Because there is that trust, dancers aren't afraid to show their vulnerabilities. They know that their coach will pay close attention to every detail, down to costumes and hair. Finding the right coach at Bolshoi was going to be crucial to any success I could hope for there.

Sergei had suggested that I work with Alexander Vetrov, known as Sasha, a long-limbed and powerful former dancer with the Bol-shoi who had lived in America for the past fifteen years. There, he had run a small ballet company and school in Arlington, Texas, becoming a U.S. citizen. Sergei had invited him to return to Bolshoi Theatre as a coach at the same time that I joined the company. Sasha spoke English, knew life outside Bolshoi as well as in, and was returning to the theater with a new perspective.

I hoped to find with Sasha what I had found with Yuri: an intimate connection with a coach who could push me beyond my limits and see things in my dancing that I could not. I knew my shortcomings and needed someone to address them honestly and devote the time it would take for me to progress past them. That was the challenge. I also needed to be paired with a Bolshoi coach who would push me to adapt to the Bolshoi style. The word "*bolshoi*" actually means "big"; the theater's stage is larger than most. To inhabit it, to leap across it, to fill it, my dancing would need more amplitude.

I WANTED TO restructure everything about my dancing, and to do that I needed a totally honest dialogue with my coach. I didn't want to be coddled or taken care of. Because self-doubt is common in dancers, they often seek to be nurtured, and coaches occasionally serve more as a supportive parent than anything else. I had witnessed those relationships. And I had seen how ego and stubbornness can become a wall between that dancer and anyone he or she worked with. Such dancers were stuck in their own way of doing things and unwilling to bring themselves to a vulnerability that let growth occur. I was determined not to tumble down that path. I needed to be told the truth.

In the studio on day one, I had told Sasha that I couldn't grow unless he gave me brutal honesty. We hardly knew each other then, and I think those words came as a shock to him. Before establishing a rapport I was encouraging him to pick apart everything about me.

"This is the only time I truly grow," I told him, assuring him that he wouldn't offend me by telling me what wasn't good enough; that in fact, the opposite would occur. The more I was told what was wrong, the more I could thrive.

SASHA AND I dove into the work immediately. There was detail in his corrections. The approach into my jumps. The attack of my arms. Even the placement of my fingers before I propelled myself into the air. My apprehensions subsided. We found our ebb and flow in rehearsals and began a natural and enjoyable banter. I became certain that we would accomplish a lot together. I soon had a deeper understanding of jumps I had executed for years. Sasha was molding me into a better version of myself, chiseling at one detail after another. A foot. An arm. An angle of the head. I realized what a uniquely gifted coach he was and that the opportunity to work so intimately with him was a major benefit of Sergei's invitation to call Bolshoi Theatre my home.

Sasha took on responsibility for everything I did; from studio to stage. When a step wasn't executed to his liking or met to its fullest potential, he would mull it over just as much as I did. Later in the year, in a mid-performance fatigue, I began to lose strength and power in my legs. I finished the show with barely enough energy to execute the variations as we had prepared them, a result of not fueling properly and rehearsing too hard the day before. Sasha blamed himself. He told me it was his fault for not stopping me the day before in rehearsal, telling me to save my strength as well as checking up on what I was eating pre-performance. His reputation was just as much on the line as mine.

A BODY OF WORK

*   *   *

TIME WAS WHAT we needed most. We had only two weeks to rehearse for my *Giselle* with Natasha and to get me ready for judging eyes: company members, other coaches, Sergei, the audience. Sasha knew their curiosity would be intense, which is why our time in the studio was so protected, valuable, and imperative. He wanted no one watching and at times would even ask other dancers warming up for the next rehearsal to leave the studio.

Sasha would tinker with and analyze everything I did: for the smallest run to a corner he noted how my hips should be placed; how I should slow down at the end of the run. To my benefit, he was the same height as me. There is a different approach to movement and execution with such height, and Sasha could relate to that and translate it. I learned from him what an advantage height could be if I knew how to utilize it properly. When not rehearsing, he expected me to fully rest my body for the following day. Because when we stepped into the studio to work, he wanted me fully recharged, ready to deliver everything I could give him.

In the course of all this, I was still a stranger in a strange town. Other than Ivan and Natasha, I knew no one. I had no friends. No social life. Nowhere to go after rehearsals had finished for the day. I had no distractions veering me away from the work. At home in the evenings, I thought about that day's rehearsal. Sasha's guidance trickled from my head to my body, away from the literal thought of a movement and eventually into muscle memory when it "gets into the body."

A one-hour rehearsal was at full throttle from beginning to end. There were days when I would start a variation and go through it in its entirety, finishing in fatigue, pacing around the studio puffing for air. Personally thinking it hadn't been that bad, I would look at Sasha for feedback. Often it didn't meet his standards. His discerning eyes saw things I could not.

As with Yuri, Sasha would spend an hour with me on forty-five seconds of material. He would endlessly harp on my turnout, the rotating outward of the legs from the hips, which is essential to the aesthetic line of classical ballet (and consequently gives ballet dancers their "duck walk"). Sasha made clear that I had been dancing many things turned in. Because of the extreme rotation of my feet, the turnout came from below and not higher up, from the hips. He would demonstrate how it looked if his hips were open when walking, preparing, jumping, running. Then he would show me what he saw when I danced. Legs turned in. Creating a feeble, powerless walk or a brittle, small preparation for a jump. When his hips were rotated out, I could see how he added power and weight to his movements. A run looked earthbound and strong. A walk looked masculine and dense. An audience member can marvel at the height of a jump or the power of a run, but generally doesn't realize that it all stems from the strength of a dancer's turnout, a largely unknown detail that affects virtually every step. Once my turnout was corrected, over and over again, I felt physically more agile and in control, which, in turn, made for a visual difference for Sasha and the audience.

NOTHING WAS SPARED a thorough dissection, which made every movement seem far more complex than it had ever seemed before, leaving me to feel I couldn't execute it anymore. Sasha broke me down to build me back up. It terrified me when simple steps that I had executed for years completely fell apart. How could a step so basic to the classical technique, like a run or a glissade, be so difficult and intricate? I would stand in disbelief in the center of the enormous Bolshoi studio, Sasha in the front facing me. I would look at him wide-eyed, panic-stricken. These were the most fundamental steps in the ballet vocabulary and there they were, unraveling at the seams. Was everything beforehand an illusion? How had I convinced myself I was giving enough previously? But still, this was my utopia: working this hard and assessing this much.

The more we pushed through the difficult moments, the better the outcome was. I could feel the hours of molding, forming, questioning paying dividends. He wanted more. He knew there was more in me. His eye guided me forward. I felt like a foal taking its first steps. But a foal who previously had a ten-year ballet career. I was adding more to my technique. I relearned habits. I felt my focus change. At times, I attained the standard that Sasha expected of me. I shed layers of dried, uninspired skin to feel a raw, focused layer underneath.

As some new approaches felt like they had started to click, Sasha would say that, in fact, they weren't where they needed to be. So I worked harder. That drive I had lost back in New York was regained. The nourishment from Sasha, his eye for tiny detail and his honest feedback, pushed me beyond my preconceived limitations. And as consistent routine bore the fruits of that labor, I could see my dancing becoming broader, bigger, more open. It had more force. A moment of preparation into a jump was used with ultimate efficiency. I felt my entire six-foot-three frame of a body used in all its height and length. Even the way I walked on the stage was different. I had weight. Purpose. I felt like a dancer equally earthbound and airy. I could find that shading between the two more easily, offering weight when I needed it but providing the lightness of jump and presence in other moments. I began to feel a rebirth under Sasha's honest watch, there in the intimacy of the studio with no one but myself, my coach, and the pianist. Every hour spent in the studio was bringing us closer to our final objective—my first performance in Moscow as a Bolshoi Premier.

CHAPTER 26

My Bolshoi debut was *Giselle*, partnering Natalia Osipova. The opportunity to dance again with her, in her home theater, was one of the biggest personal bonuses of coming to Bolshoi. I immediately immersed myself in the flow of my *Giselle* rehearsals. First, I had a solo call for an hour, when I would work meticulously on one jump and step after another. Then, time with Natasha, running the ballet from beginning to end, for an hour and a half. I was in heaven.

Sasha and I deconstructed Albrecht, the male lead. Most of Albrecht's dancing is reserved for Act II, so Act I builds his character and allows for just a few moments of expression through actual dancing. Those moments were regarded with the same importance as a major variation in the second act. Sasha explained them anew. In the climax of Giselle and Albrecht's initial flirtation there is a small moment when he playfully chases her around the stage in a series of jetés. Sasha had infinite ways of telling me how to approach this circle, a mere twelve counts that I, beforehand, didn't realize deserved such attention.

I was finding a way back into the classical repertoire. For years, I had wanted a way to make *Sleeping Beauty* or *Swan Lake* something personal, something that felt true to myself and not dictated by generations of expectation. I had begun to do that with Yuri and,

221

as I rehearsed *Giselle* with Sasha, I realized more clearly than ever that the opportunity to do so had always been there. Because it had to come from inside. My task was to find the drive and the individuality in the work, critical intangibles that Sasha fostered but could not supply. His responsibility had to begin and end with giving me the information and enabling me to make of it whatever I could. It was empowering to recognize that, ultimately, I was the one holding the reins.

WHEN IT CAME time to perform *Giselle*, the work Sasha and I accomplished in the studio had to transfer to the stage. The comfort and growth I felt in the studio would have to amount to something in public. The expectation and pressure to prove myself were enormous. I could feel it all around me: from Sergei, Sasha, the other coaches, the dancers, the media. I was scared of that first show, when everyone would judge and scrutinize.

I was lucky that Natasha would be my partner. I knew that she would calm my nerves just by dancing next to me. Still, I kept asking myself, *Will I be able to live up to expectations?*

NATASHA AND I would be dancing on what is known as the New Stage, a secondary stage that was used throughout the six-year renovation of Bolshoi Theatre. Twenty minutes before the curtain went up, Liusia, the main stylist for the male dancers of Bolshoi, put the final touches on my hair and makeup. A friendly woman, quick to laugh and try her English out on me, she chatted with me while she worked. Nervous, I just nodded and smiled, mentally miles away. I escaped into my dressing room, alone. I sat down in my chair, the bright bulbs on the mirror warming the room. I looked at my reflection, hair blown back and sprayed, eyes lined with dark shading. I knew what task was approaching, and before I put on my costume (the point of no return) I tried to find confidence in the eyes looking back at me in the mirror. I convinced myself that I could rise to this occasion.

Outside those dressing room doors, everyone waited to watch, judge, critique, decipher. My worthiness. My talent. I reached for my costume, pulled on my cream-colored tights, and made my way to the stage.

NATASHA WAS THERE before me (it's where she does most of her preshow preparation). I pranced about, warming up like a runner before a sprint, feeling calmer now than I had in my dressing room. The curtain down, I tested out certain steps, listening to the low hum of the house as the audience entered. These familiar rituals—the buzz of the audience, the notes of the musicians warming up—gave a reassuring feeling that this was just like other shows.

Just another Giselle, I told myself.

I loved those "normal" shows, the ones where no one you know personally is watching: minimal pressure, the energy around you calm. They always loosened me up, allowed me to take more risks, to feel free. But I knew, as much as I might tell myself it was just like previous *Giselle*s, that tonight was really altogether different. It wasn't the show to relax and take risks because no one I knew was watching. In fact, it was those whom I didn't know who mattered most. Moscow audiences and I would be acquainting ourselves with each other. They had yet to form an opinion of the American who'd joined the Bolshoi Ballet. First impressions are the most lasting.

AT MY FIRST entrance, as Albrecht enters Giselle's village, I listened for their reaction. I did worry that I was going to be booed. Booed for being an outsider. Booed for being American. Instead,

I was courteously welcomed. But the applause was simply polite, as if they were saying, "Okay, we acknowledge you as a member of the company, but we'll hold off on any major enthusiasm until we see you dance well."

Though performers can rarely see the people in the audience, more importantly, we always *feel* them. They could be sitting quietly, watching the action onstage, and we still sense their energy, their collective mood. In intimate moments like Romeo and Juliet's balcony scene, the most subtle movement—Romeo's touch of Juliet's finger—can cause everyone in the house to hold their breath. This you can also sense. Applause is different. There is the roar when a dancer shows the audience a blazing technical feat. The long thunderous applause when they are deeply appreciative. The thin polite clapping suggesting indifference.

FROM THE MOMENT Natasha and I were onstage together we were connected. She was with me, and I was with her. No one else could have gotten me through the pressure. Looking at her comforted me. Dancing with her propelled me. Our energy was a drug, regardless of what stage we were dancing on. I loved feeding off her. Playing with her. Embracing her.

Without her, I had moments of panic. Warming up for Act II, with the majority of Albrecht's dancing yet to come, I lost the coordination of my pirouettes. When something goes, the feeling lost, it can head south immediately. Years of drilling pirouettes can't save it. I repeated a turn over and over, to no avail. Certain elements were against me; I was still adjusting to the rake of the stage and a canvas floor (slippery), not the usual Marley (a stickier surface, easier to grip). Natasha had slipped on the canvas in rehearsal and fallen badly. Executing a pirouette on it feels like turning on ice. Warming up, I couldn't pull out three pirouettes.

Sergei was on the side of the stage and witnessed my gradual decline. Quietly, he came up to me and, in his colorful English, told me to just focus on the motion of the turn; not to pull out multiple pirouettes but to just execute three clean single turns all in one calm execution. That was enough. He refocused my energy and I relaxed. Sometimes I ask myself what the main point is. What am I focusing my energy on? What is most important? Surely not the number of pirouettes I execute. The motion of the turn is what matters. And Sergei brought me back to the honesty of movement.

Intermittently throughout the show, I would think about the magnitude of what I was doing. About the likelihood that everyone watching was deciding whether it had been a smart move to bring me into the company. Those thoughts led to instant panic, so I did what I could to assuage them, telling myself to just allow the performance to happen. *Don't force the steps. Or the acting. Trust the work you have put in. Allow yourself to have the performance you desire.*

I zoned in on my natural rapport with Natasha in order to remain focused amid the circus around me. The activity in the wings was as it had been when I first came to Bolshoi: a bevy of dancers, their friends and children, as well as the theater's babushkas and dressers, all of them so close to the stage that they were almost on it. There were intimate moments in Act II that I worried about: kneeling by Giselle's grave, remorseful and guilt-stricken by her death. Her grave was set just off the wings, and as I carried a huge bouquet of lilies to lay by her cross, it would be hard not to notice the peering eyes of wing watchers two feet from me.

I couldn't blame them. Better a sense of curiosity than not caring at all. Ultimately, I had to ignore everything around me, and try to give the most authentic performance possible.

*   *   *

AFTER THE FINAL curtain we took our bows in the Bolshoi style; something I had yet to learn. There is a specific way in Russia of acknowledging the audience, unique to a culture that respects ballet so much. Slow, studied, in the moment; soaking in the appreciation of the audience by deliberately measured gestures. There are flowers—for most ballerinas, bouquets and bouquets of them. An abundance of flowers were brought out to Natasha by the Bolshoi ushers in their maroon jackets and skirts, doing their best to wrangle heaps of bouquets onto the stage. Then the curtain was closed, full stage bows finished. The Corps de Ballet trailed offstage back to their dressing rooms, idly taking the bobby pins out of their hair.

As the center curtain parted, Natasha and I made our way out, hand in hand, to the front of the curtain. With the house lights up, the audience was in full view. It is uniquely Bolshoi to have the house lights on as the dancers connect with the audience from the first row of the orchestra to the top of the balconies. (At most theaters the house is still dark, making it hard to see the audience.) They rose from their seats, facing the stage, chanting a long "Bra-vo," making it a metered two-syllable word. The bows in front of the curtain continued . . . six, seven, eight more. Behind the curtain, we spoke to guests standing onstage; I spoke to Sasha, who gave me immediate corrections. I've always loved notes directly after the show when it is fresh in my mind. We then continued the bows, coming out until the theater held only small groups who wouldn't go home until they had shown their appreciation a final time.

"Last one?" we said to each other as we walked out to say good night to the handful of audience members still applauding.

I owed that night to Natasha. I felt as I always felt with her: as if the audience wasn't even watching. When I was alone onstage

226

in a variation I was ever aware of them. But when I danced with her it was intimate; we were in our own private world. Performing with her told me for an absolute certainty that coming to the Bolshoi was the right decision. When we danced together, I was home.

CHAPTER 27

Three days after my debut with the company, I was being interviewed by a Russian journalist who asked, "How do you feel about Osipova and Vasiliev leaving the Bolshoi?"

She was speaking in broken English, so at first I thought something had gotten lost in translation. I didn't think she meant an actual departure from the company.

But she did.

Natasha had given me no previous warning. I didn't even know it was being discussed. Although we didn't have an ongoing social relationship outside the studio and stage, it stung to hear—especially from a random journalist—that we wouldn't be able to work more together.

Natasha and I never discussed her departure. There was nothing really to say. I wasn't angry. I would have loved for her to stick around and dance with me, but, as I said at the time, I accepted that she had to do what she had to do. She had to be artistically fulfilled, and if she thought a different company would offer her that opportunity in a way the Bolshoi could not, then she should go for it. It wasn't up to me to ask her to stay solely for my selfish reasons; obviously that wasn't reason enough.

Still, Bolshoi lost two of its greatest stars. Natasha and Ivan were the fresh faces of the new generation of Bolshoi dancers, and had been nurtured and groomed in the company. They were a sensation throughout the dance world, having created an enormous success in their performances with Bolshoi of *Don Quixote* in London. Seven months earlier, when I had gone to see the Bolshoi's *Flames of Paris* and been struck by how invigorated the company looked, Ivan and Natasha, dancing the leads, had been brilliant, incandescent stars. Through their raw, urgent belief in their portrayals, I saw the necessity of our art. They *were* Bolshoi. And Bolshoi was in them. But artists must stay true to what they believe will best enhance them.

REGARDLESS OF MY feelings about losing Natasha as a partner, I had to focus on *Beauty* for the reopening of the Historical Stage. The performance would require every ounce of my mental and physical energy. With both of our *Giselle*s behind us, I was at last in the studio with Svetlana. I was immediately struck by her personal warmth. We fit well together, easing into the partnering quickly and efficiently. There was a softness to her when we were together; I sensed she was relaxed and comfortable with me. I also felt she enjoyed my foreignness, and appreciated the risk inherent in coming to Moscow and Bolshoi. And it comforted me to know she liked practicing her English on me.

Svetlana had an extremely tight bond with her longtime coach, Ludmila Semenyaka. A fiery woman, Ludmila had been one of the great Bolshoi ballerinas. She warmly welcomed me to the company in our first rehearsal together. It was the four of us in the studio: Sasha, Ludmila, Svetlana, and me. We got straight to work on *Sleeping Beauty*.

From the start, I was assured that this wasn't going to be a one-way partnership. Both Svetlana and Ludmila told me to chime in if there was ever anything I thought would work better for us; all

I needed to do was let them know. I had expected to be told what to do with little room for deviation. But I was pleased that they were curious about what I had learned previously and about the nuances I brought to the ballet. It reminded me of Makarova's words on the eve of my arrival to Bolshoi: "Don't try to be like the Bolshoi. Show the Bolshoi who you are."

They also made every attempt to help me transition smoothly to life in my new environment. They constantly asked what I needed. A good masseur? Directions? The best grocery store? Anything. They had true empathy for the fact that I had left the familiarity of home.

SINCE SVETLANA AND I hardly knew each other, our pairing, in a situation with such immense pressure, was a gamble. In our first rehearsals, I was shocked by her strength and her physique. As I had seen when she danced at ABT, she is an ideal ballerina with long hyperextended legs and arms, a short torso, and piercing, overarched feet that come to a very defined point, finishing off her line in a visually optimal way. She is lithe and thin, which in a ballerina could signal a lack of power. But as soft and ethereal as she looks, she is made of steel. She is always in control. If there was ever a moment when I had her somewhat off her leg, she conjured her strength to keep herself up on her own. It made partnering her a joy, with little stress about her abilities to hold herself up. The worry beforehand—about not being able to keep up with her, not having an artistic and personal rapport—was forgotten at the start.

Svetlana is a ballerina of two sides: A model of grace, as one would imagine a ballerina to be. Also, a strong woman who makes decisions based on nothing but her own instinct, who forms her own opinions and sticks to what she believes. For which I have complete respect. Like other successful ballerinas she is in charge of her own career and artistic choices.

From the beginning, she told me to stand up for what I believe in. I prided myself on being a team player, compromising for the bigger picture of a given situation. Svetlana would state very clearly what she needed and why. Nothing was irrational. It was never rude. Never impolite. But firm and assured.

I HAD QUICKLY learned that I'd had to be approved by a number of people before I was approached to dance *Sleeping Beauty* with her. There had been other choices, but she'd agreed when my name was suggested to her by Sergei and the former director of the Bolshoi Yuri Nikolayevich Grigorovich. I was clearly the most controversial choice, and possibly the riskiest, but she had taken the gamble.

Initially, when we were introduced in the studio in front of the other dancers, we had been like shy little kids whose parents had set up a play date. But we soon got to know each other. She had a husband (an accomplished concert violinist) and had recently given birth to a baby girl, Anna. As we rehearsed more, I came to see how serious she was in the studio, making the sharp division between work and private life. We joked and laughed from time to time, but there was always a goal to accomplish. A task at hand. She reinforced for me, by example, the absolute power of the work ethic. Not only did she work hard, but she did so day in and day out with no complaints.

Months later, when we began rehearsals for *Swan Lake* she would toil endlessly on every detail with Ludmila. She would at times be slow to start, chatting while putting on her pointe shoes, but once she was ready, her focused, deliberate energy was never wasted on anything else.

I took none of those moments—partnering her, watching her rehearse—for granted. From time to time, I was reminded of when I watched her dance *La Bayadère* at ABT, me blending in with the others on the side of the stage, all eyes on her stunning physique and polished Vaganova training. Now we formed our own bond together, embarking on a new partnership.

CHAPTER 28

At Bolshoi, I became an ever more avid observer of the company's traditions and history. They were everywhere. In class. Before performance. After performance. During rehearsal. I found personal fulfillment in adhering to customs upheld for generations. I didn't feel a need to be the American trying to break them one by one. Instead, I viewed them with fascination and enjoyed making them a part of my routine. Before one of my first shows, I sat in my dressing room and did my own makeup, just as I had countless times before. After the performance, the head makeup artist for the male dancers approached me and kindly commented that I hadn't had enough makeup on. The underlying issue, as I realized from her comment and by observing the other male dancers pre-performance, was that *she* did their makeup from start to finish. No one did his own; that was her responsibility, her job, in which she took enormous pride. She was, after all, a professional, and my amateur application would offend anyone with her expertise. So from then on, before my warm-up for a show, I sat in her chair and let the professional do the job.

THE COSTUME DEPARTMENT at Bolshoi Theatre is a part of its history that I regarded with genuine awe. When I arrived in Moscow, the costume shop occupied an entire building where dozens of women toiled away making tutus, tunics, tights, opera cloaks, tiaras, hats, boots, even pointe shoes with the stamp of Bolshoi Theatre on the sole. When I was summoned there, a curt security guard sitting in a small entry box asked for my Bolshoi identification. No smile, no greeting, no idea who I was. Like all Russian guards he treated me, or anyone, as a threat until proven otherwise. My identification accepted, he gave me a single nod to pass through into a desolate courtyard. I could see an unmarked metal door across the way. I always noticed these entrances throughout Moscow. Nothing adorning them. Nothing welcoming. I entered into a sparse lobby area. On the wall was a huge plaque adorned with a hammer and sickle and the letters *USSR* written in Cyrillic script. Around it were dozens of pictures of employees, stern-faced men and women from the 1960s or '70s. Frozen in time. From another era. Buildings like this one would become unremarkable to me during my time in Moscow, but this first impression was startling.

The building's interior had pockmarked walls and floors, as if the concrete was disintegrating. I walked up a huge staircase with massive windows looking out onto a playground. Workmen in overalls and women in blue aprons crowded the stairwell landings, where there were worn couches they relaxed on. Everyone was smoking. They stared at me as I walked, observing me coolly, not knowing who I was. I reached the fourth floor and made my way down a long hallway with a dozen metal doors, all looking exactly the same. Through trial and error, I found that inside each one was a separate department that housed costumes for the opera or the ballet, with different departments for men and women. Finally, I entered a vast room where half a dozen women were huddled together. Some were middle-aged, some were older. They all had tape measures around their necks. Their faces lit up when they saw me, and they signaled to me to walk in. I noticed that several mock-up costumes lay on a chair beside them.

There was no single source of light but many lamps and ad hoc chandeliers hanging from the ceiling. The walls were lined with mismatched couches, chairs, and tables that looked as though they'd been passed down or found on the street. Giant mirrors lined two walls, not one matching the others. One huge mirror hung in a gold-painted and elaborately corniced frame; another, unframed, leaned against the wall. Devices that looked like clip-on reading lights were attached to the mirrors and lit the fitting area. The light they emitted was bright and harsh and distinctly unflattering. Off to one corner, the changing area was designated by a piece of fabric used as a curtain. Inside the tentlike space was a single chair to sit on while trying on tights. In the back, past the fitting area with the couches, were the large worktables where fabric was cut and costumes constructed.

The ladies who worked in this room had a singular specialty: the creation from start to finish of the men's ballet costumes. There were other women in another department altogether who made the tights and the shoes, and a completely different group who made the women's costumes and their tiaras. Everything worn on the Bolshoi stage was made in this building, by a dozen different departments.

I was slated at that time to dance all the classics in the Bolshoi repertoire, so every one of my costumes would be fabricated especially to fit me. This is a major difference from many other companies, where costumes are shared by several dancers and handed down to new generations of dancers who come after them. Although it's less personal, there is a certain nostalgia when you put on a costume once worn by a dancer you look up to. For a ballet at ABT, the tag inside my costume once read *Baryshnikov*. It was such an old costume that it had completely lost its elasticity and fit me even though he and I have a serious disparity in height. Any male dancer would get a thrill wearing his costume.

Given the length of each classical ballet, there were no less than two costumes for each one and as many as four costumes for a single role. Ensuring the perfect fit and size meant I would be in those fittings for hours, spread out over a number of days. In addition to the two costumes for *Sleeping Beauty*, there would be three for *Don Quixote*, two for *Swan Lake*, two for *Giselle*, four for *Onegin*, and four for *Marco Spada*. The fittings seemed interminable as the *kostumeri* surrounded me and contemplated every inch of fabric. How it lay. How tight it should be. Patience was my ally. I had to keep in mind that the meticulous work I demanded from myself in the studio, repeating steps over and over again, was the same work the *kostumeri* expected of themselves. I couldn't rush them; regardless of how much my legs and calves started to cramp. I was used to dancing all day, but oddly enough, standing perfectly still for hours wears out your legs in a completely different way. I'd get hungry and tired. Then I'd zone out, a zombie in a prince's tunic and tights.

ON MY INITIAL visit, the first things the *kostumeri* showed me were very rough mock-ups of the costumes I would wear for the opening of *Sleeping Beauty*. Both jackets were a lightweight velvet; one in a very pale blue, the other a very pale yellow. The ladies put the mock-ups on me and started pulling and cutting and pinning. All six women surrounded me, speaking in Russian, analyzing how the costume would lie on my body. It was a science to them. I stood there for the better part of an hour and a half, legs throbbing in my white tights. When I tried to indicate certain changes I wanted, for instance to make the front of the jacket more open at the bottom, we did our best to communicate through gestures. They would contemplate what I asked and decide among themselves whether or not it was possible, a negotiation that always led to a very animated back and forth among the six women. When they reached a decision, it would be conveyed to me by

Yulia, a petite woman in her fifties with pulled-back brown hair that smelled faintly of cigarettes. Yulia became my main costume lady, partly, I suppose, because she could speak to me in very slow basic English. I would respond either *nyet* or *da*.

Most of what I suggested was put into effect. But there was one thing I wanted to alter for my *Swan Lake* costumes that turned out to be asking too much. *Swan Lake* has reached iconic status globally as the most recognized ballet in history. But at Bolshoi, where it was created and premiered in 1877, the ballet is a part of the theater's identity. I was well aware of this when I tried on my mock-up for that role. Nevertheless, I requested what I thought was a simple change. The silver-laced white fabric of the sleeves jetted out at the shoulders and resembled a white pouf that looked, to my eyes, too old-world and old-school. I asked if they could just make a straight sleeve with no ruffle at the top; trim it down to streamline it a bit. I'm not typically finicky with my costumes, and I'm usually content to go along with what the designer intended. But this was one thing I very much wanted to modernize. The women surrounding me looked puzzled and reluctant. They took the sleeve in about a centimeter.

I looked at them and said, "Can you get rid of the whole thing? I would like just a straight sleeve."

They took it in another centimeter. I wasn't getting very far. Finally Yulia said that this was the designer's wish and they couldn't do a straight sleeve. The sleeve had been that way since the original production. I could have refused and told them how I envisioned the sleeve, but I realized that respect for tradition was strongly upheld by the *kostumeri*. My costume was a part of Bolshoi Theatre history and had to be honored as such.

IT WASN'T LONG before I became comfortable with the *kostumeri*, swinging open the door to the shop and greeting them with "*Zdravstvuyte krasivitza!*" I had no idea whether I was saying "Hello, beautiful!" correctly; or was it "Hello, beautifuls!"; or "Hello, the beautiful!" But it brought an immediate smile to their faces nonetheless.

When I needed to come in for a fitting, the message would be conveyed to me by any one of a number of people: Svetlana, Sasha, the rehearsal coordinator, the assistant director. When I finally got a mobile phone, I received texts in English that read, "Please come. Yulia costume." Succinct; to the point; and, endearingly, in English.

Occasionally, I would learn what roles I was going to be dancing from the costumes for which I was being fitted. One day the women showed me the mock-up for the title role of Pierre Lacotte's *Marco Spada.* To my knowledge, it had been decided months before that I would dance the supporting role of Prince Frederici, not the main character. I told the *kostumeri* they were wrong, but they insisted they had been told to make Marco Spada's costumes for me because I was dancing the premiere. And so it was that I found out that I was not only dancing the role of Marco Spada but would do so on the opening night.

WHEN A COSTUME is made especially for you, it has the power to change the way you carry yourself. At my final fitting for *Sleeping Beauty,* I slipped on the pale blue jacket to be worn with my matching pale blue tights. Gone was the mock-up with its rough muslin. In its place, delicate velvet and ornately hand-stitched embroidery. The velvet stretched; neither too heavy and cumbersome nor too flimsy. It hugged my body perfectly. I was proud to have the *kostumeri*'s work on my body. Dancers need material that breathes well and cooperates with the extremities of movement when we perform. If the costume doesn't fit or the fabric is too stiff, we become stiff ourselves, uncomfortable in our adopted outer layer. Certain steps can also become impossible because of the restrictions of the costume. The *kostumeri* had sourced the ideal fabric to allow me the freedom I required. There was room in the shoulders for when I would lift my ballerina, and tightness in the waist to create an aesthetic line from the hips downward. The proportions were perfect, as was its detail, down to every rhinestone sewn on with absolute attention. The cuffs were laced with intricate gold and silver beadwork with more beads edging the fronts and decorating the backs. Each jacket would be worn over an embroidered vest, under which was a high-necked silk shirt with a cravat and pin. Everything was meticulous.

Costumes for a full-length ballet had rarely been fit to my exact measurements before. At times they were gorgeous to look at but difficult to dance in. But this was entirely different. What had begun as a jumble of rough fabric and straight pins had turned into the most comfortable and beautifully ornate costumes I'd ever worn. It made me happy to see the pride on the *kostumeri*'s faces, with the finished product on my body.

In the press conference just before the final stage rehearsal for *Sleeping Beauty,* I faced the cameras wearing the pale blue jacket made for me. I stated how lush the production was, down to the costume I wore at that moment. I said I was honored to be dancing in such beautiful attire. The next week, when I arrived for more fittings with my *kostumeri,* the ladies thanked me for mentioning the costumes in the media. How could I not have? Hours had gone into every detail of fabricating the best costume possible. These women were just as committed to Bolshoi Theatre as anyone who received more public accolades. They deserved as much attention as any other element of the production.

DANCERS FORGE VERY close relationships with these women who make their costumes from scratch throughout their careers.

When I first visited the costume ladies, I noticed they had hung pictures of some of their favorite dancers on the walls. Sergei Filin was there, Nikolai Tsiskaridze and Yuri Grigorovich as well. At the end of my first season, on my way into a fitting, I noticed that I had made the wall. I was deeply moved by this gesture, knowing it was entirely up to them to determine who was on the wall and who wasn't. My picture was one that had been taken in Colorado during the Vail International Dance Festival by Erin Baiano, a friend and photographer. The *kostumeri* had found it on the internet, had it blown up and printed, and there I was, in a gold frame next to some of the great dancers of Bolshoi Theatre. I supposed I might have won them over with my "*Zdravstvuyte krasivitza!*" every time I walked in the door.

THE COSTUME SHOP eventually moved from the crumbling Soviet building back to Bolshoi Theatre. Its windows were situated just behind the giant statue positioned near the top of the theater that depicted Apollo, god of music, and his chariot drawn by four mighty horses. Beyond it you could see the imposing Kremlin and Red Square. Yulia and the other costume ladies had the best view of anyone in the entire theater. They had put in the years at the "warehouse" with not much of a view, so they rightfully perched high above the theater, looking out over all of Moscow.

CHAPTER 29

Svetlana and I continued to prepare Yuri Grigorovich's production of *The Sleeping Beauty*. As in Grigorovich's *Swan Lake,* the Prince's first appearance is a series of soaring leaps, bounding straight out of the wings. The steps were not complicated. I learned them as a young student training with Mr. Han and continued to dance them my whole career. But, as at the Mariinsky, they were executed in a different stylistic manner here. Sasha's guidance, based on his entire career working for Grigorovich and dancing in his productions, was essential to my understanding the steps. Simply put, I had to learn how to take off for a jump in a way that was foreign to me. Sasha started me from scratch, teaching me how to lengthen the glissade (which is the preparation into the leap) in order to launch myself into the air. He would tell me to throw my front leg as high as it could go, even before I got off the ground, in order to generate as much force as I possibly could. Once I changed the initial propulsion into the jumps, I was able to change the jumps themselves. After a few trials with this new glissade and preparation, I had so much force going into a jump that I was startled in midair by my newfound height and couldn't land properly. But there was less grunt work involved because I was now coordinating my body in the proper alignment, using the force generated to my advantage.

Years earlier, Guillaume once passed me working at the barre in morning class and muttered, "Relax, you are turning blue in the face." This is how I continued to work for years. But when incorporating Sasha's techniques, I didn't have to muscle everything out so much. I could use the impetus gained to actually release in midair, making less work for myself.

Sasha also taught me about the illusion that I could create for the audience simply through the line of a well-placed leg. When we spoke about a tour jeté (a leap into the air springing off one foot, then executing a half turn and landing on the opposite leg), he told me that the secret was to raise my legs as much as I could midair; creating the impression that I was jumping higher, when in fact I wasn't at all.

AS THE PERFORMANCE of *Beauty* was nearing, the time came for our work to be observed by Yuri Nikolayevich Grigorovich himself. At eighty-five years old, he was one of the most lauded and prolific directors of Bolshoi Theatre. Though he was no longer the company's director, a post he had held for decades, he continued to work with dancers, staging his productions, which were now staples in the repertoire. I could sense the control he still had over a rehearsal room full of dancers. Everyone was silent and focused. He commanded the respect he deserved. A true Russian leader, he never hesitated to give a critical opinion.

In our rehearsals he would look at the dancers on the stage—then grab the microphone (the "God mic," as we call it in ABT) and spit out a stream of corrections. It was a productive way of working, but terrifying if you were on the receiving end. I understood nothing when he was shouting into the microphone in Russian. But I could feel his energy (basically how I was understanding everything at that point). One of the dancers, fluent in English, was sitting next to me in a rehearsal and told me that he was telling the dancers how beautifully they were dancing. How much he liked everything. The dancer was kidding.

ON THE DAY of my run-through in front of him and the entire company, I had yet to see Yuri Nikolayevich in rehearsal (as a form of respect, in Russia you address your elders by their first and middle names). I was aware that there was a great possibility that he had never seen me dance. Ever. I knew that, yes, he did approve of me doing the premiere with Svetlana, but he had never seen any rehearsals or coached me. So this evening rehearsal, with the entire Bolshoi Ballet watching in the wings, was my proving ground. My chance to show him, and the rest of the company, that I was capable of dancing the premiere with their prima ballerina.

Even though we were all in rehearsal clothes and on a practice stage, this sort of rehearsal, in front of the directors and choreographer and dancers who were yet to be my friends, was more intense than being onstage with 2,500 people watching. As dancers, we are aware of each other's opinions, which can be curt, even vicious. It is terrifying when you know that everyone is forming their impression. For all those reasons, it wasn't a rehearsal; it was the first in a series of performances, some of the most pressurized performances I'd ever dance.

I HADN'T FELT nerves like that—at a run-through, or even a performance—for a long time. When I started receiving featured roles at ABT—*Symphony in C*, or the pas de trois in *Swan Lake*—I would obsess over that final rehearsal, about going in front of everyone in the studio. But that had subsided as the years rolled on. At the Bolshoi, as I prepared to dance for Yuri Nikolayevich, seeing that everyone around me was nervous as well and wishing me good luck, those feelings of fight-or-flight resurfaced. I *had* to prove myself and my abilities. To everyone. To the dancers, all curious to watch me. To Grigorovich, whose production it was. To Svetlana, with whom I would be dancing on a stage for the very first time and who needed the certainty that I could partner her well. To Sasha, to whom I needed to prove that all our work and extra hours of rehearsal had paid off. Above all, I needed to prove myself to Sergei Filin, to show him that he had made the right move by giving me this opportunity. Not just the opportunity of dancing in *Sleeping Beauty* and joining Bolshoi Theatre but also of being chosen for the significant honor of dancing on the highly anticipated occasion of the reopening of the Historical Stage. When I performed, Sergei's judgment would be on display.

REHEARSAL WAS HELD on the Upper Stage, an exact replica of the main stage, located at the very top of the theater. As I warmed up, bouncing around as usual, Grigorovich walked toward me with a warm smile and a handshake. When he spoke, it was clear that he recognized exactly how I was feeling. Sergei translated as he said warmly, "Please don't be nervous for the rehearsal."

It was comforting to have his support.

But as I looked around the stage and into the wings, it struck me how few of the eighty or so people gathered there looked familiar. Only Svetlana, Ludmila, Sasha, and Sergei. No one else. Svetlana seemed nervous as well, intensely focused on her own pressures. Princess Aurora is one of the hardest roles in the repertoire for the ballerina. There is no hiding behind character or movement to mask flaws. You are raw onstage, displaying your technique and line to everyone who watches. There was just as much pressure on her as there was on me. Although this was her home, and not yet mine. She was at ease in a culture and language of her own, able to verbally express what she needed and felt. Absent that liberty of expression, I just had to dance. But through all of it I could feel the support bonding us. We would carry each other through the pressure of the rehearsal. This fresh bond as partners lent us license to calm each other in times of stress. Here was our chance to implement it.

As I continued warming up onstage, I convinced myself that the very nerves I was experiencing meant that I was in my preferred state: on the very brink of failure or success. Moments in the past when I lacked drive or inspiration came to mind. Those times of boredom in rehearsals, waiting for them to end so I could distract myself with something else entirely. Now, in my first major proving ground, I was taking the risk that I artistically craved. In the end, there is nothing more exhilarating than contending with that sort of pressure—the kind that comes when you challenge yourself beyond conscious limit.

AS THE REHEARSAL commenced, I kept reviewing my first entrance, mulling it over and over in my mind. A leap from the wings, bursting out, hopefully thrilling the audience into applause. Altogether a rousing prospect, but stressful for the performer. In other versions of *Sleeping Beauty*, I have simply walked onstage for my first entrance, calm and restrained. Nothing like at Bolshoi Theatre, where the entrance for the Prince is an explosion into midair. As I readied myself for it, I heard the buildup of the music, the anticipation ascending through Tchaikovsky's score.

I looked at the dancers already onstage, busily prepping themselves for the appearance of the Prince. They glanced at me in the wings. I made eye contact with some, nervously looking for assurance. "You can do this, David. We are on your side." But instead, nothing. Just dancers glancing back, no familiar faces showing support. I was alone in my journey.

I took my preparation offstage for that leap, my left leg extended in front of me as if readying for a sprint. It was that moment of no return. I had committed to being here. And I committed to this first leap. I gave myself over to a massive, high-flying jump and was propelled from the wings onto the stage, as if I'd been shot out of a cannon.

I landed from that first jump and immediately felt that I was going to faint. I was out of body, looking at myself jump onstage and, all around me, the Bolshoi dancers were watching. Everything went white and I was swamped by the thought that I couldn't handle the pressure. I pushed ahead as if on autopilot, executing the steps I had rehearsed with Sasha for weeks on end. This was when his dissection of every foot, finger, head movement, and musical phrasing came into focus. Those hours of practicing every nuance seemed to hold my hand and lead me forward. When the pressure is high, all you have to rely on is the work you have done previously. Because you've rehearsed so much, the steps have become steeped in your muscle memory. With that memory and pure adrenaline and grit, I charged through the first variation and finished forcefully. I could finally calm down; my initial appearance to Yuri Nikolayevich was behind me.

At that point, the fear subsided and morphed into the will to succeed. I regained my mental confidence. With the rehearsal pushing on, Grigorovich began to correct me, his Russian voice and dialect booming through the microphone.

"Stand more to the right."

"Wait for the music to enter."

"Use the second wing and not the first one."

It became an almost comical scene. Grigorovich would yell something to me from the audience; I would look at him and then his corrections to me were passed on either through Svetlana, who was dancing at my side, or by Sasha, who shouted the corrections at me in English from the wings so that I could apply the revision.

It was almost like a poorly dubbed movie with a five-second delay, the audio preceding the action.

DURING THE ACT III Grand Pas de Deux (the main show-case for Aurora and Désiré), the time came for me to perform my main solo. As Svetlana walked offstage after our adagio, I stayed center stage. The room hushed. I felt the tension in the silence.

My starting position was in the upstage corner. I took slow, deliberate steps as I traced the perimeter of the stage. Making my way, with adrenaline overpowering doubt, I thought, *Look at where you are, David. On the Upper Stage of Bolshoi Theatre. Everyone on the stage, in the wings, and in the audience is watching. You've been given this opportunity. Life has placed you here, from a distant suburban upbringing. In America, no less. But here you are, fortunate enough to dance in Moscow for one of the most revered companies in the world. And now you prepare for a solo in front of artists whom you call your colleagues. Take this moment in. Be present. This is something to remember.*

It was as if I were soaring. Really leaning into the work and not taking the easy road. That work led to accomplishment, even pride. Pride that I took not the road that was worn with experience, but a road I was forging myself.

CHAPTER 30

With only a handful of days left before the official opening of *Sleeping Beauty*, I began to feel tremendous external pressure in addition to my own self-inflicted stress. The premiere on November 18, 2011, would inaugurate the renovated Bolshoi Theatre; two days later the ballet would be broadcast live to movie theaters around the world. There was a lot at stake: a brand-new production with lavish sets and costumes, the Bolshoi's prima ballerina to support, and the reopening of the theater after its renovation at a cost estimated at $760 million. My parents were coming to Moscow for the opening. Dmitri Medvedev, the president of Russia, would also attend, officially opening the theater with other members of the government. Every dancer of the company and the entire staff and administration of Bolshoi Theatre, all three thousand employees, had been waiting for this premiere. Their beloved theater had been brought to new splendor. They all were proud, as I was, to call this new shining gem home.

My nerves and confidence fluctuated hourly. *Sleeping Beauty* was a ballet I had danced around the world, but now I felt as if I had never danced the role. Once again, Sasha analyzed every step in my final rehearsals with him. And again, no step was spared.

Svetlana worked on her variations endlessly, every day toiling away. On the eve of the premiere, she took me into the corridor for a pep talk. In her studious English she told me not to worry, that everyone in the company was supporting me and liked me. That I didn't need to stress about proving myself. All I needed to do was to show people my talent and simply dance. I was touched that she took the time to settle the nerves I thought I was concealing. The intimacy of that private moment and her words of support seemed to connect us more.

I would be onstage for a total of an hour and fifteen minutes. But in that time there was a fork in the road. One way led to failure, buckling under the pressure that was so palpable to me. The other way, to conquering that pressure and using it to my advantage. Although I doubted my own abilities, the prospect excited me. This back-and-forth mind game of doubt and excitement was a familiar feeling. I loved the pressure, thrived on it. But I also hated it. I wanted it over. Yet I wanted to savor it. I wanted to crawl into a hole and disappear. I wanted to succeed.

I WAITED IMPATIENTLY in my dressing room during the first part of the ballet. I didn't make my first entrance until Act II, long after Svetlana had gotten her nerves out of the way and was into the flow of the performance. The wait was by far the worst part. In my dressing room alone, with my makeup and hair readied by Lena and the music of the Prologue reverberating through the closed door, I felt as though I were in a pressure cooker. It was unbearable. I couldn't sit or stand still. I closed my eyes, visualized my breath, and felt the ground below my feet. It brought me back to Svetlana's talk with me and her assurance that all I needed to do was show the audience my dancing.

In the moments before my first entrance, I prepped myself in the wings. I was finally ready. I knew it. The music built. That first grand leap approached. As I propelled myself onto the stage, I heard weighty applause, which meant that the audience was with me, ready to see "this American," "the gamble," "the risk." I fed off their energy, and it sent me hurtling forward scene by scene. When the Act III pas de deux ended, Svetlana and I took lengthy bows to the audience and to each other, hearing the unison clapping that no other opera house in the world replicates. Then I sent her offstage, watching her sprightly exit into the wings. Slowly, deliberately, I made my way to the top of the stage. As I walked the audience was hushed, expectant. I looked around at the company members seated onstage in their costumes. The same emotions that had engulfed me during rehearsal on the Upper Stage came rushing back. I absorbed the moment. I never could have imagined that I would be where I was standing. Dancing this ballet with this company and its prima ballerina. I took a deep breath and assumed my starting position. The beginning notes of my solo sounded. It was time to do what I had done many times before. And so I danced.

AFTER THE FINAL curtain, Svetlana and I gasped enormous breaths of relief. We hugged in elation. We couldn't form words. We didn't need to; we both knew it had gone well. Every aspect of the production was like nothing else I had witnessed. The scale of the set design. The beauty of the costumes. The quality of the dancers. Everything had come together to create a spectacle suited to the grand reopening of the Bolshoi's magnificent theater.

Backstage, a slew of people rushed the stage. Yuri Nikolayevich expressed his happiness and proudly told me that Medvedev had expressed similar compliments. Honestly, Grigorovich's opinion was more important to me than the president's. He embodied Bolshoi Theatre's history and identity. It was a great honor to dance in his production with his company.

When the Russian president swooped onto the stage, the entire company flocked around him. Svetlana sought me out of the crowd, calling, "David, come here!"

She pulled me forward by the hand, urging an introduction.

"My congratulations," said Medvedev in English. "I hear you don't speak much Russian."

"*Tolka chut-chut*," I replied. *Only a little.*

"Well," he said, "it may be only a little, but it's with no accent at all."

His remark evoked laughter from everyone, myself included. We formally shook hands as he walked off the stage surrounded by security.

But where were my parents? I didn't see them yet but knew they were going to be brought backstage. The cover to the pressure cooker had been lifted, and all I wanted was to hug them. To see their faces and celebrate this incredible occasion. As they finally approached the stage I ran toward the two people who had always supported the risks they knew I loved to take.

TWO DAYS LATER we were ready to repeat the entire performance. This time it would be seen by tens of thousands of ballet enthusiasts around the world, relayed live into cinemas in fifty countries. I had the same doubt. The same fear. It would not be any easier because Svetlana and I had already danced the opening. In fact, it was a completely different sort of pressure. There were cameras everywhere capturing every nuance and bead of sweat.

For the cameras we wore less makeup and adjusted our movements and acting for close-ups, as opposed to the acting one does to engage audiences in the far reaches of the theater's balconies.

That evening, I was putting on my costume when I heard a frantic knock on the door. Someone from the camera crew feverishly explained that I had to get ready right away for a live interview in four minutes. As quickly as I could, I pulled on my pale blue tunic and tights. When I slipped on my left boot, which belonged to the pair I had painstakingly broken in, it suddenly burst on the side seam right on the heel. Every dancer has his or her own way of breaking in shoes. Some, like myself, prepare their shoes days before a show. This was my one pair for the filming. The pair that felt most comfortable. I had no choice but to switch to shoes that were stiffer and not broken in. In rehearsal, I would have been given the time to fix the problem. But no matter what, the curtain always goes up as scheduled; especially if it's a live performance being conveyed to audiences around the world.

WITH THE MUSIC for my entrance nearing, I stretched my left leg in the wings and prepared. When the time came, I leapt onstage just as I had done before. I jumped. I jumped again. Then, as I pushed off my right foot for a double saut de basque, I felt a sharp strain in my right ankle. There was no stumble, no trip of any sort; the audience would not have noticed. But I knew immediately what it meant: I had sprained the inner part of my foot.

Everything became crystal clear. The pain of the sprain, with a sold-out Bolshoi Theatre and countless people watching live in cinemas around the world, forced me to focus inward. I could not, would not, reveal what had happened. So I danced, thankful for the adrenaline that kept me going and masked the pain. When I eventually went offstage and waited for my next entrance, I told no one what had occurred. There was nothing anyone could do. It would only engender chaos and create an unnecessary negative energy throughout the entire company. I performed each painful leap or step as I had rehearsed them. I didn't hold back. In the third act variation I jumped just as high as I had before and executed turns with the same force. I concentrated on the goal of finishing what I had set out to achieve and what everyone around me expected. But I could barely step onto the foot during

255

curtain calls. No one suspected anything had happened until I was hobbling offstage after our bows.

When reality set in, I took this as a sign. My gut told me I had hit my limit. My limit of pressure, of expectation, of mental and physical focus. I needed a rest.

It's hard to imagine now how I even got through the pressure of that month, from the initial preparations of *Beauty* to the two high-wire performances.

My ankle sprain was temporary and kept me away from rehearsing and performing for only a couple of weeks. But what I had gained through those pressurized weeks of rehearsal and on the stage was permanent. The heightened stress had taken me further into my dancing and pushed me into another realm of artistic fulfillment. This was a peak in my life as a performer. I felt I was on the cusp of understanding the meaning of life. The pressure that I overcame during the lead-up and eventual performances of *Sleeping Beauty* was something I needed even more of. I had gotten that first dose of an addictive drug.

Because once I had faced the pressure, experienced it, and gotten through it, I craved another hit.

CHAPTER 31

After a brief trip to New York where my sprain healed, I returned to Moscow. The city was more familiar to me now, but Muscovites would at times try my patience. I didn't have the pushiness of most Russians. When others told me to assert myself, I found it unnatural. Russians conducted their lives, at times, in a way I couldn't comprehend. I couldn't relate to the curtness of the deli clerk who was annoyed at my request for sliced meat or the waitress glaring at me because I didn't have a reservation.

The foreign daily life. The loneliness. They were aspects of the challenge I had professed I so needed. Consequently in my life outside Bolshoi Theatre, I had no choice but to lie in the bed I made.

Taking the Metro to the chiropractor, miles outside the city center, I would sit on the loud, hollowed-out train with its brown plastic benches and look around in fascination at the evening commuters. The women in the furs. The men, with their brusque macho air. The young women with their long blond locks and sky-high stilettos, even in the winter snow and ice. I was sure they could sense that I wasn't one of them.

Globus Gourmet, a grocery store across the street from my apartment, was often the true test of my patience. The Russian way of shopping and of "customer service" was altogether different from anything I'd experienced. Shoppers asserted themselves through the aggressive use of the metal shopping carts; just as travelers did at Domodedovo Airport. They would press forward in the checkout line, blocking as many people as possible from moving in any other direction. I could never countenance the inability of Moscovites to stand in a single-file line. *Damn it!* I'd think, *get off my ass and wait your turn!* Instead they would ease closer and closer without making eye contact. With no choice but to push forward myself, I would make my way up the line to the cashier and silently hand over my various items. Rarely a smile from the checkout clerk.

One time, as I attempted to swipe my credit card, it was declined. I swiped again. Declined again. The woman behind the counter looked at me stone-faced, annoyed.

"*Ni Rabotaet,*" she said. *Doesn't work.*

"*Da, Rabotaet (Yes, it works),*" I said.

"*NYET! Ni Rabotaet! (No! It doesn't work!)*"

She swung the machine around, rolling her eyes, and tried it herself, touching the card as if it repulsed her. When, for a third time, the card didn't work, another clerk came over, pressed a button on the cash register and the card was accepted. The first clerk glared back at me. Never would she apologize or take any responsibility.

At times like this I would think, *You've chosen this life. These things are passing moments. And you will come out stronger.*

IN TIME, I learned to acclimate. I became more practiced at that Russian hello with its curt nod and possibly the merest shadow of a grin. Nothing like those effusive American greetings with smiles, teeth, hugs. Going back and forth between the two countries was like living two lives. In that sense, I did feel like a "double agent," as Stephen Colbert jokingly accused me of being.

In one life, my New York life, I was at ease, traversing the streets of a city I knew well, socializing with friends, speaking my native language, and living a full, busy, chaotic, stimulating existence. In Moscow, though my dancing life provided all the stimulation I could wish for, the rest of the time I was the reserved, quiet, focused dancer. No one truly knew me, and I truly knew no one.

Of course, I was acquainted with a few people there. I could see that some of the other dancers were slowly warming to me, as some would even practice their English in passing. Others were not welcoming.

There was Nikolai Tsiskaridze, for instance, a longtime Bolshoi Premier dancer. I was fifteen when I first met him, and he had taken an avid interest in my dancing. When we were both performing on the *Kings of the Dance* tour, he would laughingly call me "my Adonis" and "my little baby." So I had assumed we were friends. But he no longer treated me as such when I came to Bolshoi, passing me by in the hallways with barely any acknowledgment. When I was home, I learned that he had spoken to a reporter from the *Los Angeles Times*. "I like David very much," he had said, "and respect him as a dancer, but [his dancing at Bolshoi] is an insult to the entire Russian ballet, a demonstration of indifference to the rich Russian tradition and culture."

In fact, I could appreciate why anyone might criticize my position at Bolshoi: an American joining their revered theater, bypassing the school that hones the dancers and upholds traditions of the company. But all I could do, now that I was ensconced at Bolshoi, was remain diplomatic. Keep smiling, work hard, handle the pressure, and do my job.

MY FIRST DAY back at Bolshoi, I had a rehearsal for *Swan Lake* with Sasha in which everything seemed to click. We fed off each other's energy. His corrections. My applying them. The cabriole

derrière, one of my weakest steps, needed special attention. To execute it, the working leg is thrust into the air while the underneath
leg follows and beats against the first leg, sending it higher. The
landing is then made on the underneath leg. All of this happens in
about two seconds. An intricately complex two seconds, analyzed to
death by Sasha and myself. He told me to propel my first leg high
up in the air before I even took off for the jump. This allowed me
time in the air to properly execute a double beat.

He was pushing me far beyond what I thought I could do.
He asked for two double tours in a row in the coda (something I
never thought possible), and in my double tour to arabesque he
gave just the right correction to land it on the spot, absolved of
hops, which ruin the effect of the landing. Each time I applied
what he said, I found myself frozen in shock over the newfound
feeling. A rehearsal like that one was enough to outweigh all the
discomforts of the move to Moscow.

THERE WAS LITTLE comparable to dancing *Swan Lake* with
Svetlana in the theater where it was created. I was conscious of
being a minuscule addition to the ballet's long lineage at Bolshoi
Theatre.

One particular moment is embedded in my memory. Prince
Siegfried finds himself between two rows of swans at the lake as
he searches for Odette. As I made my way through the swans,
I noted that I was walking through one of the most celebrated
Corps de Ballet in the world, thirty-two perfectly synchronized
Swans, with Tchaikovsky's Act II music rising from the orchestra
pit to the stage, the same stage and the same pit for which the
ballet and its music were written. I had never even imagined
being surrounded by such history and beauty. It wasn't that I felt
I deserved to be there; I simply felt I was lucky enough to have
been invited to experience it.

*　　*　　*

MY FIRST SEASON with Bolshoi, 2011–2012, was also my first full winter in Russia. Dull gray clouds blanketed the city. The nights became longer, easily edging into early afternoon and late morning. Fur coats were worn everywhere. The first snowfall came at the end of October, just when I was preparing for the opening of *Sleeping Beauty*. No one seemed surprised by such early snow, but everyone's mood changed.

I noticed that people grew more and more solemn. Their faces dropped and an internal spark seemed to fade. The grayness of the days became all-encompassing. It's dispiriting to see the sun disappear by four in the afternoon or to wake up at eight thirty in the morning and look out your window at a pitch-dark world.

The dancers risked becoming vitamin deficient in those short winter days and long nights. Sasha told me to keep eating vitamin-rich foods so I wouldn't lose the energy needed to keep dancing at peak level. He had danced through many a Moscow winter in his career, and knew full well what charged a dancer's body in weather like this. I listened to what he told me, eating red meat and *kotletki*, the delicious breaded chicken. The three canteens at Bolshoi Theatre served fresh food at a next-to-nothing price. The recipes had been, I was told, unchanged for forty years. Typically simple Russian cooking. Meat, potato or cucumber salad, soup, *kompot* (a pureed juice made from cranberries or cherries). I'd hoped the food in the canteen would keep me rightly fueled, and it did.

MY OFFICIAL INTRODUCTION to the infamous Russian winter was a trip to the U.S. Embassy to renew my passport. I had allotted one morning only to run this errand, a task I assumed would take no more than an hour. It was –25 degrees Celsius

(−13°F) as I charged out of the subway, face down, leaning into the frosty wind. It is a running joke with friends that I go out in the depths of winter wearing just a thick sweater and scarf, no coat. So, typically, I had moved to a city synonymous with icy winters without adequate protection. I didn't do furs, but I definitely needed a warm coat. I'd wrongly assumed I was equipped to handle this journey with gloves (too thin), a hat (too thin), and my new winter coat (stylish, but again, too thin).

Moscow streets are notoriously large and deceiving. A small distance on a map can turn out to be miles on foot. There is no way of crossing the many lanes of traffic. You must always use underpasses, which can throw off your sense of direction.

Soon, I began to panic when I realized I had been walking for fifteen minutes in the wrong direction. I raced back to the metro station as quickly as I could, regrouping and trying my best to thaw out a bit. Again I looked at a map to try to direct myself, puzzling over street names written in Cyrillic. I had gotten used to street signs in an entirely new alphabet, making distinctions by the way the first letter was written. But at times, this being one of them, I completely lost my sense of direction.

After figuring out which way to go, I charged back into the frigid wind. I had never been so cold in my life. My toes tingled with what I feared was the beginning of frostbite. I had no sensation in my limbs. My gloves were so ineffective that I took them off, pressing my fingers close to my palms, trying desperately to regain feeling. My eyes watered so badly I felt like I was crying. My nose was dripping so constantly that it wasn't even worth the effort of wiping it.

At last, in the distance, just before losing all hope: an American flag. I bolted toward it as quickly as my numbing legs could manage. Inside, I collapsed on a chair, unable to focus on matters of official business. I could hardly breathe. I needed to thaw my nose, my toes, my fingers, my ears. Finally I was able to stand up and find a place in the long line. When I got to the front I was still so frigid I couldn't feel my fingers and was unable to take my passport out of my jeans pocket.

YET APART FROM the grayness and bitter cold of Russian winters, there is a romantic side to those long months as well. I knew about this Russia from novels and movies, and now I experienced it firsthand. I found the beauty of Moscow as I walked through the streets in the black of night, bundled up as I went home from a dinner or a performance. You could almost hear the silence through the frigid air. What snow there was would be soft and pillowy on top and frozen underneath. I will never forget that distinctive crisp crunching sound the snow makes when you walk down the street, or the soothing hum of heating systems in the buildings I passed. On bitterly cold nights, walking home from a restaurant, that crunch became etched in my memory.

AS EACH WEEK marched on, my body would be brought closer to deep fatigue. By my day off, which came on Monday, I would feel overcooked, dried up, and in desperate need of rest. I couldn't plan anything on this coveted free day. I would be incapable of errands, lunches, whatever might force me out of the apartment at an allotted hour. The only thing I wanted to do on a Monday turned out to be the ideal curative.

The *banya* is a traditional Russian sauna. Perfected over hundreds of years, it provides a mindless utopia and by far the best way to cure overworked muscles and exhausted brains. I was introduced to the *banya* by Semyon Chudin, a Russian Principal Dancer who joined the company the same time I did. He became one of my dearest friends at Bolshoi. He had gone to the *banya* for years and swore by its time-tested remedy.

Semyon brought me to the best *banya* in the center of Moscow, Sanduny, a vast bathhouse spread out over the whole of a long city block just five minutes' walk from Bolshoi Theatre. Since 1808, Sanduny has been Russia's most luxurious and renowned bathhouse. Its carved and domed ceilings, elaborate gilt work, stately columns, and vast rooms are stunning works of art that give the sense that you've gone back in time to the profligate era of the tsars. Though it's grand, it also shows its age: the worn cornices, with their varying layers of colors peeking through, betray how many times they've been painted over.

A bell on the wooden exterior door sounds your arrival. In the spacious entry hall, there is a large winding staircase and an attendant in a small glass booth waiting for you to pay. The ground floor is cheaper and more barren, with only the necessities of hot sauna and cold plunge on offer. The pricier upstairs area has the sauna, a large heated pool edged with Roman statues, a cold plunge, and waiters attending to your orders in a vast room with rows upon rows of large red banquettes to lounge on. Semyon and I would check our coats and head up the marble staircase. At the top of the stairs, we pushed open an outsize, heavy door into the main room with its red banquettes. We would find an empty space and a waiter to take our order: a green terry-cloth towel (to dry off), a red sheet (for the sauna), a felt hat (to shield our heads from the extreme heat), plastic sandals, and *morse*. We always started with *morse*, a puree of cranberry juice, served freshly squeezed in a large stein, full of pulp and always chilled. The other men frequenting Sanduny drank large beers to wash down their food. Semyon and I were in recovery mode so beer was never part of our routine. But beer with your friends at the *banya* is a true Russian pastime.

Sanduny was and still is a social hub where Russian men come to socialize and solidify business deals. Like Americans suited up for a power lunch at the Four Seasons, Russians clad in green towels and white felt hats make an amicable deal over beer at the sauna.

Once we installed ourselves, we got undressed. Nudity is not an issue at the *banya*. Russian men and the attendants all walk around completely nude, chatting and laughing with their friends without any sense of modesty or embarrassment. Because of our ballet physiques, Semyon and I stood out next to hairy-chested Russian men with enormous potbellies. As Semyon introduced me to some of the attendants, I naturally became known as the American.

The sauna was an education in Russian culture. You could take in the heat of the sauna and sweat everything out, then plunge into the ice-cold wooden baths, and finally immerse yourself in the large swimming pool. Or you could purchase a bunch of fragrant oak or birch leaves called *venik*. These leaves, which can also include eucalyptus or juniper, are soaked in a bucket of water, then used by a naked attendant to stroke and tap and beat you (mercilessly) from head to toe. It's an extreme and sometimes painful measure. I rarely did it, but when I did I felt that my entire body had been given a new blood flow.

Whichever method I chose, when I had had enough I would go back to the banquettes and order more food and *morse*. The same cycle could be repeated for hours on end.

THE OTHER BATHERS soon learned that Semyon and I were Premier Dancers at Bolshoi Theatre. Telling men in a sauna that you are a ballet dancer might not go over so well in other parts of the world—including America—but it's altogether different in Russia, where there is immense respect for ballet dancers in general and Bolshoi dancers in particular. As I went more frequently with Semyon, I got to know the sauna attendants. One of them, an exuberantly friendly man named Genia, became fascinated that I was an American dancing at Bolshoi Theatre. His face would light up when американец, "the American," walked in. He would ask me, "What are you dancing? Who are you dancing with? Do you miss New York?"

We would stand there, naked, chitchatting as well as we could. He spoke no English at all. I spoke minimal Russian at best. So we tried to converse in Russian. I would understand about half of what he was saying, and at times we would have the awkward blank stare, neither of us having any idea what the other had said.

Eventually, Genia mustered up the nerve to ask me for tickets to one of my shows. For many people in Russia, going to Bolshoi Theatre, a place of pride for any Russian, is an unattainable dream. I could sense that Genia had wanted to ask me this for some time but was too shy or modest to ask a favor of someone he barely knew. He explained to me that it would soon be Woman's Day in Russia and it would be very nice if he could take his girlfriend to a performance. Something special for her on her day. It was an endearing request and I told him that I would try to figure something out.

When I came to Sanduny with the tickets for *Swan Lake*, large red strips reading большой, *Bolshoi*, in big gold lettering, Genia couldn't contain his excitement. Like many Russians, he had been told as a child that maybe one day, instead of watching Bolshoi on TV, he could actually see a live performance, at the historic theater. I had never witnessed such gratitude for the opportunity to attend a show. It gave me as much fulfillment to give Genia those tickets as receiving the tickets gave him. I can only imagine how proud he was to give them to his girlfriend for Woman's Day.

THE MONDAY FOLLOWING Genia's visit to the Bolshoi, my reputation at Sanduny had instantly changed. Genia had come back to work and told everyone that he had seen *Swan Lake* with Svetlana Zakharova and that I had danced the Prince. Now that they had connected me with Bolshoi Theatre, which they had fantasized about since they were little kids, I had, in a way, become a childhood hero come to life. As an American, whose own childhood imagination had run to heroes like John Elway of the Denver Broncos (even while idolizing Fred Astaire), I was astonished to see them with such deep respect for a ballet dancer. What Genia, and so many others at Sanduny, felt about ballet deepened my understanding of Russian culture.

CHAPTER 32

Giselle, which I first danced with Natasha, would become the ballet I performed the most at Bolshoi Theatre. As a company member I would dance the Grigorovich version and get to know it intimately. Most intimately with Svetlana.

The leading character of Albrecht is young and feckless. He is a nobleman who spots Giselle, a naive peasant girl, and quickly becomes smitten. The ballet takes place centuries ago, when class divides were rigid. For Albrecht, courting Giselle is impossible, so he masquerades as a country boy named Loys. He sees little consequence in his flirtations. But Giselle falls passionately in love with Albrecht. She discovers his deception only when his fiancée, Bathilde—a beautiful noblewoman—arrives unexpectedly in her village with the rest of his court. When Albrecht affirms his betrayal of Giselle by kissing Bathilde's hand, the sensitive and delicate Giselle collapses, and dies. In many productions, just as the curtain is falling on Act I, Albrecht, ashamed and grief-stricken, flees the village, followed by his dutiful manservant. The impulse to flee the scene, and by extension the tragic consequence of his actions, has always seemed the right artistic choice to me: Albrecht has done a terrible thing; the villagers, witnessing the death of their friend, rightly blame him; his perfidy is exposed and his cowardice shows through.

But Yuri Nikolayevich saw it differently. His production calls for Albrecht to stay onstage, holding Giselle in disbelief and shock. I assume he felt that Albrecht fully apprehended what he had done, and realized that he had truly loved Giselle from the beginning. So he remains among the accusatory villagers, embracing the dead Giselle until the curtain falls.

For the most part, I was given a measure of artistic freedom with my interpretations of repertoire at Bolshoi. But certain aspects were set in stone. For my debut in *Giselle* with the company in November, I fled the stage at the close of Act I. Sasha came to me the next day and said that Grigorovich wanted me to stay onstage. When there was a specific request from Yuri Nikolayevich, there was no negotiation. It did make for a dramatic end to the act, with Albrecht cradling Giselle in his arms with the villagers surrounding him. And after all, I was at Bolshoi to absorb these cultural and artistic viewpoints.

PREPARATIONS FOR *GISELLE* with Svetlana were condensed into a mere three-day period. It was one of those rare times when scheduling, in between one ballet and another, afforded us only a short stint to work things out. She was easy to read as a partner, though, which gave us the time to look past technicalities and on to artistic rapport and interpretation. Her Giselle was shy, frail, lithe. I fed off that, feeling as though it was natural for Albrecht to not only be attracted to the vulnerability she exuded but to use it to his advantage in his disguise as a villager.

Svetlana's coach, Ludmila, sat in the front of the room, enthusiastic about our interpretations, offering notes and small anecdotes, some from her personal experience as one of the great Giselles of Bolshoi Theatre. The energy in the studio was inspired and positive, devoid of stresses.

I never doubted the role of Albrecht as much as others in the repertoire. The steps are manageable, nothing like *La Bayadère* for instance, where Solor's steps are so difficult that Marcelo Gomes and I coined the phrase "six steps," meaning that to get through the ballet we had to do a series of six combinations of steps, all extremely daunting.

The real challenge of dancing Albrecht was his character. Apart from Romeo, there was never a character that I felt deserved a more humane and complex interpretation. I didn't want to play him too soft, head-over-heels in love with Giselle (my natural inclination and much how I fall into an all-consuming infatuation in real life). But I also couldn't play him solely as a cad, unaware that his actions could have serious consequences. It was a difficult balance to find. After a particularly emotional *Giselle* with Natasha at ABT, Natalia Makarova came to my dressing room and told me that in Act I, I had been *too* emotional, oversaturated. I realized then that a dancer's personal experience in a live performance can be vastly different from that of the audience. We, as dancers, can finish a show and think it was one of our worst, failing miserably at every level, while our coaches think it was one of our best. Or we can think we did a great job, maybe nailing a pirouette or something else that is technical but essentially vapid, and our coaches think the performance was lacking true risk or sufficient artistic interpretation. This is an *art*, after all, not a circus.

THE PERFORMANCE BROUGHT Svetlana and I together in palpable ways. She was vibrant and alive. From our first encounter she responded to my gestures, my looks, and I did the same in return. We played. And the fact that we didn't rehearse very much gave us a great spontaneity and helped us in the end.

During the intermission, Sergei and Sasha came backstage to tell me how passionate the first act ending was, when I had been following orders and cradling the dead Giselle in my arms.

CHAPTER 33

I left Moscow the day after I closed *Giselle*. No time to waste. I returned to New York to work with Alexei Ratmansky on his new *Firebird*. This was the first time I would be working with him since I joined the Bolshoi, where he had trained and been Artistic Director. I sensed I could understand his heritage a bit more, the way he communicated, anticipating his expectations as a creator after being on his old turf. As with many dancers who come from historic institutions like Bolshoi, the theater he was brought up in never truly left him. I could now more deeply understand his language as a choreographer.

Alexei was reworking *Firebird*, a ballet choreographed by Mikhail Fokine with a score by Igor Stravinsky. It was a huge undertaking. Alexei was creating more ballets that had historically significant scores and iconic choreography. I thought it was a daring move. Instead of creating something completely new, which audiences cannot compare to an existing work, he was reinventing something that had withstood the test of time. After all, *Firebird* was first premiered in 1910 by Diaghilev's Ballets Russes, one of the most innovative companies in ballet history. But Alexei was a responsible reinventor who didn't seek to forget the past but rather wanted to add to it.

Alexei's casting for *Firebird* was completely out of the box. I wasn't scheduled to dance the young Tsarevich Ivan, who would be the perceived typical role for me. Instead I was cast as the evil sorcerer, Kaschei. I loved putting my mark on roles that didn't involve being a prince, on dance characters like Basilio in *Don Quixote* who went against my natural demeanor.

Alexei gave me the freedom to experiment. I have seen dancers transform themselves when granted that leeway. They open up and allow themselves to move differently; they discover new ways of attacking movement. It's almost as if they shed a layer of skin. The skin of inhibition. Gone is the confinement of keeping turnout, pointing your feet, producing technically proficient steps, or shaping your legs in a certain way—freedoms, in other words, that classical ballet usually doesn't permit. My idea of freedom doesn't exist in the prince roles. For me, true freedom will always flourish in the creative process with a choreographer whose work grows from a seed of an idea and fully blooms on the stage.

ONE MIGHT THINK that *Firebird*, a ballet that audiences know so well, is exactly the kind of work that leaves me feeling the sort of confinement that I have tried desperately to escape. But Alexei's approach to Kaschei, the story in general, and the music were completely different from any production I had seen before. While he respected the story and the style in general, his ballet had a modern freshness. Alexei gave me the liberty to discover my character. At first all I knew was that Kaschei is a sorcerer who imprisons the Firebird in the confines of his garden. He controls everything within its walls under a mysterious spell. In the past, the character has usually been played as an old bearded man, a very Merlin-type person, in classic villain form. Alexei completely stripped away the previous perceptions of Kaschei. Instead, we made him a younger, sinister, slimy sorcerer, more mad than old and dusty. The character evolved through the movement. There was both a freedom and a restraint. I felt I could try things out on my own without looking to him for every direction and nuance. Each rehearsal in the studio became a test of my imagination as I experimented with the many different colors added to my interpretation of the role. Alexei gave me the sense that it was my job to make the part my own, knowing all the while that if he didn't like something he could honestly tell me. It truly was empowering. I felt I could go anywhere I wanted to go because the role was created for me. Gone were the comparisons to previous Kascheis. Alexei had taken music and a story created more than a hundred years ago and made something completely new. I was taught, yet again, that to be that dancer at the inception of a work is to be a collaborator in the process, and this is the ideal form of artistic expression.

For instance, Yuri Grigorovich's *Spartacus* was created on Vladimir Vasiliev. Every step was selected with him in mind and reflects the tremendous depth and breadth of his emotionality and technique. He had a colossal jump and a dramatic flair that exemplified the modern Bolshoi style. In making use of Vasiliev's strengths, Grigorovich created Vasiliev's signature role, as well as one of the greatest roles for a male dancer of that style. Others have performed the role of Spartacus successfully, but Vasiliev's performance set the standard.

The same goes for Balanchine ballets created with a certain danseur or ballerina in mind. These ballets were geared to the specific talents of the stunning dancers in his company: Edward Villella's masculine vigor will forever permeate the leading male role in "Rubies"; Suzanne Farrell's cool elegance and effortless fluidity defined the lead role in "Diamonds." Although roles do evolve, and I have wept at the sight of Sara Mearns's interpretation of "Diamonds," it was created with Farrell in mind. The role must evolve, though, to stand the test of time. There's no point in saying "No one will ever exceed Gelsey in this," or "No one will ever match Fonteyn in that . . ." if these perceptions are being invoked to stubbornly dismiss the brilliance in *this* generation.

I think any dancer would agree that nothing equals the thrill and the honor of having a role created on you. In an art whose impact comes from live performance, it is ballet's truest form of artistic immortality. Years after your career has ended, whenever that role is danced, your own unique stamp will always be on it.

ALEXEI'S *FIREBIRD* PREMIERED in Costa Mesa in a frenzied atmosphere. There is always a certain buzz on opening nights, in the audience but especially backstage within the crew and dancers who have been working on this creation for months. From the moment we dance the first steps in the studio, a bond begins to form in an unforced, natural way. Over time the bond strengthens (the more colossal the work, the stronger the bond), right up to the eleventh hour when steps are changed or finished, stress levels mount, and everyone has opinions on everything. Moments before we go onstage in front of an audience for the first time, when we stand in costume before the call to "places," everyone is in it together and we wish each other the very best show. We huddle together, with the curtain down, and collectively agree to commit to the work we have created. Such was the experience the night *Firebird* premiered. Natasha danced the title role. Marcelo danced Prince Ivan. I danced Kaschei. And we presented Alexei's ideas to the audience.

CHAPTER 34

Quickly back to Bolshoi. I was anxious about returning. I was still new and barely knew anyone in the company. I hadn't been there on a continuous basis, so every reentry was a shock to me, like starting over once again. I felt a growing pressure of expectation (whether imagined or actual). I worried that people's perception of me was greater than the reality. I felt vulnerable and susceptible to mistakes, just like every other dancer in the company. But this vulnerability was an impediment to growth. I knew this. My work at Bolshoi wasn't a reinvention of the wheel; it was just a different way to drive with the wheel. It gave me texture. More depth. A richness as an artist because of new absorbed experiences. The outcome was always worth the pressure and anxiety.

This time I tackled another icon of the repertoire and of Yuri Nikolayevich's productions: *The Nutcracker*. This ballet was precious to me as the spark that ignited my life's pursuit. My passion for *Nutcracker* has deepened as the years have passed. The music is Tchaikovsky's familiar score. I have listened to parts of this ballet as I walked down the street in New York or Moscow, far away from the rehearsal studio, intensely moved by sections of it. I was ready to take on one of the most recognizable productions of Tchaikovsky's music.

The Nutcracker is a staple of the repertoire at Bolshoi Theatre. The dancers know the ballet so well they need few rehearsals to get it into performance shape. Much like *Swan Lake* and *Giselle.* But the ballet was a debut for me, like learning to ride a bike without training wheels.

Shortly before my premiere, the entire company was called to a rehearsal just to give me a run-through from start to finish. The last thing they wanted to do. I walked in focused, ready to tackle new territory, and feeling bad for bringing in the dancers solely because of my inexperience. Their stoic stares didn't help my nerves. We walked through the spacing; I mapped out where I should be and with whom. The dancers marked their steps, waltzing about at half energy as I tried my best to replicate a performance atmosphere. It was essential that I subject myself to every element of a real performance, experiencing it in all its aspects before the point of no return. That unique, collective energy I felt in performance was missing in the studio. I tried to engender some sort of stimulation. Because there was nothing from the other dancers. No matter how much I tried to give, they stayed at base level. I didn't blame them. They were in full swing for the season, exhausted from the relentless performance calendar.

When I began the pas de deux with my partner Nina Kaptsova, the company lined the circumference of the studio and watched. I looked around the room and saw all eyes directed toward us. My solo felt almost like an audition. It pushed me to produce work that could be deemed worthy by these dancers I greatly respected. I was, once again, in survival mode. I had no other option than to succeed, through sheer grit and determination. To prove myself to my new peers. At the end of my solo, there was a polite round of applause, but as I looked around, I saw the same stoic faces as before. It was a far cry from dancing with ABT, a company where I felt I could potentially fail and wouldn't be judged for it. At Bolshoi I still felt I was being judged the entire time. Because I was the new kid on the block, I had to push past my fear of failure and call upon every bit of energy and skill I possessed to dig deeper, go further, and find more of the will to succeed that is essential to any striving artist.

CHAPTER 35

My life outside the Bolshoi walls remained lonely. After Natasha and Ivan departed, other than Semyon I knew only three Bolshoi dancers, and, even with them, the connection was professional rather than personal. There was Sergei, of course; and Sasha, my coach; and Svetlana. They were never less than kind, attentive, and helpful, offering up whatever they could to make my move and transition as smooth as possible. Still, I was alone after hours. When rehearsals finished, I would go home and settle into a solitary evening. Even on the rare occasions when I went out to a restaurant, I was alone. I passed the time with movies, Skype, books. In New York, the need to run the race of shows, dinners, concerts, museums was relentless. It was easier to simply hibernate in Moscow, a city whose environs still intimidated me. As I had in Paris, I was sacrificing a social existence for an artistic one.

EIGHT MONTHS INTO my time in Moscow, a New York friend suggested I meet a Russian designer he knew from the fashion world. Vika Gazinskaya is a tall blond Muscovite with a severely cropped haircut. As I watched her bound up the Bolshoi steps for our date to the opera, I was stunned by her original sense of modern Russian style. Vika is a passionate, quintessential Russian soul. Her love of art and fashion go hand in hand with her emotions, which she sometimes has a hard time keeping at bay. We clicked immediately. She inhabited a part of Moscow I had yet to experience. I knew Bolshoi and only Bolshoi. She knew the modern art and fashion crowd; artists and designers who were making lives and careers in modern-day Moscow.

Vika invited me into her life. She introduced me to artists my age, whose passion, much like that of my friends in New York, was to create contemporary work. It was refreshing to meet people who, like me, were wholly committed to a vision, a lifestyle, an art.

GOSHA RUBCHINSKIY, A talented designer and photographer, was one of these friends. Gosha, with his trademark laugh, an impeccably buzzed haircut, and a methodic grasp of the English language, documented the diverse aspects of Russian life: the young boys and girls of Russian skate culture and the raw energy of Russian youth in the cities he visited.

He is a proud Russian who regards it as a personal mission to show the modernity of his country to the world. We immediately began talking about working together. The idea was to make a documentary-style portrait of me living in Russia and working at Bolshoi Theatre. I had had people photograph me at Bolshoi for certain publications but never over a period of time. So there would be a photo onstage, another in the wings, another wearing clothes from certain designers. But our idea was to create a portrait of the American in Moscow. It wouldn't be the pretty shots taken for the glossy magazines but something sweaty and realistic. The in-between shots. The images in which the subject looks imperfect, which are usually edited out. Unlike most ballet photographers, Gosha wasn't at all interested in the perfect jump or pose. He wanted to find images that revealed the dancer. He didn't know the ballet world and hadn't ever imagined he would photograph inside Bolshoi Theatre. I loved that. This collaboration, I thought, was exactly the sort of fusion between the traditional and the new that Bolshoi Theatre was becoming.

Throughout the year Gosha shot countless pictures, and though the project never fully came to fruition I was still glad we did it since it grew out of a desire to explore an idea. I fed off the work of others, especially those from completely different artistic mediums. I always believed this kind of process benefited both sides of any project. I opened up the ballet world to him. And he shared his artistic and aesthetic eye with me.

VIKA INTRODUCED ME to a new group of people when she invited me to a party at Simachev celebrating the birthday of one of her friends. Sima, as it was called, was the local restaurant/bar/club frequented by the art crowd of Moscow. I'd never set foot in it, knowing little about what was considered cool in the city.

I felt self-conscious about crashing a Russian party where I didn't know the birthday girl and spoke only morsels of the language (uncomfortably forcing others to use what they knew of English with me). But Natasha Turovnikova, whose birthday it was, welcomed me warmly by telling me her greatest gift that night was meeting "her prince from Bolshoi Theatre."

Throughout that evening, people grilled me, seeking an inside perspective on my move to Bolshoi Theatre. Why had I decided to come? How had the company and audiences accepted me? What did I think of Moscow? They knew how tough the city could be at times, harsh and unwelcoming, and were curious as to how I got on living here. I had the sense that they wanted to help me as much as they possibly could. By the time the party had ended I knew I had met a group that would become my family in Moscow.

My newfound friends eventually came to see me dance. It was a joy to be able to give tickets to people I knew. Like Genia, my friend from the *banya*, they viewed it as a special honor to come to the ballet as invited guests. Little did I know that the vibrant social scene they were all part of had made them well-known Muscovites. After the show, when they came backstage, certain dancers in the company knew who they were. I, on the other hand, was oblivious to the "scene" in Moscow (having spent the last year hiding in plain sight at the theater).

Backstage, my new friends would present me with beautiful bouquets of flowers. In Russia, flowers are readily used in celebrations or as tokens of thanks, much more so than in America. Americans don't usually present flowers to a man; it's considered emasculating. But Russians present men and women alike with beautiful flower arrangements. Onstage, during bows, Svetlana is given so many flowers that she cannot even attempt to carry them all, and places them by her feet. It is a long-held tradition and a touching show of appreciation. And after a year of never having anyone I knew attending a performance of mine, I adored having my Russian friends come see me on the Bolshoi stage.

HAVING FRIENDS CHANGED the way I viewed Moscow. Before, it had been a foreign place to work in and be challenged by. But once I met true friends, the city opened up its arms to me. I discovered more places to go. I would see familiar faces everywhere. When I returned from travels, I no longer approached Moscow with that feeling of dread. I was not even close to fluent in Russian, so my closest friends, Vikusa, Natash, and Kozak, would speak English and subtly remind those around us to speak it as well. That suggestion, although generous in its intention, embarrassed me. It didn't seem right that Russians would have to accommodate me by speaking my language on their turf. But no one seemed annoyed and all simply wanted to bypass that barrier of language and converse freely.

Bolshoi Theatre had an allure and mystery for the Russians I met through Vika and Natasha. Everyone was curious about what it was like to be a dancer with the theater. The reality is that dancers from Bolshoi Theatre, though well known and respected in Russian society, are insulated from the rest of the culture as a result of the necessary and unending commitment required by their art form. For better and for worse, this is true of dancers all over the world. I've always thought it important to stay open and curious to whatever is happening culturally in the world. It does the ballet world a disservice to stay closed off and insular, ignoring what is happening and what is changing in any given field around us.

BEFORE I MOVED to Russia I already knew how negatively some in the nation viewed homosexuality. It was far more conservative than the United States, and especially New York, where the openness to all lifestyles made it easy for me to live an honest life. Being gay in New York is such a nonissue that one tends to mistakenly assume that this acceptance prevails in the rest of the country and the world.

Yet I can truly say that, in Russia, I never had to lie to anyone about who I was. I never felt uneasy while walking down the street or in any social situation. But I did become aware of certain stories: friends of friends were beaten up, harassed for being gay and out. Though I was always aware of who was around me late at night when I was leaving Simachev, it was nothing like what Americans imagined when they'd ask things like "Are you safe walking down the street?"

For one thing, the way I walked down a Russian street was no different than the way I walked down the street in New York. In fact, the only place I have heard antigay slurs in the last eight years was in Cleveland, Ohio, when I was on tour with ABT, and walking to meet some friends at a restaurant near my hotel. It was Saint Patrick's Day and drunken college kids were pouring out of bars, pissed out of their minds. As I walked past a group of frat boys, one looked at me and, apparently showing off to his friends, shouted at the top of his lungs, "LOOK! It's a FAGGOT!"

I simply kept walking. But the shock and remembrance of being called something I was constantly called in my early teens hit a nerve that had been dormant for years. This happened in *America*. Surprisingly enough, it never once happened in Russia, where my circle increasingly came to include dancers of Bolshoi Theatre in addition to the designers and artists I'd met through Vika. None of those people cared about my sexual identity.

CHAPTER 36

I was ignorant of the traditions of a Russian Orthodox wedding until Evgenia Obraztsova, a charismatic ballerina at Bolshoi Theatre and a frequent partner of mine, asked me to attend her ceremony in Moscow. "Few people are invited," she told me, "but I want you there."

I was keenly aware that Genia was devout in her faith. But having been brought up in the Lutheran religion and deemed a "sinner" because of my homosexuality, I instinctively rejected any religion whose dogma dictated right and wrong, black and white. Yet Genia's beliefs, which permeated her thoughts and actions, had a compelling spirituality. I would observe her praying before a show. Or catch a glimpse of the icons she displayed at her home or on her dressing room table. Genia didn't judge. She simply believed in the help God gave her.

She once told me, "God will guide you throughout your life. He will give you strength and courage."

Even if I didn't share all of her beliefs, I admired her conviction and understood the benefits that such belief can instill.

RUSSIAN ORTHODOX CHURCHES dot the Moscow sky-line like gleaming golden onions with crosses on top. Genia's

287

ceremony was held on a bright spring day at a church just outside the center of the city. I felt honored to be there. I knew it would be a unique experience, like nothing in the United States, for the beliefs and traditions of this church are older than America itself.

Ballet dancers typically make beautiful brides. Genia was no exception. Her fiancé, Andrei, a sculptor, stood by her, beaming his smile at everyone. They were a young, vibrant couple.

At the appointed time, the priest, draped in a gilded white robe, instructed us to enter the church behind the bride and groom and make our way around the center of the nave. We walked slowly, all of us quiet, focused.

The church was gilded from top to bottom, scented by burning candles and the smell of damp earth. Icons of saints and wooden frescoes adorned the walls on all sides. There were no chairs, only an open space with areas to the left and right for specific icons where you could pray. Worshipers lit candles and crossed themselves, always touching the right side of the chest before the left, as opposed to the Western way of touching the left side first. That was one thing with which I was vaguely familiar because, in rehearsals, when dancers had to cross themselves onstage, the correct way to do it always depended on the part of the world in which the ballet was set—a significant detail discussed by many a coach.

We progressed into the nave and formed a semicircle just a few steps from the bride and groom. To the right of the nave, obscured by a column, was a quartet who began to sing Orthodox chants a cappella. The clarity and pure tone of their voices echoed through the church. It was devotional perfection.

When the ceremony began, I stood as still as I could, fearful of disrupting these deeply held traditions. I was keenly aware that this was something I might never experience again. By then, I felt even more honored to have been invited, as an outsider, to observe. The priest chanted and prayed. Some of the Russian words sounded familiar, but the majority were foreign to my ears. When you understand nothing of a language, it is body language that speaks to you. The belief and reverence of everyone involved in the ceremony was palpable. Some friends whispered to me that they had never seen an Orthodox wedding themselves. Throughout the entire ceremony, a little over an hour long, Genia and Andrei each held a slowly burning thin white candle. After standing facing the priest and the altar, with their candles burning down, they walked in at least a dozen circles around the center of the nave, regally and slowly, grounded in concentration.

They remained still when attendants to the priest raised ornate gold crowns above their heads. Genia, lost in the moment, stood with tears streaming down her cheeks. This is the image that is seared in my mind. Genia, her tears, in her white wedding dress, an ornate gold crown held over her head, holding a burning white candle in her hands. It was extraordinary to witness a dear Russian friend and partner taking such belief and joy from this ceremony and the covenant with God and her beloved that it signified.

The experience left me profoundly moved. My daily life inside the walls of Bolshoi Theatre was why I had come to Moscow. But it was the other experiences, unlike any in my life thus far, that made every risk and sacrifice well worth it.

CHAPTER 37

I n my first season with Bolshoi, Sergei and I balanced my ABT
commitments with those at Bolshoi Theatre. (I later decided
that the schedule we'd built was unrealistic.) Although there
had been ample rehearsals at Bolshoi for my first *Giselle* and
Sleeping Beauty, now my time to prepare roles was cut to days,
not weeks. My free days, which were meant to be spent relaxing
and recharging my fatigued body, were passed flying thousands
of miles from one continent to another. My idea of a day off was
stepping onto a plane and having ten to twelve hours ahead of
me with nothing to do but eat, sleep, and attempt to mentally and
physically recharge while seated in a pressurized cabin 35,000
feet in the air. I was oblivious to the consequences, ignorant
of the effect this whirlwind schedule had on my body. I would
dance one week in Moscow, three weeks with ABT, two and a
half weeks in Australia. Rinse and repeat.

I became accustomed to the endless treadmill I was on: the
physical exhaustion at the end of each show, the late-night finish
with adrenaline still pumping as I headed home to pack and prepare for a six a.m. flight for which I would trudge to the airport
at four a.m., eventually sleeping in my seat, only to wake up when
landing in another city, where I would head to rehearsals and

confront a completely different working environment, a different style of dancing, and a different ballet.

Throughout my first year at the Bolshoi, I felt the pressure to be at the absolute top of my game. I had relearned and been recoached in the classical ballets. This intense work was invariably draining; the Bolshoi style pushed me beyond anything I'd attained before. Though my learning curve was fast and steep, I struggled to stay on top of all my responsibilities as I began to ping-pong around the world, trying desperately to keep up with what was expected of me. The prospect of letting these opportunities pass terrified me. I felt an adrenaline rush journeying to one company after another, each vastly different from the previous ones. It was destined to take its toll.

IN MAY OF 2012, I was scheduled to dance my debut in George Balanchine's "Diamonds" at the Bolshoi. "Diamonds" is the magnificent third movement of *Jewels*, one of Balanchine's masterworks, which many regard as the first full-length abstract ballet. Tchaikovsky's soaring score can forge a deeply intimate connection between the two leading dancers and the audience. But my task in creating that moment, as the dancer, was much harder than I had imagined. It was a debut for the company as well, and the final big premiere of Sergei's first season as director of Bolshoi.

I wasn't in Moscow during the initial teaching of the ballet. The rest of the dancers cast in leading roles learned the piece from a former Balanchine ballerina, Merrill Ashley. I had worked with Merrill before at ABT in another Balanchine work, *Ballo della Regina* (created expressly for her). Her ability to catch the pairing of musicality and attack were a great fit for the Bolshoi dancers. She pushed them deeper and deeper into the Balanchine style, which she had learned from Balanchine himself. And she did so without interfering with Bolshoi technique.

When I eventually came to Moscow to learn the ballet with Merrill, I was far behind everyone else in the cast, including my partner Svetlana Lunkina, a long-limbed ballerina with a pure, refined Bolshoi style. Svetlana and I knew each other well enough, having danced together in *Swan Lake* earlier on in the season. I had heard through the grapevine that she was uneasy about the amount of time I was committing to rehearsals, although she never expressed any frustrations to me directly. My plan was to learn it in December for a week, revisit it when I was back in Moscow in February for another week, and then arrive with a couple of days to prepare before my premiere in May. I knew it to be an intricate and delicate work; although only thirty-one minutes in length, it was filled with many subtle nuances and discreet shadings. Learning anything that possessed such fine details always took a great amount of time and work, refining and finessing each step day in, day out. It takes months for the steps to settle into the body, eventually becoming second nature so the artistry can dominate. Foolishly, I assumed that it would not take long to prepare for a new ballet of which I had no prior knowledge.

WHEN I FLEW in two days before the premiere for the final dress rehearsals, I hadn't even passed the most basic hurdle of memorizing the steps and focusing on my partner's needs in the pas de deux, the most iconic section in the ballet. It was apparent to me, and no doubt to everyone else, that the ballet hadn't been properly absorbed into my body. You need that absorption in order to be open enough onstage to take risks and move freely and confidently. I wasn't near that point.

During the dress rehearsal I was also horribly jet-lagged. In one of my solos, as the company looked on from the wings, I landed from a jump on an angle and slipped on the floor, going down on my butt loudly. I still remember the gasps from the dancers, all looking at me as I peeled myself off the floor of the Bolshoi stage.

The night of the premiere, my usual nerves were laced with fear. There is a big difference between the fearful nerves that come from being unprepared and the normal nerves you feel because, after all your meticulous preparation, you hope to show what you've achieved through the process of rehearsal. All I could hope for that night was that nothing would go terribly wrong.

There were no awful mishaps during that show, but it was clear to the audience, myself, and the other dancers that something was amiss. To me, my performance felt empty and cheap, devoid of the depth one hopes to find in any ballet. Dancing to Tchaikovsky's music, on the Bolshoi's stage, aware of the dancers who had performed this work, I could only feel weak and thin and subsumed in a sense of disappointment and failure. My commitment to the role hadn't waned, but it looked like I didn't care because I gave a vapid performance. I had compromised the outcome of "Diamonds" because I wanted to do too much in too little time. The fact is, no matter how much you prepare, there is no guarantee that you'll go out onstage and dance the way you dream of dancing or how you have rehearsed in the studio. But being inadequately prepared is inexcusable.

I WALKED AWAY from that performance having learned a vital artistic lesson. Never again would I take a choreographic gem and deny myself its deserved preparation time. I couldn't, nor can anyone else, just slap a premiere together. It was no one's fault but mine.

I returned to New York thoroughly chastened, knowing that I owed it to myself, the dancers I worked with, and the audience to never allow a performance like that to happen again.

CHAPTER 38

That spring, as I prepared for another *Romeo and Juliet* at ABT with Natasha Osipova, I realized how much my attitudes had changed since the first three times we danced these roles side by side.

In earlier days I was still chasing the idea of perfection that had attracted me to ballet at the start. I had thought that this search for perfection, in the studio and on the stage, would make me a better dancer. In some ways it did, but it also had left me in mortal fear of making mistakes. By this point, I had had enough positive reinforcement and, perhaps more important, enough disappointments to fully comprehend the benefit of mishap. There is a great story about George Balanchine and the legendary ballerina Gelsey Kirkland. During class, Balanchine told the women to perform a diagonal of grand jetés. Gelsey stepped out to do them and fell flat on the floor. None of the others fell, but Balanchine said that Gelsey was the only one who had done them right because she was the only one who really went for it, risking everything. I felt too safe, too calculated. I craved that same fearlessness, the willingness to discover an emancipation from caution. I witnessed it in others. And I had come to strive to attain it myself. To this day, it is something that I wish I had aspired to sooner, and given myself the freedom to explore much more.

As a young dancer, when approaching a step or lift or turn I deemed hard, I would say to myself, *Don't fuck this up.* I vividly recall thinking those words on countless occasions, even in performance. At times I wondered if it was a form of superstition, that the very act of thinking *Don't fuck this up* would protect me from any and all regrettable mistakes. But I had come to realize that the common thread among the disparate artists I admire most is that they do not protect themselves at all. Sure, they may question in the studio or doubt just before a performance, but when the moment presents itself they appear fearless. I think of artists in any medium who boldly eschew established norms and notions because they have that burning desire to express themselves in the only way they know how, and from that deep, compelling instinct comes their vision. Francis Bacon and his angst-filled canvases; Willem de Kooning and his singular interpretation of the woman's body; Lady Gaga and her electrifyingly versatile voice; Hiroshi Sugimoto and the overpowering Zen stillness in his photographs of seascapes and theaters; Jenny Saville and her abundantly fleshy human figures.

Their fearlessness and, in turn, originality, became the qualities I prized and desired above all.

From a young age and well into my professional career, I had been obsessed with executing a perfect tendu. The word "tendu" means to stretch; in execution you slide your foot outward, away from the body, keeping the tips of your toes on the floor as your foot arches. It's visually simple and one of the first steps you are taught in ballet class, but it's so imperative to dancing that Balanchine said if you could do this one step correctly, everything else would fall into place.

When I first moved to New York, I would watch Wendy Whelan, an inimitable ballerina with New York City Ballet, execute that very stretch of the foot in Willy Burmann's advanced class. I thought it was the perfect tendu, but as my perspective shifted I realized that it wasn't. What made it *seem* perfect was that it was emphatically *her* tendu in all of its uniqueness and individuality. She gave the illusion of the perfect tendu because no one else was creating a movement quite like hers. So in the end, a form of perfection was attained.

Similarly, I continued to learn from Gillian Murphy's willingness to test new ways of executing steps and to gracefully bear the success or failure of each gamble. When something didn't work, she shrugged it off with a giggle. It was fascinating to witness. I would agonize over one jump while she would easily launch into something and see what happened, which consequently made her dancing fresh. I wanted to emulate that ability to throw those dice and not obsess over the perfection of it all.

More and more, I sought to follow the example of great artists like Alessandra Ferri and Julio Bocca, two incredibly supple, intense, and romantic dancers who let natural emotion infuse every step they took. They would go so far into their characters' feelings that they risked looking over the top. But they never did. They were alive, vibrant, full-blown. Not only fearless but natural. Watching them made me want to be more of a natural interpreter, to go onstage and forget about technique and truly embody a character. To have the role I portray come pouring through the steps that can embody love, passion, fear, jealousy. Emotions we all feel easily in life can feel anything but natural when you have to conjure them on the stage.

ONE OF THE most significant, and truthful, critiques of my generation of dancers is that we focus too much on the technique of dance. It's so easy to get caught up in that idea of achieving "perfection" and to forget that being "perfect" can drain your dancing of the force and fire that makes art expressive. Steps are not art. Technique is not art. What you do with them becomes art.

Yes, the audience wants to be thrilled; they love witnessing those superhuman feats of multiple turns and huge jumps. But a performance of pure technique leaves them empty. Like eating candy all day and nothing else. Ultimately they come to ballet to be moved, to be transported. Only artistry, and the emotions that undergird it, can bring an audience to rapture or tears.

I had come to believe something Nureyev once said: "Perfection is sterile, unattainable. You have to match your own ideal. My ideal is not everyone's perfection."

My own ideal had become to have the courage, to play, to experiment. Take fear out of the equation. Seize the opportunity. Spend it. Save nothing. Push myself to limits I didn't think possible. And that could only happen when I stopped telling myself, *Don't fuck this up.*

Instead: *Risk it all and potentially fuck this up.*

EVERY *ROMEO* WITH Natasha became more intense than the one that preceded it. I was apprehensive, knowing that because the first one took us by such surprise, this one could potentially not live up to it. We knew what this ballet did to us personally. It allowed us to sink so deeply into the roles that the lines blurred between reality and performance. We were left stunned at the end of each show, still clinging to each other even long after the curtain had gone down. Now, three years after we first danced it together, I was determined to not attempt to repeat past performances. I wanted to approach each performance as if it were completely new and let it unfold on its very own terms. I didn't want to fall into one of the greatest perils for a performer, which is to look back thinking, *I know what works, what they want, let's do the same thing again.* That slope is slippery: you give the audience what you think they want so they'll like you once more, scream for you once again, cause the theater to erupt in applause. The greatest duty to yourself as an artist is to push beyond expectation. I wanted our *Romeo* to stay alive, like a new discovery each time.

ON THE NIGHT of the show, I felt the expectation of the audience across the orchestra pit. In Act I, with the scene change complete, the front cloth rose and Juliet's balcony was revealed. The moment arrived: our balcony scene. The hush of the audience is what I always tune in to the most as I wait in the wings. The theater was completely silent. Then the organ softly broke that silence as Juliet stepped out dreamily onto the balcony, high above the stage, and basked in the moonlight.

In the wings, with my long brown cape draped over my shoulders, I reminded myself, *Just let it happen. Don't force anything. Let us fly.*

I bounded out and a moment later stood center stage, my back to the audience, beholding her on the balcony. Standing so far from her in such dim light, I could not see the details of her face, only her silhouette, which appeared both frail and powerful. She turned toward me, her face now illuminated by a warm, dim light above. Our eyes met and locked. We gazed intently at each other; we breathed as one. Every move we would make after that was intimate, impassioned, conjoined. I danced for her, completely entranced, each step pouring out of me.

She ran to me, gazelle-like, and we merged. It was as if I could do anything to her: carry her, turn her; she had total trust in my movements, she was supple in my arms. I fell to one knee, stared up at her, and took the hem of her dress to my cheek, pressed the soft fabric to my face.

Moments later, we faced each other. Our hands met; just a soft touch of our fingers was enough. The sensation was euphoric. We *were* Romeo and Juliet. For us, for them, it was like nothing we'd

299

ever felt before. The surge of emotion being too much to handle, she ran from me. I pleaded for her to return. She bounded back into my arms and as she sought to dash away once again, I grabbed her hand. This touch meant something else entirely. We became still, an arm's length apart. She slowly turned to me. We gazed at each other. Without doubt or question, as if drawn by magnets, I walked slowly toward her and our lips met. Then she broke away, dazed, and dashed up the stairs to the familiar safety of her balcony. I watched her run, then raced to the foot of the balcony, arm upraised, reaching for her, seeking to prolong that singular euphoria as the curtain fell.

These intense, genuine emotions were played out in front of a vast audience at the Metropolitan Opera House. Like voyeurs, they watched our every move. We were so deep in our own connection we completely forgot that those 3,800 people existed. There was only Natasha, my Juliet, the movement, the emotions, the music.

At last, I thought, what I felt onstage was total honesty. No pretense of what I thought something *should* be. How I *should* walk. How I *should* stand. How I *should* react. It was no longer a question of should; it simply was.

When the curtain closed, Natasha made her way down the steps. We could hear the audience applauding as I hugged her tightly, thanked her for the first act, then watched as she walked away to her dressing room. Normally, I go straight to my own dressing room to rest (Act I of *Romeo* is a marathon) but that night I chose to linger on the stage. Panting, breathless, I needed to savor the moment that had passed too quickly.

On the other side of the heavy gold curtain the audience continued to applaud as the house lights came up slowly, signaling intermission. Through the curtain, I could feel the weight of their clapping. It didn't let up but sounded stronger by the second. As the crew began preparing the stage for Act II, I heard continual shouts of "Bravi!" As deeply as Natasha and I felt the balcony scene, was it possible that the audience was as moved as we were? At times they aren't quite where the dancers are. But this response was affirmation that they went on the journey with us. They remained in the theater, still applauding. There were no planned bows for Act I. The custom for dancers portraying Romeo and Juliet is to bow only at the end of the ballet. An earlier bow would essentially break the fourth wall, that invisible barrier that divides performers from the audience. But as I made my way to the first wing to look across at the stage managers, they stared at me, uncertain. Should they pull the curtain back and let us step in front of it, even though this had never been done before? Or should they just ignore the audience's apparent desire and continue on with the interval? Minutes passed; the applause continued. The stage manager determined that we indeed should take a bow. My dresser (who stayed with me onstage after the act) made a frantic dash to Natasha's dressing room. Natasha ran to meet me. We looked at each other, stunned. The curtain was pulled aside. Slowly, holding hands, we inched in front of it. The audience, on their feet, responded. We were frozen by the cumulative effect of our shared moments onstage and this unexpected one in front of the curtain. I held her in my arms as we humbly bowed.

Live art, live performance, can be euphoria. We had given every fiber of ourselves to each other onstage and shared it with the audience. As we bowed again, tears welled up in my eyes. A moment like that is as rich and fleeting as a dancer's career.

CHAPTER 39

ABT's spring season calls for an exhaustive level of physical, emotional, and artistic commitment. But the plate was never full enough for me. As usual, my too-easily-bored self needed to augment my primary endeavors by having numerous other projects. So when the season ended and the company was on hiatus, while many other dancers were getting much-needed and deserved rest, I was committed to dance a wide variety of ballets throughout the summer and fall in Taipei, Buenos Aires, and Australia.

In addition, I had developed a subtly powerful piece with a friend, Jonah Bokaer, a modern choreographer who had danced for Merce Cunningham. We were scheduled to premiere it at the Festival d'Avignon in the Provence region of France, one of the world's most revered and important contemporary arts festivals, and also to bring it to Jacob's Pillow in Becket, Massachusetts. I was convinced I could do it all. And then do some more on top of that.

MY ABT SEASON concluded with several shows of *Le Corsaire*, a ballet I had danced many times before. The day after my final show, I was in rehearsals for ABT's Taipei tour of *La Bayadère*. My friend Reid Bartelme, a former dancer turned costume designer, came to the Metropolitan Opera House to watch my solo rehearsal onstage. I wanted him to have the experience of watching from a seat in the vast, empty theater, so I led him down a dark, narrow staircase to the pass door that leads from backstage to the front of house. As I reached the bottom and pushed the door open, I stepped on something in the middle of the landing. I slipped off it. My ankle twisted sharply. I heard a snap. Startled, I turned and walked back up the tiny flight of stairs into the wings and onto the empty stage to test it out. Reid followed me in shock.

"I think I'm okay," I told him.

I bounced around on both feet and jumped up and down to make sure everything was in order. But as I tested it more, my right foot began to swell. In a matter of seconds, it ballooned out to the side. Within a minute I couldn't walk on it. "Oh my God. Oh my God," was all Reid could say.

I became calm and focused, just as I had when I'd sprained my ankle during the global broadcast of *Sleeping Beauty*. Knowing that something significant had happened, I limped offstage and headed up to the physical therapy room. There, I lay on the table and told the therapist, "I think I broke my foot."

Then I fainted.

ABT has two physiotherapists, Julie Daugherty and the chief therapist, Peter Marshall, whom Mikhail Baryshnikov dubbed his "angel savior." Once I regained consciousness they put me on crutches and escorted me, via taxi, to the office of an orthopedic surgeon. He had my foot X-rayed and told me I'd broken my fifth metatarsal. It was a clean break, meaning I didn't displace the bone so I wouldn't need surgery. But it would require months to heal.

It wasn't until the next day that it really sank in. I was immobile. Injured. I made the calls needed to cancel months of upcoming performances. Most presenters were sympathetic, understanding that injury is a hazard that comes with the profession. But some were less accommodating. I understood why. They'd already announced my performance; the public was expecting it.

I felt horrible about canceling the piece I'd made with Jonah. At the festival where it was to premiere, Jonah had an established reputation and people were anticipating his return. He suggested that I fly to Avignon, perch on a chair with a microphone, and speak the whole time. I would have gladly ventured there and to Jacob's Pillow to salvage whatever we could of the months of intense work we'd put in. But I had been ordered by the doctor not to travel anywhere. There was no way around my broken foot and the healing process.

I kept thinking back to the moment the accident happened, castigating myself for how carelessly I had bounded down the stairs and reached for the door to the theater, my movements guided by a sense of invincibility that had built up over time. I had had such a huge year, on a global scale, with previously unimaginable attention and praise, that I couldn't disagree when a close friend said this fluke accident was not only telling me to slow down, it was also showing me that my ego had become too inflated and I needed to be brought back down to the ground.

I had definitely been brought down.

The following day, Ethan Stiefel was retiring from ABT. He was an exquisite dancer and someone I'd looked up to since high school, when I'd determined to follow him and Vladimir Malakhov to ABT. His farewell performance, as the slave Ali in *Le Corsaire*, was one of the most anticipated events of the season. I couldn't miss the last show of someone who had been such an inspiration and had an enormous influence on me.

I forced myself to leave the apartment and head to the theater, the last place in the world I wanted to be. But I was happy to see one of my idols dance in such a virtuosic way and to see the company and audience honor him after the performance with flowers and applause. Immediately thereafter, I went into my shell. And stayed there.

Weeks passed. The longer I was separated from the fervor and energy of my work, the more I became frightened to return to it. It was a struggle to imagine myself back in it, racing all over the globe, trying to beat some internal clock ticking relentlessly away. I had just turned thirty, the age generally regarded as a male dancer's prime. This was a time I could not afford to squander. But the recovery process was infuriatingly slow. It was two months before I could walk without crutches. By then my right leg had shriveled up; I'd lost muscle definition from my thigh to my toes. I no longer had the fat pads that protect the bones on the bottom of the foot; as I walked I could feel my bones pressing against the ground. I had gone from peak performance shape to lacking basic muscles that nondancers take for granted.

But I was desperate to dance again. I pushed myself physically, which led inevitably to more setbacks and disappointments. Four months stretched to six. Then, finally, I was healed.

CHAPTER 40

When I was finally able to return to the dance studio, I worked once again with Alexei, who was creating a new full-length work, *Shostakovich Trilogy*, which would become a masterpiece for ABT.

During a five-minute break, I lay on the ground, feet elevated against the mirror. I idly scrolled through my Twitter feed and saw a series of tweets in French stating that Sergei Filin had been attacked in Moscow. I assumed I didn't understand them correctly, but then more and more came through in other languages and confirmed what I first read. Something about a substance being thrown at him outside his apartment building. My initial reaction was that these "reports" must have been exaggerated. I couldn't possibly believe that someone would have attacked Sergei maliciously. Safety can be an issue in Moscow, so I assumed that he had been mugged. As I kept reading what was becoming a torrent of tweets, it became clear that something terrible had happened. With rehearsal recommencing, I was certain Alexei hadn't heard any news of an attack, for he was in the thick of creating.

I paced from one side of the studio to the other, unable to concentrate as Alexei worked with other dancers. His wife, Tatiana, was in the front of the studio, watching quietly. I made my way over to her and asked if she had heard anything. She hadn't. When I told her what I'd been reading, she looked at me in shock. She had known Sergei for a long time, as he had been a Premier Dancer with the Bolshoi throughout the years that Alexei preceded him as the company's director. I waited until the moment rehearsal finished to look at my phone again for any news I could garner. By then, the entire horrific story had been confirmed.

Sergei had been heading into his apartment building late at night, after a performance, when someone came up behind him, called out his name, and then threw in his face a bottle of acid mixed with urine. The perpetrator ran. Sergei knelt down and shoved snow into his eyes and face to keep them from burning, an instinctive gesture that would partially save his eyesight. He shouted for the security guard to summon his wife. She rushed him to the hospital, where he was treated for major burns and eye damage. The image of Sergei's completely bandaged face, first seen when he gave an interview from his hospital bed, remains etched in my mind.

In the days following the attack, the global media latched on to the story. Not only the dance world was shocked. It was headline news everywhere. How could something so violent and vicious happen within a world known for control and restraint? It brought the gorgeous, fantasy world of dance crashing down in the wake of a hideous crime. In that sense, the attack was a betrayal: first and foremost of Sergei and secondarily of the world of dance and its audience.

WHO COULD BE vicious enough, I wondered, to do such a thing? And what could possibly be the rationale for doing it? Those were questions that everyone in the ballet world was asking. To attack someone, anyone, in such a beastly and archaic way was beyond comprehension and had no place in the sort of world I wanted to live in.

Sergei is a visionary, a dreamer, propelled by his devotion to this art form. At times he had been a controversial figure with a fiery demeanor. But more often he was an impassioned leader revolutionizing the Bolshoi and bringing it into the current day. Along the way he was required to make decisions that some found distasteful or even enraging. Strong opinions are the sign of a strong director in ballet and in other major art institutions around the world. Though he did not lack detractors, an attack of this nature was unthinkable.

Since I was in New York, reaching Sergei was almost impossible. He was bombarded by good wishes, as were his family and the entire Bolshoi Theatre. I sent him my support through others who were close to him, but I felt very separated and distant from my director and friend. It would be weeks before the truth was known. In the meantime, troubling facts seeped out, one after the other.

Sergei had been receiving threats prior to the attack. The tires of his car had been slashed, he'd had repeated nuisance calls, and his email was hacked. Just prior to the attack he had told the Bolshoi's General Director, "I have a feeling that I am on the front lines." The Bolshoi's spokeswoman, Ekaterina Novikova, said the suspicion was that he had become a casualty of the infighting between rival groups of dancers and managers. She told the press, "We never imagined that a war for roles—not for real estate or for oil—could reach this level of crime."

It finally emerged that Pavel Dmitrichenko, a dancer in the company, was angry because his girlfriend, Anzhelina Vorontsova, had been passed over for certain roles. He had planned the attack and hired two hit men to carry it out. I was stunned when I heard this. Pavel and I had danced together; he had been Von Rothbart when I danced Prince Siegfried in *Swan Lake*. It took me quite some time to get to know him and become friendly with him, but eventually we established a chummy rapport, easily joking about things in rehearsal or onstage. He had a fun sense of humor and seemed to be liked and accepted by the other dancers. It was a shock to learn that this horror had originated with him.

Pasha, as Russians called him, would later say he intended to "rough Sergei up." In his courtroom testimony, he insisted that he never imagined the attack would turn out as it did. He was sentenced to six years in prison, and released midway through that term.

THOUGH I WAS aware that the company had a long-standing reputation for scandal and intrigue, this was a side of Bolshoi Theatre from which I was generally protected. Whether it was because I didn't speak the language or because I inevitably remained the "American at the Bolshoi," I didn't see the deep inner workings of the company. I didn't have to fight for roles or go through the arduous and often dispiriting process of working my way up. I came into the company supported by Sergei and the Bolshoi's general manager. They backed me and stood by my reason for being there.

Once again, I wouldn't be surprised if some of the dancers secretly resented that my presence in the company had deprived them of certain roles; some might have even been annoyed that I was American. But if that was the case, they gave no signs of it. The interactions I had with everyone had been increasingly friendly and warm.

While it had been hard to get to know my colleagues at first, beyond that nod of acknowledgment in the hallway, within a year my rapport with the dancers at Bolshoi Theatre rivaled my rapport with the dancers of ABT. We established a banter in daily class that was jovial and lively. I never once had even the slightest sense that I was in danger or that my safety was compromised. What I saw inside the walls of Bolshoi was a collective effort between dancers, musicians, singers, stagehands, and administration, all of whom were united by their pride in the work presented onstage and through their conviction that Bolshoi was the crown jewel of Russian culture.

I was once giving some American friends a tour of the theater. They walked around amazed by the ornateness of the lobby and sheer size of the backstage area and studios. Finally, I brought them onto the stage to show them the interior of the theater, the beating heart of the entire building. But the theater was completely dark. Onstage, a group of designers, stage managers, and workmen were lighting the stage for the new production of *Marco Spada*. As usual, the house lights were completely out and the stage lights were on. My friends, edging out of the wings onto the empty stage, peered into the vast darkness, trying to catch a silhouette of the chandelier, seats, anything. Then, in a flash, the house lights were brought to full strength and the interior of Bolshoi Theatre was revealed in all its glory. The stage managers, working in the audience, had seen me with my friends on the side of the stage peering into the dark theater. They halted their lighting call to bring up the Bolshoi house lights, just to allow my guests to see the astonishing interior. It was a thoughtful gesture, especially since they were crunching out long hours, lighting a ballet to be premiered in only a few days. That was the type of Bolshoi Theatre I knew.

I WAS AWAY from Bolshoi for thirteen months. I didn't want to be absent from the company I had grown to love, but I was forced to heal my fracture under the guidance of my team in New York. I wanted to come back stronger, ready to pick up where I had left off. Still, my return intimidated me. I had concocted many theories of how the dancers and staff perceived my absence. I pictured the dancers blaming me for it. Consequently I felt some guilt about having been away. Because the last thing I wanted to do was fail to fulfill my end of the arrangement I had made with Sergei.

When I finally returned to Moscow, the company welcomed me warmly. It was more like home than ever before. Svetlana became my most frequent partner, though I started to work with other ballerinas within the ranks. I would slave away six days a week, toiling with Sasha on whatever upcoming ballet I had scheduled, and on Mondays, like clockwork, I would head to Sanduny with Semyon. I looked forward to the mental and physical break Sanduny afforded me, with one of my best friends in Moscow. My Russian was still minimal at best, but the burgeoning friendships I had with other dancers developed into genuine mutual affection. This truly gave me a sense of place. At last I was comfortable.

I WAS EAGER to dive into the work with Sasha again. I had missed it greatly, and once we commenced I could sense that I relied on him more than ever before. I was struck by the fact that no matter how far a dancer progresses in his career, he remains dependent on the feedback of his coach, that seemingly omniscient figure watching from the front of the room. The coach is essential. But along with the luxury of having a personal coach who tells you what looks good and what doesn't, the work process—even for a very experienced dancer—can become more about pleasing someone else than about trusting your instincts as an artist. It's all too easy to cede authority and judgment, to let your coach be the sole determiner of what is good enough. Often when I ask a dancer how a performance went, the answer will simply be "My coach was happy." I wanted to find a balance between trusting my own ideas and relying on the opinions of others. Even though Sasha was so important to me, I wanted to trust myself more.

While I had hoped my injury would cause me to settle into a more sensible work pace, I could feel the addiction to work yet again. And I was hungrier this time. Having tasted my dance mortality, I was wholly resolved to dance as much as I could. Given the time I had lost, I wanted to accelerate full throttle.

CHAPTER 41

I looked at Svetlana in disbelief when she invited me to dance *Sleeping Beauty* with her at the Paris Opera Ballet in December 2013. I was terrified by the prospect of seeing *them* again—the students who had been so dismissive of me and made my year there a misery. Still, I accepted the invitation.

The opportunity to return to Paris and prove my worth was something I had hoped for. And to return with one of my favorite Bolshoi partners seemed all too appropriate. Fourteen eventful years had passed since I was *"L'Amerique"* training at the school. In the intervening years I had built a professional life that I was proud to have worked so hard for. I knew who I was as a dancer. This time, I would not let myself be distracted by the casual cruelty of others. There was an enormous task at hand, and it was to dance as well as I possibly could and by so doing defeat the memories that had plagued me since I'd left Paris.

The Paris Opera's version of *Sleeping Beauty* was choreographed by Nureyev. It was like no other version I had ever danced. Performed not just in Paris but in cities around the world, it is a marathon of solos and subtle character development. Although I had danced other versions of *Sleeping Beauty* with the Mariinsky, Bolshoi, and ABT, this felt like a completely new ballet. When I first looked at a YouTube video of the variations I would dance,

I couldn't believe how taxing they were. Staring at my computer screen, I felt my confidence plummet. But I began to chip away in the studio, alone at first, then eventually with a coach. Day after focused day. Step after step. Clearly, it was a role that would swallow me unless I took everything I had learned over the years of dancing around the world and applied it.

MOST VERSIONS DEPICT Prince Désiré as merely decorative, dancing around like a Disney-esque nobleman, looking terminally fraught and puzzled while searching for his one true love. In the past, I had always enjoyed the display of pure classicism in the Grand Pas de Deux at the end of the ballet, but the Prince had remained two-dimensional, devoid of true human emotion. Nureyev forced me to rethink the role entirely. He pushed every character in the ballet to the extremes of technical capacity, adding steps on top of steps in lightning-quick succession. He had tailored the role of Prince Désiré to his own romantic, virtuosic style and created three extra solos that gave the character depth and range and elevated him to a figure who, like Albrecht and Romeo, experiences honest human emotion. There is an arc through the ballet that brings him from melancholic solitude to a triumphant climax.

When I started to rehearse the ballet in Paris I realized that this version asked a different approach to my technique. This seemed to me the essence of the famous Nureyev style. Earthy, speedy, using both the melody of the music and the supporting notes. The undercurrent of an oboe. The subtle pulse of the strings. Some steps were "en bas," below the movement, creating a style that allowed me to move faster yet express more intricately. I was working with Clotilde Vayer, an expert of this style who had worked with Nureyev and danced his versions of *Beauty*, *Romeo*, *Swan*, and *Bayadère*. Critics have complained that Nureyev's ballets have too many steps, are too busy with excess. When steps are so taxing, they can control the dancer, as opposed to the dancer controlling them. It is easy to see when that occurs. The dancer struggles, lagging behind the music, unable to gain the edge. The more I rehearsed these bewilderingly challenging steps, the more comfortable they became.

I found that his *Beauty* allowed for deeper questions and more meaningful answers. There were nuances and shadings for me to convey and profound, interesting connections between everyone onstage.

OVERALL, MY SCHEDULE was madness. In the four weeks leading up to Paris, I danced in Moscow, then in Singapore with the Bolshoi for *Swan Lake*. Back to Paris to rehearse *Sleeping Beauty*. Sydney to rehearse and dance Alexei's *Cinderella*. Moscow to rehearse Alexei's *Lost Illusions*, based on Balzac's serial novel *Illusions Perdues* and finally back to Paris.

I rehearsed *Sleeping Beauty* in every city I went to regardless of which ballet I was dancing there. When I had no one to rehearse me, I worked alone in the studio, going over everything by myself. I was running myself down again, but I never lost sight of the fact that, by dancing in Paris, I was returning to the place that had rejected me. Most of the students who had made fun of me when I was a teenager were still there. Some were Étoiles. Most were in the Corps de Ballet. I was being given the chance to face classmates I had tried so hard to forget. They had plagued my dreams for years: apparitions standing before me in a group, as I came to dance with the company or revisit the school. Always, a feeling of rejection pervaded. I was determined that when I shared the stage with them, I would dance the best I possibly could.

*   *   *

WHEN I WALKED into the vast Studio Balanchine at Opéra Bastille for class at Paris Opera, a few dancers were warming up on the sides of the studio. The room was enormous, with grid-like windows looking out onto a view of residential Paris. I took a place in the back of the room and began to stretch and warm up, consciously ignoring the dancers I recognized from years earlier. In walked Alain, tall, and as lanky as before; the leader of the school in my day, now a Premier Danseur. In walked Sophie, same blond hair, slinky walk; the girl who had made no secret of her distaste for me when she laughed out loud after I slipped on the stairs. Her rank, Quadrille, was akin to being a member of the Corps de Ballet. I felt no reason to acknowledge them. I was there to do a job. I was back to dance as a professional. I had no need for their approval.

None of them came to say hello. Maybe some didn't recognize me. Maybe some didn't care. There was a younger generation I hadn't gone to school with who knew me as a dancer from ABT and Bolshoi, not as "l'Amérique" at the school. They greeted me. Talked to me. Told me they were excited to have me there. What a difference that was.

But as my shows approached and I started to share the stage with dancers from the past, Sophie slowly came around. Gil Isoart, one of the company's ballet masters, was a mutual friend who had worked with me at Bolshoi Theatre. He knew of my past experience with Sophie, and after he left Bolshoi he became an indirect liaison between her and me. Because of him, Sophie started speaking to me in class and even quietly supporting me as my performances approached.

During an early rehearsal, as I walked onstage for my entrance in Act II, there was Sophie. Her eyes connected with mine. We were now professionals. Life was moving on. The past was becoming exactly that.

A BODY OF WORK

*　　*　　*

OUR TWO PERFORMANCES were scheduled just after Christmas and just after New Year's. My schedule left no time to celebrate the holiday season. On Christmas Day, Svetlana and I went to the empty Opera House to rehearse our solos and pas de deux. Everyone else at Paris Opera was home, feasting, opening gifts, enjoying the holiday. But there we were, sweating away in the quiet of the theater.

THE WORST PART of *Beauty* had always been the wait for my first entrance. But the nearly unbearable degree of pressure I felt before the performance in Paris was something I had experienced only once before, as I waited in the dressing room for my first entrance of the same ballet at Bolshoi Theatre. Waiting in Paris, anxiety got the best of me. Every second would inch by, and within every second, I analyzed step after step. I put the final touches on my makeup, sprayed my hair one last time, and buttoned up the beautifully embroidered costume the wardrobe department had made for me. I closed my eyes, alone in my dressing room, and took three deep breaths to settle my nerves and ground myself. I walked down the long cement corridor, into the wings.

Dancers around me were preparing themselves for Act II as well, tying their pointe shoes, rosining up, bouncing up and down to warm their bodies. I walked past the wings and onto the stage. A thirst for what was to come finally enveloped me. As the time drew closer, more and more dancers came onstage for the beginning of the act. The director of the company, Brigitte Lefèvre, came up and wished me "*Merde.*" Dancers who passed me wished me the same. Dry ice gave off a vapor that filled the air, representing the morning mist in the woods. I practiced some steps, warmed my body even more, fed off of the energy of the few dancers and crew milling about the stage, glancing my way.

The moment had arrived. I felt as though the only choice for me was to release everything and let the adrenaline propel me forward. I had ridden a roller coaster that, after the laborious and jerky climb to the top, was peaking, and now there was nothing left but a thrilling ride.

The curtain rose and I stepped onto the stage at Paris Opera with the confidence that I could do what I needed to do because I had doubted and questioned it all. After the sheer grit of work, I was able to execute those daunting steps and put my stamp on this role.

AS I TOOK my final bow, the entire company stood behind me applauding. I had danced *Sleeping Beauty* with Paris Opera. I had faced one of my greatest fears. I had realized a goal I had harbored for the better part of fourteen years. I had risen to the pressures. It was an absolute peak.

Later, after meeting scores of people backstage, I walked back to my hotel alone, carrying my bags full of cards from well-wishers, makeup, warm-ups. I thought, *At this moment I could retire.* I could stop dancing. I felt like I couldn't get any higher. Not that I couldn't get any better, because if I looked at a video of the performance I had just danced, I would find enough flaws to want to retire for a very different reason. Still, I had that rare feeling of being pleased with the outcome.

But, as always, I wanted more. I was aware that everything that preceded this point had gone by so quickly that, in a flash, this time—the prime time—would be over.

CHAPTER 42

The sense of completion, however colossal, quickly became hunger yet again. My addict self took over. I was running on pure adrenaline. Fatigued and malnourished. The day after *Beauty* ended, I packed everything at Bastille and carried it all to Paris Opera's other theater, the august Palais Garnier, where I joined the Bolshoi and commenced rehearsals for my debut in three days' time in Alexei's *Lost Illusions*. I couldn't say no to dancing at both opera houses within a week.

I will never be given this opportunity again, I thought.

And so I danced, the sheer elation of what I had just experienced driving me forward. But I became aware of a slight sensation in my left foot. Like an itch that came when I pushed off of it into a jump. It quickly went away after the initial propulsion, but in the takeoff, it persisted. No matter, I thought. There was too much to do; too many places to dance; too many debuts to prepare for.

I ignored it. It wasn't much at first, and the thought of it sidelining me, even for a couple of weeks, was too much to fathom. I didn't have time to listen to my body. After Paris, I was back at Bolshoi preparing for another live broadcast, this time in a title role created for Nureyev and choreographed by Pierre Lacotte, *Marco Spada*. The very next day after the broadcast, I was flying

321

to Milan to make my debut with La Scala, another dream stage and company that I'd never thought attainable. I couldn't and wouldn't stop. I didn't pay attention to anything except my desire to dance.

LA SCALA HAS been influential in the opera and ballet worlds for generations, and an invitation to dance there was an honor not easily afforded. I was asked to dance Nureyev's *Swan Lake*. As I'd discovered with his *Sleeping Beauty*, the variations were more challenging than any I had previously known. Again, it was another approach altogether, not like Bolshoi at all. With new intricacies came a new taxation on my body.

In rehearsal I experienced the same consistent pain in my foot, sharp and deliberate on takeoff. I could execute the required steps regardless, but every day I had the same uncomfortable sensation. The itch-like feeling was now more like a piercing needle. Wherever I traveled I would see the physiotherapist of that company, asking where she or he thought my pain was originating from. There was never a diagnosis, usually just a simple massage and brief chat about what I could do to remedy it for now.

I was far from home and under too much pressure to give my foot any serious consideration. Instead, I distracted myself with Milan. It was my first time in the city, so I became an avid tourist. People had warned me about Milan, saying, "It's not like the rest of Italy" or "It's too industrial." That's what I fell in love with. The imposing, grand stone buildings towered over me as I walked down the streets. It had an importance and a buzz. And in the middle of the city was the great Teatro alla Scala. I settled into the company well; the dancers, mainly Italian, were warm and welcoming.

I also knew about La Scala's infamously opinionated audiences. They loudly bravoed when performances moved them, and loudly booed when performers didn't meet their standards. I worked with that in the back of my mind. It was the first time I was appearing in Milan, and I had the whole scenario mapped out:

Curtain up. I would dance. They would boo.

Simple.

In fact, there were no boos. The public was generous, and while a theater of such importance as La Scala made me nervous, I still liked the pressure to produce. The audience and La Scala's director, who had hired me as a guest artist, expected me to dance well. To a standard. My expectations were as high as theirs. Those two sets of expectations had to be met.

I RETURNED TO Moscow to learn the most iconic ballet in the Bolshoi repertoire. I had never been sold on *Spartacus* as a ballet; I thought it dusty and dated—until I watched it in the vast Bolshoi Theatre. I was sitting in the center of the house, and when the overture started it had so much might and conviction that it felt as if the orchestra was blowing the walls off the theater. From that moment on, I was sold on the power of *Spartacus*. The dancers also validated why this work is still relevant. I was proud, sitting there, to be a part of a company of such quality and vibrancy.

I began to prepare one of the most iconic roles in the Bolshoi repertoire. The rehearsal process for Crassus, the morally corrupt Roman consul in Yuri Grigorovich's *Spartacus*, was intensely satisfying. Crassus's character borders on the insane. He loves war, power, sex, violence. He craves bloodshed. A deeply complex role that holds extreme weight in the Bolshoi's history, I was learning it from one of the great Crassuses, my coach Sasha. We took every moment we could get to work on the role, staying late in the evenings. The steps were foreign to me. This *was* the definition of the Soviet Bolshoi style, where the movements were bigger than the dancer, calling on me to expand my body in a way I never had before. Sasha explained each phrase in total detail: the way to bend the body to create the arc in a pas de poisson; the preparations for jumps that defied the cleanliness I had honed for years. In this role, I would take off for jumps in the most efficient way possible, regardless of form. It was all to create an illusion in the air; the taking off was purely a means to an end.

WORKING ON CRASSUS took a toll. I was being pushed beyond what my body could handle. I was already running on empty, but the difference in style was (as I look back now) potentially the tipping point.

My foot started to hurt more consistently. The pain was always there when I took off for a jump. Crassus has a huge diagonal of sissonnes, half-bent fishlike jumps in the air, which showcase him initially on the stage. The entrance creates gasps if done properly. We worked this diagonal endlessly. And each day, each time, my foot produced a sharper and sharper pain. I assumed it would go away eventually. So I continued on. After all, the stimulation of Crassus and other approaching opportunities were too great to pass up.

BETWEEN NOVEMBER 9, 2013, and January 18, 2014, I flew a total of 45,231 miles. I learned and danced four new productions. I translated four different styles of choreography, all in full-length works. Pushing through, remembering the choreography, executing the steps fully. Once again, my days off took place "in the air," meaning that the day that it took to fly from point A to point B was my rest. I would board a plane, veg out in the seat, and try to relax mentally and physically, only to hit the ground again running.

Here is what I wrote at the time:

Some would think my schedule is absolutely crazy and a recipe for disaster or dare I say injury. But it keeps me ticking. It keeps me interested. Makes me feel that I am living this moment in my career to the absolute fullest. When I feel I have to justify things, I say to myself or others that this career span is minute. It's over in a blink of my eye. And when all is said and done and I cannot dance anymore, I want to feel that I did everything in my power to have lived this dancing career to the fullest. Hence the crazy schedule. There is so much to do. So much to get done. I can't sit somewhere and do one thing at a time, waiting patiently for the next thing to come. It just can't happen like that. It's not in my DNA. One of my mottoes is "I'd rather be busy than bored." Boredom is a curse that makes me feel I have no purpose in life. Boredom rots inspiration and slowly eats away at me. So there must always be projects on the horizon, things to rehearse, projects to consider. When there is too much is when I feel at home. When I feel that I can prosper and thrive. There is never enough. But this is the curse of the hungry artist.

That is why I have to do as much as I can right now, be completely busy and frantic and stressed and overscheduled. So when I have finished with this period in my life I can look back and know that I have done absolutely everything I could have done. That I tried my absolute best.

My guiding principle has to be: Work hard. And then work fucking harder.

When I read this now, all I can say is that these are the words of someone who did not give thought to consequences. But it perfectly describes my state of mind when I still believed I was invincible.

CHAPTER 43

I had been waiting for a tour like this since I became a dancer with the Bolshoi: a tour during which I would come back to the United States with the Russian company I had joined. In 2014, I finally came home.

My most recent performances in Moscow had been hard to get through. I would come offstage feeling that I had barely been capable of finishing the show. I knew these upcoming performances would be difficult too, but I was determined to do them. It was a huge homecoming. Though American audiences knew I was dancing in Moscow, they hadn't seen me dancing live with Bolshoi. So the chance to perform with them in Washington, DC, and in New York, where audiences had seen me grow as a dancer, was meaningful and important.

It was a three-week tour. The company was scheduled to perform *Giselle* at the Kennedy Center in May, and then, in July, to offer a slew of standard Bolshoi repertory for the Lincoln Center Festival in New York. Svetlana and I were to dance the opening night in both cities. This was the complete circle. I was coming back, three years after I "defected," to dance in my home country; to show American audiences what I had been learning in Moscow and how I had acclimated to the Bolshoi Theatre style.

As I flew to America with the company, I felt that I was

welcoming them to the United States. It was a complete reversal of my situation in Moscow. Because the uncomfortable divide between us had dissipated, I was a genuine part of the group. I could introduce them to the security guards at the stage door. The spoken language and signage were exclusively in English, but I could translate. When I talked with the dressers and stagehands, they told me their impressions of how they felt the company was run (with order and purpose) and the differences culturally between "us" and "them" (Russians tend to be more direct). I felt like I was mixing my two lives into one. Russian culture on American soil.

I HAD MADE so many debuts as a budding professional at the Kennedy Center. My first leading role in Balanchine's *Symphony in C.* My first *Romeo.* My first *Swan Lake.* My first Solor in *La Bayadère.* And now, in my American debut with the Bolshoi.

As at many shows before this one, Mr. Han would be watching. As I prepared with Svetlana and the rest of the company, I pictured him sitting in the dark theater.

What would he be thinking, I wondered, as he watched? He still occasioned the same stress in me as before.

Yet during the performance I felt calm. Once the curtain fell and I had made my way back to my dressing room, I heard a knock on the door. Mr. Han greeted me dryly, as was his way.

"Hello. Good job tonight."

We shared a long hug, happy to see each other after so long.

"Tell me what you thought," I said. "How was my cabriole?"

That question brought us back into the routine that would be eternal between us. I, the pupil, and he, the teacher. My curiosity to hear his critique. And his brutal, dry honesty. He began a dissection of my performance, just as I wanted. I could feel that he was happy for me, proud of the work we'd put in so many years before.

Everything had changed and yet it seemed that nothing had changed: I was still the boy he trained and he was still "Mr. Han."

MY FOOT WAS becoming a major issue, something I knew I couldn't ignore for much longer. I was consistently in pain, and when I tried to push off, the pain worsened. But I chose to dance, paying no attention to what my gut was telling me.

In Washington, I could make only one attempt at rehearsing my variation for *Giselle*. After jumping so much the pain would be too great. It was horrible knowing how few moments of true strength I could muster up. But I was in no position to cancel performances. I didn't want to let ABT down. Nor Bolshoi. Nor the audiences expecting me on the stage. I willed myself to push through it all.

A week after the Bolshoi engagement ended, I was back in New York, dancing with ABT. When another dancer became injured, I picked up an extra show of *Giselle* with Alina Cojocaru. Alina and I had danced together previously but never formed a consistent partnership. For this particular show, the last-minute change left us with less than a day to prepare. We quickly rehearsed and hoped for the best, trusting that our experience would guide us in a spontaneous performance. It did. Our minimal preparation paid off.

Deep in Act II, I slowly walked out onstage for the main variation, to the hush of the audience. I paused, shifted my weight to my right foot at the start of the music, with my arms raised toward the sky. I took a large glissade, reaching my right foot out, propelling myself forward. With my left foot trailing behind the right, as I was pushing myself into the air for a cabriole, I felt a twist and pull in my left ankle. I knew something had happened. Adrenaline yanked me through my variation in front of 3,800 audience members; my mind raced. I knew I had hit a pronated downward angle in my left ankle and sprained it. This had happened before. I was all too familiar with the feeling of a sprain. In pain, I finished the variation. Eventually the curtain went down on a *Giselle* that was memorable for two very different reasons. One: Alina and I had danced together in unity and spontaneity. Two: It was the start of the downward spiral that would deprive me of the ability to push on through anything. I was at my breaking point. It would only get harder from here.

THE NEXT DAYS were a blur of failed attempts at keeping my scheduled commitments. Though my foot needed time to heal, time was something I could not afford without foregoing certain performances. I came into a studio at the Metropolitan Opera House a week later to test out my steps for *Swan Lake*. Kevin tried to guide me along. With my foot taped up, I tried to ease my way through, but I couldn't push off my left foot properly. I knew I couldn't continue. I canceled the rest of my ABT 2014 season.

The New York performances with Bolshoi in July were coming up in a matter of weeks. I would again dance at Lincoln Center but this time with my Russian company. I felt a responsibility to lead them into this season; it was an important tour for Bolshoi. So I rested and tried to heal the sprain as quickly as I could. A week later I was back on a plane to Moscow to rehearse *Swan Lake* for New York. I entered the studio with Sasha and told him where I was physically. We dissected every jump that took off from the left leg and tried to relieve the pain by changing them to the other leg. This unsettled us both. I didn't want to alter the steps that Yuri Nicolayevich had choreographed and that I was used to. But there was no other way through. I had healed enough to be able to dance, but not to dance the exact steps. In a series of jumps, at my entrance, I would push off the right foot instead of the left. The beginning of my Act III variation would start on the other side of the stage, so I could push and land on my right foot. We changed everything we were able to. Certain steps couldn't be changed because they involved other dancers, and they brought on the pain that had increased to a debilitating degree. I just gritted my teeth and danced. I knew I was on empty, but I felt I had no choice.

ANTICIPATION MOUNTED AROUND me as the two New York performances of *Swan Lake* loomed. More than thirty of my family members were in town for the opening, as well as family friends and fans from around the country. There was a discernible buzz. But through all the attention and anticipation, I was distracted. I felt a mounting unease about the pain that would not subside.

On the first night, as the lead-in to my entrance swelled from the orchestra pit, I stood in the wings praying I could get through each jump. I just hoped that whatever was causing that pain wouldn't produce a snap, or a crack, or a pull on takeoff or landing, leaving me unable to finish the few performances I had left in that season. I willed myself to get through those two shows, knowing I wasn't offering my best on the stage.

Those last performances of *Swan* were not me. I danced protected and reserved. Before each entrance, I hoped for the best. After each exit, I was relieved to have gotten through another section of the ballet. There was so much distraction around my homecoming (dinners, cameras, articles, previews, reviews) that I almost thought the public hardly noticed the actual dancing. But as I knew from before, when an artist's work starts to slip, even an untrained eye can see it.

I felt like a fraud, a fake, in the world I respected. I wasn't giving the art what it deserved. My inner circle knew how I felt. Sergei, having danced Yuri Nikolayevich's *Swan Lake* more than I ever had, noticed the steps I had changed to protect my foot. Sasha, I could sense, just wanted me to get through it.

There are some photographs, captured by a friend who was documenting me in the lead-up to the tour for *Condé Nast Traveler*, that show my last few performances before I stepped off the stage. Henry Leutwyler is a photographer who can reveal the essence of a dancer in his or her domain. In one of his pictures, I am midair in a Moscow studio, Sasha behind the camera coaching me. In what seems like a perfectly captured moment, with photographer and subject clearly synced, there is a detail that tells the true story. The image shows the jump at the start of my Act III variation. I am jumping in the opposite direction from that which the chore-ography calls for. Henry's image brings back painful memories of my physical shortcomings at that time and the subsequent pain.

In another, I am in my Lincoln Center dressing room, putting on my white tights, hair and makeup ready, a face of pre-performance concentration. But what is on my mind isn't the usual nerves of the looming show, it is the doubt that my foot can handle the stress I am about to inflict upon it. You can see an eerie despondence in all of these photos.

After the performances were over, Henry captured Svetlana and I hugging onstage. There is such relief in my face, a happiness that I made it through without major mishap.

Though internally, I knew I was broken.

CHAPTER 44

At last, at the end of the New York performances, I was on a much-needed vacation. I had made it through, without my best work onstage, but at least from start to finish. I was desperate for a rest. I needed to get away from everything and everyone. A solitary road trip was my remedy. I began just outside my hometown of Rapid City, South Dakota, at an idyllic cabin owned by Sam and Karen Mortimer, very close family friends since my birth. After a few days there, listening to the rushing stream just outside their house, I headed straight down the border of South Dakota and Wyoming. I crave this part of the country. It is quiet, underpopulated, and vast. During the drive, I would step out of my car onto the side of the road and listen to the near deafening silence around me. It was the opposite of the chaos I had just left. Under the seemingly endless sky of the place where I was born, I was at last calm.

And with that calm came clarity. As a pedestrian, I was pain free. I could walk as much as I wanted. But I knew that when I needed to return to dancing, the pain would return as well. I cut my vacation short to fly back to New York, where my surgeon decided that an acute injection of cortisone into the damaged area might relieve enough pain for me to go on dancing. It wouldn't be a permanent fix, but it might provide temporary relief. I would know the results immediately. The plan was to inject the foot using sonogram guidance and test out right there in the doctor's office what produced pain. If there was none, the cortisone would have done its trick. If not, I was told the sole remaining remedy would be surgery.

The operating room was cold. The doctor's assistant (a Russian) asked me to lie on the table with my foot perfectly positioned for the injection. She covered my whole leg with sterile towels, sanitized and numbed the area of the foot, shut off the lights so the doctor could see the screen, and coated the sonogram wand in cold gel. I thought, as I lay there, how depressing it all was. From the initial elation of my return to the States with the Bolshoi until now.

After a prick and a dull sensation in my foot, the injection was over.

"Now, try to test what would produce the pain," the doctor told me.

I eased myself off the table, stood on my foot, and started the suggestion of a glissade. I still felt the sharp sensation. Or so I thought. I wasn't totally sure.

I tried again, pushing a little harder this time.

I felt it.

The pain wasn't gone.

But it was a little less intense.

I lied and nodded to the doctor that it felt a little better.

"Good," he replied. "Take it easy the next few days and then in a week test it out in the studio."

I EASED INTO dancing the following week. I didn't push much by way of jumping or using the foot to its fullest, but after a week it was time to see whether or not the injection had worked its magic. On a rehearsal day, toward the end of morning class, I slipped out of the studio full of sweaty dancers and into an empty one. I tried to replicate, at about 60 percent of my fullest push, some of the *Swan Lake* steps that had been so painful previously.

Glissade cabriole.

Oh fuck, I thought.

Again.

Glissade cabriole.

Fuck.

It hadn't worked.

A sense of dread came over me. A feeling of surrender. A despondency that I was done. I had tried everything I could to avoid this decision but alone in that empty studio, hearing the music from the other room as dancers surged into the air freely, I decided the fight was over. Surgery was inevitable. What a bitter contrast: dancers in the adjacent studio bounding in the air to the sound of a big sweeping waltz and me alone, grounded with the knowledge of my inescapable future.

I ATTENDED MY scheduled rehearsals during that day, remaining quiet about my decision to my colleagues. After all, I wasn't incapable of dancing. I just couldn't fully do what was asked of me.

ABT was preparing Jerome Robbins's *Fancy Free* for its fall season, a ballet about three sailors on evening leave in New York City. It had been a personal triumph for me when I debuted it. I had warmed up to playing the "shy" sailor, though it had taken some convincing that I could dance a role so different from my usual fare. The répétiteur led the rehearsal with another group of sailors and I stood in the back with the dancers in my cast: Marcelo Gomes and Craig Salstein, a close friend since ABT summer intensive years. We were a good pack together.

This would be my final rehearsal.

Although I wasn't aware at the time of how long it would take to recover, I was told it would take at least four to eight months. I observed the room. The dancers who had no idea that I was bowing out. The atmosphere of the rehearsal, some dancers stressing, others working hard, others phoning it in. The pianist, pounding away at Leonard Bernstein's score. Silently, I was saying goodbye. But I felt calm at last. Reserved. Affirmed.

And at the end, as the dancers went on to another rehearsal, I left the studio with no sense of when I would return.

CHAPTER 45

In August, two weeks after my last rehearsal, on the eve of my operation, my mother flew into town to take care of me. We went out for a "last supper" at Strip House, a traditional steak house in the heart of New York. With martinis we toasted the decision made and the road ahead. At least Mom would be there for the first crucial week; the drugged-up, incoherent post-op week filled with stone-cold nights and dazed Percocet days.

On my way to the hospital, I had a hunch. A strange feeling about the operation. There was nothing specific about it, nor anything that I could put my finger on, but there was something off inside me. By then, I was a pro at ignoring gut instincts, so I did as I usually did. I brushed it off. I remember thinking, *It's too late to cancel it anyway.* The decision had been made.

I RODE HOME from the hospital with my mom. The surgery had taken four hours, and we had been told that when they opened my foot up it was a mess inside. I had a damaged deltoid ligament with a bone fragment embedded within it. While the surgeon was in there, as a precaution, he shaved off some bone spurs at the top of my talus.

I was still in a post-op stupor as the driver pulled up to my apartment building. I took my time getting out of the cab, unsteadily crawling onto the support of my crutches.

"What happened?" exclaimed the doorman. "Oh, man! This means you won't be dancing for a long time!"

One of the more obnoxious tenants in the building, who looked like he was a little too close friends with the drink, was leaning against the front desk in a lazy slump.

"Not again!" he barked at me.

I stared at him and didn't reply.

"Oh, oops," he muttered. "Did I say the wrong thing?"

"Yes," I said as I hobbled to the elevator.

MY MOTHER WAS an amazingly attentive caretaker, but after a week she was gone. I attempted to stay positive. I wanted to see the experience as one in which I could learn and grow and do things that I didn't have time for when I was going four hundred miles an hour. But despair crept in and settled there for the long stay. The walls of my apartment seemed to get closer and closer together. My thoughts veered from panic to utter disbelief. *How am I here . . . ? Again?*

Days passed as I sat on my couch, foot completely bandaged and elevated. I binge-watched *Six Feet Under* on my laptop for the second time. The goals for this newly allotted free time went by the wayside. There were too many hours in the day to fill. I gazed around the apartment. I saw corners that I didn't finish decorating, empty spaces that were supposed to contain furniture I never bought, a piece of art I'd always hated and now had to stare at all day. I told myself that injury happens to almost every athlete or dancer in one form or another. But it still ate at me and left me worrying about the people I had let down.

*   *   *

EIGHT WEEKS AFTER the surgery, the doctor gave me the go-ahead to start rehabbing the foot. The cast was sawed off; under it was a red, swollen foot and an atrophied calf half the size that it had been previously. "It shouldn't be this red," my physical therapist told me.

Never mind, I thought.

I needed to get on with rebuilding the calf, and strengthening the newly fixed ligament.

I was determined to do it properly. I didn't want to rush it or cut corners. I knew that if I took the fast track to getting back onstage, I could very well risk a major setback. Slow and methodical was going to get me there faster.

Before I could even think about starting ballet, my foot had to recover and be integrated back into the simplest activities: walking, climbing stairs, standing. New York life posed a substantial problem. In New York, you walk everywhere, and climb up and down subway stairs constantly. As a New Yorker, one takes that for granted. But for a recovering dancer on crutches, every step, every stair, is a challenge to a healing foot.

After the cast came off, another eight weeks passed before I finally started remedial ballet. I quickly realized that even remedial work was far too much too soon. A basic stretch of the foot. A bend of the knee. Even a rise onto demi-pointe. I had to accept it. Everyone who has been injured likes to tell their own story of time off, an anecdote to give you perspective on the hardship one goes through while learning to dance again. Clinton Luckett, then Ballet Master at ABT, shared with me the story of his own recovery process. As time passed after a first knee surgery, it became clear that he needed a second operation; the worst-case scenario for any surgical outcome. As he talked, emphasizing the tough fight that would be required for me to get back to dancing, I felt a piercing sense of dread. I suspected right then that I would need another operation.

*   *   *

THE DOCTOR HAD told me my estimated recovery time would be four to eight months. As each day passed into the next, I thought I must be making some sort of progress. But from the moment my foot was revealed from under the cast, it was bulbous and red. Like a balloon that never lost its helium. I assumed it was all part of the reaction to surgery and would eventually go down. It never did. It persisted. Red. Obtrusive. Almost angry. I had sensations of nerve pain on the side of the ankle, again like an itch that wouldn't go away. It appeared if I walked too much or stood for too long. I couldn't fit my feet into anything but large supportive Nikes, which I had to use even as dress shoes. I showed up in black Nikes during the celebrations for the Kennedy Center Honors, which I had to attend as a member of the Artists Committee. I even wore those Nikes at the White House when meeting President Obama.

The months of recovery time slipped away. One by one, I canceled performances. Commitment after commitment. La Scala. Bolshoi. ABT. Japan.

I was making some progress in class. But while I was able to execute more steps, something held me back. Something I couldn't yet explain. I could only push my body so far before it blocked me, telling me it wouldn't go any further.

COMPLICATIONS PILED ONE on top of another. My Achilles tendon started to produce a very sharp pain at the base of my heel. It would come and go, never producing the same pain consistently. But it hurt just as I pushed off for a jump, when the heel raises ever so slightly. The pain built and built. The more I tried to push through it, the worse the sensation. Like a knife stabbing my tendon.

The itching I felt in my deltoid ligament whenever I walked too much was a potential sign of complex regional pain syndrome (RSD). A colleague was diagnosed with this and explained it as the most debilitating pain she had ever experienced. "I'd rather be in labor again than have RSD symptoms," she told me.

My doctor wanted to nip it in the bud, so I was put on Neurontin, a medication used to treat nerve conditions and seizures. The nerve specialist warned me, "Ask your friends to keep an eye on you. If you become withdrawn or emotional they must tell you and then you need to stop the drug immediately."

A month into taking it, I was at my wit's end. One evening, I sat on a stoop near my apartment and began to wail. I sobbed so hard I couldn't breathe. It was as if there were no more filter left in me. I was lost in a thick forest with no idea which way was out. I had felt that way for the six months since my operation. One week dragged into the next. I'd wake up in the morning light, stare blankly at the gray walls in my bedroom, and find barely any impetus to continue fighting.

ALL THE COMPLICATIONS stemmed from one overriding issue: I still couldn't plié properly. Every other symptom (my Achilles, the nerve pain) was caused by the blockage I felt when I needed to bend my ankle into a range that is crucial to dancing. My lack of plié had produced all these other problems.

As the 2015 Met season rolled on without me, I stood just off stage right with my friend Craig, one hand holding the portable barre. Craig has a natural instinct for the needs of dancers in class and he gave me barre and strengthening exercises when he had a break from rehearsals and shows. As he tried to push me through an exercise, I struggled yet again to find the proper depth in my plié. The more we pushed, the more stuck it got. I was exhausted. At last, I broke. Something was functionally wrong.

Instinct told me that there was no way I could push through; it was like trying to push a door open with no idea of what's blocking it on the other side.

I stopped, overwhelmed. After ten months of the fight, I was done. I stood there, numb, in the wings at the Metropolitan Opera House, on just a strip of dance floor. Around me was the vast backstage area of the Met, the worn wooden floors, and the stage just to the side. There was such a divide between what was happening offstage and what was happening on it. My colleagues, riding the wave of the eight-week Met season. And me, panicking, distraught that I just couldn't join them.

A NEW MRI gave me the answer that instinct had been telling me all along. I had a glob of scar tissue embedded in the top of my ankle where the doctor had shaved off my bone spur as a precaution. This was precisely why I couldn't plié. There was an extensive thickened callus of scar tissue across the entire front of my ankle joint, which was blocking that movement. It seemed that the surgery had required two completely different recoveries. The deltoid ligament repair, which had been successful, needed immobility to heal. Hence the hard cast and the crutches for eight weeks. But, unbeknownst to me, healing the talus shaving had required mobility from the outset. Continuous movement would have told the body not to lay down that scar tissue.

I knew that the one way to achieve functional freedom was to get rid of the scar tissue. Surgically. A new doctor confirmed this. He bluntly stated, "The only way you will be able to do what you need to do at your level is if I go in, as noninvasively as possible, and remove what shouldn't be there."

My physical therapist, Michelle Rodriguez, was by my side in the doctor's office, asking the questions I didn't know to ask. Once the appointment was over, we got in a taxi. As we rode, I sobbed. The worst-case scenario had become real. Eleven months after my first surgery, I needed another.

THE NIGHT AFTER my second surgery, I lay in the hospital bed, my foot again wrapped in bandages, just like a year before. My disbelief and despair were temporarily replaced with optimism and relief. I was taking care of the problem at last. *Once I get out of the hospital it will be smooth sailing,* I told myself. *I'll pick up where I left off and get quickly back to rehearsals and full class, making up for the time lost.*

The only perk of possibly having RSD (my nerve pain) was receiving ketamine to mask any symptoms. Naively, I asked what the drug was.

"Don't you know about Special K?" the nurse asked me.

"Of course I know what it is. I was a raver in the late nineties."

Though my teenage raving days were spent sober, everyone on a drug around me was taking either Ecstasy or Special K.

"Well, now you can do it legally," the nurse said as he inserted the needle into my arm.

As the ketamine filtered through my body, my hospital bed became part of a lively circus act.

The nurses came in to ask how I was doing.

"*Great!*" I told them.

The sliver of the East River outside my window became a sea of glitter dancing before my eyes. The Kardashians, on TV, became my instant best friends. They were a family I'd loathed for years, refusing to watch them until now, when I was fully drugged and loving them.

At two a.m. the night nurse interrupted my mental plans to conquer the world, asking yet again how I was feeling. I looked at him, bug-eyed, beaming. "I *still* feel great!"

"Maybe we should give you something to help you sleep. I think you'll feel better in the morning if you have some rest."

I didn't want to end the trip with my newfound best friends, but I knew morning was coming soon enough.

BLEARY-EYED, THE NEXT day I woke up to the reality of post-op handicap. I looked down at my swollen foot, hidden beneath bandages. I was eager to leave the hospital, fast-forward through the weeks of rest, and get back into the studio. I'd already wasted enough time. My new doctor beamed with optimism, telling me that he wanted me walking on it in a week, giving it just enough time for the incisions to heal and the sutures to be taken out. The "mess" inside the foot had solidified his hunch that surgery was the only way. There was scar tissue all around the ankle, blocking almost every part of the natural glide of the talus when I would try to plié. He'd methodically gotten every bit of unwanted tissue out of my foot. It had been a success.

As I rode to my building in a taxi, my armor came up once again. I knew I would have to confront the same comments as the first time. Cue inquisitive doorman. Cue neighbor's shock and abrasive questions. Cue looks of confusion from everyone with whom I came into contact. After this second surgery, I knew the question they were secretly thinking but didn't dare verbalize.

Why don't you stop?

I was coming to that question in my own time. But not just yet.

CHAPTER 46

Once I was given the go-ahead to walk and then to start push-ing the foot through dancing and exercise, I returned to the studio. I worked alone. My plié was certainly better. I had a range of motion that I hadn't had before. But with this new range of motion came fragility. My foot was weak. I was able to move it in directions I hadn't in over a year, but it didn't have the muscle to support that movement. It felt like a flat tire.

I just wanted to dance.

I'd try to do a little more each day. With frenzied determina-tion I attempted steps that my body wasn't strong enough to do. I was delirious with the desire to get back as quickly as I could. I thought, *Too much time has already been lost.*

I had no methodical approach. I had physical therapists, mas-sage therapists, acupuncturists, Gyrotonic teachers, and personal weight trainers, but no one to help me in the studio. I would take any class that was available, and what was available was usually way too advanced for me at that moment. I needed slow, studious work and repetition, not what was given to healthy dancers in a daily company class.

In Craig's morning class for ABT, I tried to execute a speedy diagonal of piqué turns, pushing off the left foot onto a straight-legged right foot. I tried to keep up with the dancers circling

345

around me, but my foot was too weak to handle the fast tempo and such quick transitions. When I pushed off the left foot and felt it, I knew I had done something. There was a sharp twinge right by my ankle. I stopped and went to the side of the studio while the other dancers continued on. I had gone too far without realizing it until it was too late.

That was the start of a series of harsh realizations that the environment in New York, rehab in New York, and my life in New York wasn't working for me anymore. I was pushing myself too far, too fast, too frantically. From that moment in class, with the feeble ankle joint pinched together, unsupported because of a lack of strength around it, a constant pain was induced. Each time I tried to plié there was a sharp pinch, like a dull needle being stuck into my bone.

AFTER THE FORCED positivity following the second operation came an all-too-familiar despair. By the middle of fall I had lost control yet again. I had no end goal to look to anymore. I knew I was completely floundering. I couldn't go anywhere without people asking me what was taking so long.

Mornings were the worst time. Sleep seemed a preferable state to waking life. As I came to, I would feel a sense of utter disbelief. I would get out of bed, an emotional weight already on my shoulders, and shuffle through the day in a thick haze. A dull numbness. I sank deeper and deeper, caring just enough to complete the day's routine of physical therapy and class. But not enough to be proactive about bettering my mental state.

I would show up at Michelle's office for my physical therapy appointment, sit on the treating table, and cry. I couldn't hold it back. As hard as I tried to get on with business and take care of the problems, the real problem was that everything that mattered to me was spinning wildly out of control. I was more and more paralyzed. But Michelle always pushed me forward, even when I didn't have the energy to do so myself.

I STOPPED CONNECTING with friends. Never a smoker before, I took up the habit, and passed time with my legs up on the windowsill, blowing the smoke out my window, staring down at Twenty-Second Street below me. I enjoyed this. It felt like rebellion.

From my window I could see people passing by with purpose. Rushing with the workday energy that only New York City can conjure. I photographed the people I saw, interacting with life not as a participant but as an observer. I watched the world go by without me. I was avoiding the problem. I refused to admit that the routine I was in wasn't bringing me toward recovery. The physical therapy. The class. The environment. My gut told me otherwise. It told me that nothing I did was working. But I was in denial. Ultimately this taught me to always listen to my gut.

CHAPTER 47

Wherever I went in New York, people would ask how the recovery was going, expressing concern that it was taking far too long. Diana Vishneva came to me, tears in her eyes, worried as to why I wasn't getting back onstage, eager to do anything to help, suggesting a specialist in Germany. Alexei Ratmansky, propelled by the same concern, cut right to the chase: "Are you jumping yet?"

We both knew that jumping is the greatest stress on the body and the true test of progress.

"I'm not even close," I answered.

Alexei's wife came to me one afternoon, gazing at me, saying, "You look different. I cannot tell why, but you do."

I knew why, deep down.

I was beginning to let go. Give up. Remove myself from the world that defined me.

I had never been fearful that I would have to stop dancing at some point. That was an inevitability and a fact from which I had never shied away, one that made my dancing life all the more present and precious. Now I could see the increasingly real possibility that this debacle could be the end of my career. Suddenly, a possibility I had never considered loomed before me: that all the years of work and dedication would come to an end not by my considered choice but due to a series of events that were out of my control. I'd be finished by a "career-ending injury." These, of course, are not unheard of. But dancers and athletes tend to assume they will happen only to other people.

I FELT I had two options. I could retire. I had been approached about opportunities to transition smoothly into a nondancing role that would assure that my commitment to the art and what I had learned as a dancer would not be wasted. I had a fervent desire to give back to my art form everything that I possibly could. I had experienced inklings of what this felt like: mentoring a young dancer through a scholarship program I'd established at ABT; discovering new creators through a choreographic program, also at ABT; envisioning what style of repertoire to commission and how best to nurture dancers within a ballet company; imagining how best to nurture yet challenge audiences. These were far more appealing options than being just another desperate artist clinging on to the scenery for one more show. I felt like I had more to say, not just as a dancer but as a champion for the art form.

My dancing career had been more than I ever could have dreamed. I remembered walking home after my shows with Paris Opera, thinking, *Yes, I could retire at this moment.* So why not let it all go and rest assured that I had done everything I could until the very last exit off the stage?

My other option involved a fight. I could battle this plagued injury head-on, but somewhere else completely. I could place myself in the hands of what I had heard was one of the best rehabilitation teams in the world of dance. Dr. Sue Mayes, a physiotherapist at The Australian Ballet, presided over a department of specialists she had developed over the span of a twenty-year tenure with that company. She was Sylvie Guillem's personal physiotherapist, and I had met her in Japan, when Sylvie and I were dancing in the same gala. I had witnessed firsthand the work that Sue and her team did when I guested in Melbourne. I had always felt welcome down under. But it would be a gamble. I would have to leave everything behind and put my entire career in the hands of people who were strangers to me.

I contacted Brooke Lockett, a dancer with The Australian Ballet and a dear friend who was just coming back from a knee injury. When we connected via Skype, she was shocked by my appearance. "You look lifeless," she told me. I couldn't help but cry. She was kind and encouraging and explained the details of her rehab schedule there; how they built her up, what they focused on, whom she had helping her. It sounded idyllic and safe. She was completely in their hands. We made a deal that she would speak to Sue privately the next day and ask if she would be willing to take me on.

Brooke relayed to me Sue's reply: "How soon can he get here?"

I WENT TO Kevin. Always one to offer grounding advice, he had seen me grow into the artist I had sought to become. I was ready to present to him what seemed the only two options: I could seek a different perspective from the rehabilitation team at The Australian Ballet widely believed to have the finest program for dancer injury prevention and rehabilitation. Or I could retire.

I sat across from his sturdy oak desk on the third floor of ABT, the large windows behind him revealing the familiar view of New York. I held back my emotions. Although he knew I had cracked long before, I wouldn't let him see me cry. So, with a mixture of begging and asking, I posed the two options.

"What do you think I should do?"

I held my breath as I waited for his answer.

"Leaving a career behind in the state you're in isn't a solid decision. You haven't tried everything. Go to Australia and see what they can do for you."

He then finished with something direct and frank that I have carried with me ever since.

"You are at your lowest right now. You cannot make a decision as momentous as that of retiring when you are in this state."

THAT WAS IT. The moment when I decided to leave New York and see what could be done for me elsewhere. I was certainly not a stranger to this sort of move. Paris. Russia. Now Australia. I seemed to thrive in the unknown, in distant places. My gut told me the same thing Kevin had. *Go and seek.*

I booked a one-way ticket to Melbourne. I now had a plan. I could look forward to something. Immediately I experienced everything around me through different eyes. ABT. The streets of New York. The bustle. The energy. My diner. My routine. The stoop I would often smoke my rebellious cigarettes on. I was somewhat nostalgic, but I couldn't wait to get on that flight away from all of it. It was time to move on and give this one last effort. I was vanishing, in order to come back with an answer to the oft-repeated and terrifying question: *Will I ever dance again?*

WITH MY BAGS fully packed, the last thing I did in New York, hours before my flight, was to go to a no-frills barbershop on a side street in my neighborhood. A Dominican man sat me in his chair, placed the robe over my shoulders, and asked what I would like.

"Shave it all off," I said.

He looked at me, puzzled, apprehensive to take the razor to my long blond hair, essential for my princely roles.

"Are you sure?" he asked.

"Yes, a number two."

"Let's try a number four first."

He shaved, one lock after another. I stared at my reflection, watching every chunk fall to the floor. It was incredibly cathartic. When he completed the number 4, he asked my opinion.

"More," I said.

He meticulously shaved almost to my scalp.

I walked out free. Free of everything behind me.

I TOOK A photograph of myself on my normal smoking stoop, with head freshly shaved, cigarette in hand. I posted it on social media with the words "Goodbye, New York. There's some stuff I have to take care of once and for all."

CHAPTER 48

In November 2015, I began my first meeting with the rehabilitation team, lying on the floor of their treatment room, head freshly shaved and foot a swollen red ball. The three people who met me that day would watch my every move and dictate what I could and could not do for the duration of my stay. Sue Mayes. Paula Baird Colt. Megan Connelly. Respectively, Principal Physiotherapist, Body Conditioning Specialist, Ballet Rehabilitation Specialist. They would keep me from doing too much. Or push me if I wanted to do too little.

When I had worked briefly with Sue some years before, in Japan, I'd found her to be gently confident, strong, and warm. She was of medium height with a welcoming smile and a striking bob of blond hair held back by a trademark headband. In Melbourne, Sue was in her element, treating dancers of the company and managing its entire program of rehabilitation. But I hadn't gone there solely for Sue. I came because of what she had created. The team. The success rate. The individual plan for each and every dancer.

Sue assessed the foot for a long while. I had previously sent her my most recent MRI results, X-rays, and doctors' notes, so she had an idea of the course of unfortunate events. She had me plié (pain), tendu (blocked), and relevé (stiff). She looked at my reddened, bulbous foot and asked if it consistently looked like this or if it was just swelling from the flight.

"It always looks like this," I said.

AN HOUR LATER, Sue made the plan of attack. It was clear that my symptoms were not new to the team. I hadn't come to them with an ailment they hadn't dealt with previously.

"We're going to start you over. We will start cleanly with incremental progress from the beginning.

"You won't be doing ballet for a little while. We want to begin by building the strength you have lost. This is paramount. You'll build up the chain to strengthen the support you will need for the foot. We won't actually be concentrating on the foot for a while, just the strengthening you need above the foot. That strength is crucial in the entire chain leading down to the ankle: hip flexors, quadratus femoris, gluteus maximus/minimus/medius, quadriceps, hamstrings, adductors, gastroc, soleus. You'll be working with Paula for five hours a day. There will be no work with Megan, no ballet, at the beginning. But likely, after we assess the progress in six weeks, we will see if you are ready for some floor exercises with her. For now it is all about strength. I am not concerned with the foot and the pain it produces when you dance. This will be looked at later."

Sue would not give a time frame for when I would start ballet class, or when I would finish my rehab here and head back to New York or Moscow. No matter; I was there for as long as it took. It was a one-way ticket, after all. Sue conditioned me from that first meeting to know that we were, from this moment on, working from a clean slate. She didn't concern herself with what happened before, what had gone terribly wrong or who had been involved. It just didn't exist for her. What existed was what was in front of her. Me, head shaved, foot swollen.

I said I would do everything they told me. No more, no less. I cautioned them that they would have to keep me busy. I couldn't have idle moments and time to think. Idleness was toxic for me. I would descend into my thoughts, ruminating on how and where it went so wrong. It was a habit I'd developed in New York, back in the days when I was smoking and gazing out my apartment window.

"You'll be busy," Sue said. "Don't worry."

Most important, I was comforted by the three of them, all equally attentive and focused on my problems, I felt assured that I was in the right place. Far away from the people asking when or "if there is any hope." Everything in New York became a far-off memory. I had flown to the bottom of the world. Now I was in it for the long haul. This was the last-ditch effort.

PAULA AND I started work the next day. I was rested from a good night's sleep after my twenty-one-hour flight. We began with her hovering over me while I executed the most minute exercises. Paula had been a dancer in the company for more than a decade, transitioning to a teaching role afterward. She translated Sue's methods of rehabilitation into a language that dancers understood. A warm presence with a quirky sense of humor, she was petite with a black pixie cut and a thick Aussie accent. The majority of the Aussie-isms I would pick up came from Paula.

PAULA'S ROOM WAS an open square with a wall of windows looking out to an enclosed balcony. It was spare and plain with no fancy machines that sparked awe. On warm days she would open the door, letting a light breeze carry into the space. Pilates equipment, weights, and small knickknacks for performing the most minuscule of tasks were neatly placed around the room.

Tucked in the back of the sixth floor, it had a calm, nest-like quality, with no external noise. The dancers of The Australian Ballet were in their two-month end-of-year Sydney Opera House season. There were no dancers at the company's base in Melbourne. I was grateful to have them gone. I couldn't deal with the prospect of interacting with dancers. Although I was away from the constant questions from people I knew well in New York, I was aware that I would hear those questions again when the dancers returned to Melbourne. I wasn't ready for that. For the next ten weeks, Paula and I could work quietly and diligently for hours.

Paula had names for every exercise she taught me:

Side lie (adductor)
J-Lo (QF, hamstring, glute)
Ins and outs (ankle)
Fronts and backs (ankle)
Tower (adductor)
Air bender (upper body)
Nobby's landing (metatarsals)

Among many, many more.

In my daily sessions with her (three hours in the morning; two in the afternoon) we moved slowly, as she detailed each exercise and colorfully explained its purpose and how it should feel to me. She used analogies like "Think of churning butter" and "It's like a rabbit hopping in the garden. Hop, hop, hop, hop."

We had a lot of ground to cover. The team's initial and over-reaching goal was to give me the education I needed to be able to troubleshoot any physical hiccup myself. I had no prior education in this regard. Like many dancers in New York, I had always expected to have someone else fix me. I felt for Julie and Peter at ABT when a dancer would hop on their treatment table and lie there idly scrolling on an iPhone while they massaged away.

This "fix me" mentality also led to surgery. Americans view surgery as the fix. "Fix my torn ligament." "Fix my scar tissue." In Melbourne, the team's philosophy was that surgery was practically never an option (they'd signed off on only five ankle surgeries in thirteen years).

In their eyes, an injury could be successfully rehabilitated by proper, methodical strengthening and manual attention. Not by connecting the injury to a machine for relief or interfering surgically with the body healing on its own. Sue taught me the power of the body's natural healing process. The body can rehabilitate itself when an injury is approached thoughtfully, and we can aid that natural process (i.e., strengthening) as opposed to interfering with it in an operation. She did believe in surgery, but only when nothing else produced results she deemed sufficient.

Sue also hypothesized that, for me, surgery hadn't been an inevitability.

"Sure, deltoid ligaments are fraying with what you put your body through. Every athlete of your level has fraying ligaments, among many other issues," she told me. "That's why I don't like to look at MRI tests anymore. They show you everything that is wrong in the area tested. It gives you an unrealistic picture. I like to decipher only by symptoms. Not by test results."

"So if I didn't have surgery, how would you have rehabbed my foot?"

"Exactly as we are doing it. No different. But what has happened in the past is gone. We deal with what is in front of us now."

AND SO MY education started. I'm baffled as to why I hadn't already known what Paula was teaching me about my instrument. I had expected my body, the vessel of my artistic expression, my livelihood, to function properly with little understanding of how it works and what I need to do to make it work.

I learned all the body's muscle groups through the exercises she taught me. Strengthening was not defined by the grunt it produced; I barely worked with any weights over twenty pounds. It was defined by an understanding of the precise activation of each muscle and how it served a purpose to offer support. I was taught to understand why I did a given exercise. Only then did I have the knowledge to use a particular muscle to its fullest advantage. For hours, in "side lie," I lay on my side, foam mats and rollers propped up under my body, activating my adductor longus. Or, with one foot on a rotating disk and one leg propped up on a Pilates reformer, I hovered in between, activating my quadriceps and quadratus femoris. This was the "J-Lo" (named after the butt we would develop from doing this exercise).

Throughout the work, following the team's suggestion, I diligently jotted down my own interpretations of the exercises into a small yellow notebook, the act of writing helping me to absorb them more.

I was happy to be where I was. Happy to be in isolation. Happy to take in the information Paula gave me. Happy to be far away from the life I had grown to loathe. These hours on end, coaxing the body into strength, represented a fresh start with a fresh outlook.

ON THE FOURTH Thursday in November, three weeks into our work together, Paula and Megan were troubleshooting an exercise called "Spanish seat belt." With rope wrapped around my knees, hinged backward into a counterbalance, I paused as emotion suddenly overwhelmed me.

"Today is Thanksgiving in the U.S. And typically we go around the table stating what we are thankful for. As I'm here, far away from my family, I'm thankful for the two of you and Sue. I'm thankful for the care you have shown me."

I teared up, but Paula, who was not one to wallow in emotion, replied, "Okay. Now back to your Spanish seat belt." There was work to be done.

Later that day, as a token of appreciation, I gave them a pumpkin pie I had baked the night before using my grandmother's recipe.

BUT MY THANKSGIVING was also a lonely one in the absence of friends or family. I was determined to celebrate it somehow. I researched restaurants that offered a "Thanksgiving dinner" and made a reservation for one ("Yes, one," I repeated to the host over the phone). I'd been alone for many a holiday around the world. On this occasion, I was seated next to the waiters' station and the water jugs at the bar. The dinner was dry meat, a sliver of "corn bread," watery gravy. I looked around at the other Americans trying to force Thanksgiving in Australia. They shot pitying glances back at me, sitting alone by the water jugs.

I SPENT MY free time alone as well. In New York I would have been attending performances, dinners, events, openings. In Melbourne I commuted to the studios in the morning and headed back home when I finished.

Previously, I thought that physical rest was a waste of time if I wasn't dancing. Now I rested at "home," in an apartment I was renting from a friend who danced with The Australian Ballet. I took my time with everything; coffee in the morning, walking to the train, arriving at the building for the daily work, taking the train home, cooking myself a simple dinner of meat, veggies, and potatoes. To my surprise, I was calm. I found a new sort of contentment. It was equally blissful and lonely.

But I knew I had to heal alone. I had no energy to answer the usual questions of when and how: When will you be back onstage? When will you dance again? How did this happen? So I didn't reach out to anyone from home. I shut off email, social media, most contact with the outside world. I stopped responding to messages and got an Aussie mobile number; my American cell phone became inactive. I committed to nothing but my rehab. I had no desire to see the latest play, or to be a tourist in Melbourne. I cocooned.

As content as I momentarily was, the idle time did, as I anticipated, contain moments when I felt complete loss and despair. Especially when I had finished my rehab for the day. I would climb on the tram with the late-afternoon sun shining through the windows, sit down, and look around me.

I would wonder, *What went so wrong that I ended up here? How am I in this moment? How did I go from such heights and artistic fulfillment to this, begging on the floor for this team to give me an answer? This one last effort to see if I can ever get back from this never-ending ailment.*

Yet as the weeks wore on, the daily accomplishments began to outweigh the loneliness and unhappiness I felt at night.

PAULA AND I worked for three months straight. In that time, I gained a new perspective on the strength within my body. With progress made and strength built, I was finally given the green light to start a small barre. In New York, when physios would say, "Take a barre and see how it feels," I'd had no idea of how much or how little to do. So I'd do what I was used to doing, and it would set me back weeks if not months.

Now I was watched closely by the team, and nothing would be left to chance as it had been before.

Those first "dancing" days were the most raw. I hadn't been in a studio for months. Megan waited for me inside. A sense of dread came over me. And I was angry. I didn't want to be there. Instinct told me it was all over. That what I was about to embark on—dancing again—was in vain. That it wasn't going to work. I internalized all those emotions, bottled them up and hid them inside me. I wasn't going to waste Megan's time with my feelings. I was just going to get on with it. As angry and miserable as I was.

She placed a long foam roller on the floor and told me to lie down on it.

"First I want you to feel your deep rotators," she said, "so put your feet on the ground and your back on the roller."

"Aren't we going to do a barre?"

She chuckled. "Not for a couple weeks."

My hopes had gotten the best of me. Instead of dancing, I was lying on a roller in white socks and tights, sliding my legs backward and forward to the sound of her counting. I did what I was told to do. I had surrendered from the beginning to their method of rehab, so I would not object. But I was crestfallen. And I wanted no one to see me in this state. Megan and I were in the smallest studio on the lower floor of the ballet building, away from the main traffic of rehearsals and ballet classes of the school. I was thankful that I could do this without people looking in and seeing what I was up to.

In later sessions, we were at times on the building's main level, along the long corridor of studios. I closed the blinds to every window and closed the doors. No one was going to gawk at my condition, remembering how I had been and comparing that to how I looked now.

MEGAN, A PETITE, intense woman with short brown hair, has a strong drive. She is resolute and focused in her commitment to help dancers, be they injured or healthy. She desperately wanted my rehabilitation to be a success and from the outset approached me with every ounce of energy she had. It was too much for me to digest. It was too full-on. I had moments when I thought it wouldn't work out between us.

I resented her. Her corrections irritated me. I was unwilling to drop everything I thought I knew about myself as a dancer. She touched my body where my weakest points were (typically just under my butt), poking for signs of activation. Internally I fought her words but knew that it wasn't what she said that annoyed me most. What annoyed me most was my ego.

I never verbalized it, but we could both feel the tension in the studio. I wanted to rip her to shreds. Anger oozed out of me. I wanted to scream not only at her but at life, my situation, my reality. She was having me execute absolutely everything differently. I did a relevé with my adductors and gluteus minimus instead of my feet. I did a tendu using the same muscles, activating the tops of my legs and not just presenting my pointed foot. She was challenging everything I knew. And I didn't want to hear it.

Megan assured me it would help me in the long run, creating more longevity and safety for my body. I felt like my ass was sticking out. I was totally turned in. There was no aesthetic anymore. No presenting of line.

But deep down I knew that this was the only path toward health. I couldn't dance the way I had previously. I needed to hear her words in order to properly rehabilitate my foot and return to the art it was my duty to portray. There was no other way. Well, there was one other way, the way out, and I had chosen not to take it before I got on that plane.

Megan fought me fighting her. I would talk to myself, saying, "David, what you were doing beforehand clearly wasn't working. Why are you fighting this so much? Give yourself over to her."

I had seen dancers before who never allowed themselves to be corrected by anyone. They are the stalest of artists. Always having an excuse as to why what someone is telling them won't work. I refused to be this kind of artist. I didn't know better than Megan. I did know that ego is the ultimate killer.

And so, day after day, something inside me pushed on, kept me going.

My parents called it courage; the courage to continue and believe in the outcome. I didn't see it as courage at all. As it was when I started dancing, it was just what I had to do.

CHAPTER 49

In the beginning months, the work with Paula and Megan was mentally hard but not physically demanding. I finished the day with energy to spare but nowhere to spend it. I tried to avoid idle time, but I couldn't run away from it entirely. I knew that I needed it to process the work and heal the deep wounds that still stung. But my weekends were entirely idle. I had no motivation to do *anything*. Saturdays and Sundays I was on "forced rest." I wasn't allowed to do class, exercise, or exert myself physically. In the early stages, walking was monitored as well. Sue would say, "Enjoy the weekend. Drink a few beers. *Relax!*" In other words, "Be *happy*!"

ON SATURDAYS AND Sundays I woke up at noon, if not after. (In New York I was up by nine thirty at the latest.) Bringing my coffee back to bed, I'd waste time online or on Netflix until around three o'clock. Feeling peckish and thirsting for my first beer, I'd finally head out to the pub, order a pint, and smoke a cigarette outside. After a burger and fries, and three pints, I'd stumble home, crawl back in bed, and watch more movies.

I knew I was being self-destructive. And I didn't care. I would spend whole days just lying there, or sitting outside the pub alone, in a daze, watching the traffic go by, drinking beer after beer. I would imagine running into someone I knew. That they would see me in this grungy state, in the middle of the day, that stereotypical drunk. I knew I was depressed. I knew I wasn't helping myself with my mental health or recovery. Still, I indulged.

I became a regular at specific watering holes, that American sitting alone at the bar. One was the Prahran Hotel, my weekend midday haunt. I'd head over there around three and order lunch and a beer at the bar. While I waited on the food, I'd go out for a smoke with a Carlton Draught, my beer of choice. Aussies considered it a cheap, trashy beer, but I've seen them enjoying a Bud, which they think is a high-quality import.

Another haunt was the Flying Duck, a pub minutes from my apartment. I didn't care that I was alone there on a Saturday night, when all around me were men trying to impress women in short skirts. Again I was that loner in the corner.

On Friday evenings I'd go to a beautiful park where dog owners would take their pets for a run. Growing up with golden retrievers, I found joy in watching the dogs dashing around frantically searching for balls. I'd buy a six-pack of Carlton Draught and settle onto a bench and watch. I'd sit there for two or three hours, calmly sipping beer after beer until the sun had completely set and everyone had gone home but me. I became that man seated alone in the park until after dusk, drinking beer. The one whom everyone would fear and take pains to avoid.

At the Flying Duck, it was seldom busy midweek so as I drank my beer alone, the staff would come over for a chat. They'd ask me what I was doing in Melbourne (my accent a dead giveaway). I'd fill them in. One thing would lead to another, and after a couple of weeks, I knew most everyone who worked there.

Instead of "knowing" them the way I would in New York, which would only ever amount to saying a cordial "Hello," "You good?" "Yes, and you?", I made the effort to really talk with these people. The same went for Alex, my morning barista. I didn't have seven places to be at once, like New York makes you think you do. I set aside the urgency and self-importance that come with an overly committed lifestyle. In New York I would feel that I couldn't be bothered speaking to people uninvolved in my everyday tasks. But in Melbourne, being in these places *was* my everyday task. It felt honest and true. And I liked stepping back and experiencing the people around me. It contributed to the rehabilitation I was just barely beginning to experience.

CHAPTER 50

Sue, Paula, and Megan saw that the way of working I practiced since I was thirteen years old had slowly chipped away at me and led me to injury. It wasn't that I had been taught improperly. The exact opposite. I had had the best of teachers during my adolescence, led by Mr. Han. The body I was given made for a symmetrical and flowing line, but what gave me my line when I pointed my foot also gave me a certain vulnerability. When I landed from a jump, my foot could go in any direction. And if the foot isn't well supported by strength above or around it, it can slowly wear down, or even break, as mine had at the Met back in 2012.

Now that my foot had succumbed to injury, I was open to the strengthening exercises that Paula gave me. But ballet with Megan was different. I had spent my entire career perfecting my technique, and I didn't want to consider new ideas that would change what I felt I had done reasonably well. I didn't want to question or challenge. I just wanted to "get better."

The work became more focused and intense. Six months in, I was with Paula every morning and afternoon for two-hour-long sessions. After my first session with her, Megan was waiting to teach me class.

371

Always, when I stepped into the dance studio, anger would envelop me yet again.

Anger at Megan.

Anger at myself.

Anger at my inability to be the dancer I used to be.

We were making progress, though slowly, and Megan could see that. I couldn't. All I saw was weakness, pain, swelling, tightness. Darkness. An inability to execute a proper plié. A bulbous ball on the top of my ankle, perpetually swollen and red.

At night, at home on my balcony, I would look up at the sky and beg the universe, *You have me. You've brought me to my knees. There is nothing else to strip from me. Please, give me some light. Build me back up again. Just so I can manage daily life.*

I PUSHED ON, against my own desires to break everything in the studio and scream at Megan.

I didn't want her touching me.

I didn't want her correcting me.

I didn't want her imitating my weaknesses.

The energy in the room was tense; my questions about her corrections were terse and tight-lipped. We were not working with each other.

I was content at my local, drinking a beer alone. I was content in my apartment, watching a movie. I was not content in the studio. Should anyone ask me about my foot, I quickly shut them down. The only way through was to grit my teeth and work. It didn't matter that I wasn't happy. It didn't matter if I wanted to quit. Or that I was enraged. All that mattered was the work. I would tell myself, *Get on with it, David. Shut up and do what you are told.* But I still resisted her.

* * *

A BODY OF WORK

THE TENSION GOT to be too much. Megan couldn't progress with me. She didn't know what to do or say because I met everything with resistance and nonverbal conflict. I wasn't telling her anything.

But my internal dialogue was pitiful:

You are worth nothing anymore. Look at where you were and look at you now. You did this to yourself, thinking you were invincible. You worked yourself too hard, too fast, trying to take on everything that came your way. It's over. You've ruined your body. Your ego killed you. Rotted you. You let it ride away, taking you from what is actually important. You're far from a true artist. You're a sellout. All this work won't get you anywhere. It's over and you can't admit it. Life was giving you other opportunities that you ignored. To transition out of this elegantly and smoothly. You are becoming exactly what you didn't want to become . . . an old dancer trying to hold on to the past.

IT TOOK ME weeks to muster the courage to make myself vulnerable to Megan. Though I still couldn't confess everything I was feeling, I told her as much as I could. I said that I didn't believe in myself and didn't believe I would ever accomplish what needed to be done. I told her I couldn't get past my anger. At her. At myself. At the situation.

And I told her about the demons I fought internally. That's what I had begun to call them. *The demons.* These were demons that coaxed me into believing that I would never dance again. Or that the pinching in my foot or the perpetual swelling at the top of my ankle would never subside. They were the ones that made me think about how my career came to a shrieking halt and about all the people and theaters I had let down in the process. The guilt of canceling shows. The stress of imagining what people were thinking.

Megan was calm and kind. "We are now making true progress," she said. "Up to now you have been clocking in and out. You tick the boxes. But that isn't going to make you heal. You have to give yourself over. Leave your old self behind and realize the virtues of starting over. You have the chance to rebuild yourself. You can be something completely different than you were before. You can reinvent yourself. But to do that, you have to make yourself vulnerable. Let me in. Let me teach you. Let me guide you. *You* don't know best. *I* don't know best. But together we can pave the path and find our way. As of now, we are not progressing. Not in the way I know you can. It's your choice. You don't have to be here. We're not forcing you. You came of your own accord. So why are you here? Why do you keep showing up? Ask yourself this. I think you are here because beneath this internal anger there is someone desperate to get out. Someone new and not yet discovered. If you surrender to this and make yourself vulnerable, when all is done, you will be renewed."

She had said the words I needed to hear. The next day I walked into the ballet studio and stared at Megan. I said, "I'm ready to be a dancer again."

AFTER THAT, A shift occurred. I realized that anyone who was interested had to see me in my current state. The real state of where I was: socks on, out of shape, barely able to plié. So I opened the blinds and the doors to the studio and let the dancers and the students of the school watch what we were doing. No, I wasn't the person they saw on YouTube or in performance. But it was reality. The reality of a dancer who had to do everything facing away from the mirror because he couldn't stand the way he looked. The harsh reality that anyone can get injured, and this is what it looks like to try to climb back up from nothing. I wasn't going to hide it anymore.

CHAPTER 51

Now that I had unburdened myself to some extent, the major obstacle was pain. The pain came whenever I pliéd. Dancers need their pliés in almost everything they execute. From the first exercise at the barre to the push needed to propel yourself into a jump, a plié is the most crucial part of dancing. It creates the flow and ease of one's jump or a transition from one thing to another. The more brittle the plié, the less fluid the movement. My deltoid ligament and its surrounding bones pinched when compressed into a plié. At times it was simply a manageable dull ache; at other times, a debilitating shock to my foot. This was the crux of my misery. How could I execute what was demanded of me if I always felt this discomfort? I didn't think I could.

The team had a different way of looking at it (as they possessed something that I would learn to aspire to: perspective). When I couldn't see any solution to the problem, they said there were ways through the pain. That I had to train my focus elsewhere and not obsess that "I can't plié without pain." I needed to train my mind to focus on the surrounding areas that could support the foot and therefore not rely so heavily on the ankle.

My legs would need to take the pressure I had put on my foot for years.

Beyond that, I needed to ignore my pain. Which is why, as Sue stressed to me, my happiness was paramount. She coaxed me into thinking that pain was foremost a mental issue. That I had become so accustomed to pain that I recognized it even when it might not be there. I had babied my foot for a year and a half and set up a coping mechanism to deal with its disability. I would limp when I didn't need to limp. I would walk on the outsides of my feet rather than use the whole foot. Anything related to the foot resulted in a negativity that colored my entire outlook. I would have to focus my energy elsewhere and let the pinching resolve itself by way of a detour.

ONE OF THE many complex aspects of my foot injury was an insertional Achilles tendinopathy. In a nutshell, I had a hole in the lining of the Achilles tendon right at the base of the foot, just above the heel. It had caused a consistently sharp pain brought on by anything that involved a burst of a takeoff or a landing: running, jumping, landing from a turn, landing from a jump. This was a problem that arose during the rehab process in New York. To treat it previously, I had had injections and high-voltage shock wave therapy. I had tried everything to rid myself of this debilitating pain.

The treatment for an insertional Achilles tendinopathy, according to the Australian team's plan, was stairs. No injections. No interruption of the area with "remedies." As prescribed and monitored by Paula, I was to walk up and down a stairwell on a half demi-pointe (on my toes, not on a full flat foot). Stepping to the sound of a metronome, adding more steps every other day. At the start, it was simple enough. Paula had me climb up and down a mere twelve stairs. It was curiously conservative. *Surely,* I thought, *I climb more stairs than that in a day. Why not go for the full flight?* But each added step would be properly monitored every other day, so we knew exactly what might be too much if I woke up sore the next morning.

The metronome app I had downloaded onto my phone was initially set at 140 beats per minute. I felt the tendon off and on. But I was being taught that pain wasn't necessarily a bad thing. Pain sometimes meant strengthening. So I stepped. Over and over and over. Each day, I'd walk into the stairwell off the long corridor of studios at the ballet center and set my metronome, letting the tick echo throughout the entire four flights of concrete. Dancers, administrators, or building superintendents would pass from floor to floor. Some had no idea who I was and why I was on the stairs every day. I would see the confusion in their faces when they'd enter to the echoing of the ticking, seeing my tall figure fast approaching to the beat. They'd flatten themselves to the wall to let me pass.

So the methodical ticking wouldn't drive me mad, I'd change measures. Some days a ¾ time, others a ⅝. Eventually I was up to fifteen minutes of stairs, twice a day, skipping steps at 164 beats per minute. I would finish, exiting the concrete bunker desperate for air, sweating profusely. Dancers looked at me like I was mad. Surely I wasn't dancing anything so tiring yet. But once they witnessed the workout in the stairwell, they'd simply say, "Stairs?"

Traversing those stairs became as taxing as dancing a variation and coda. It would take an entire nine months to arrive at the full regimen I would employ for the rest of my time. Sue wanted me bounding up the stairs, a step at a time, sometimes two. It then made complete sense. Leaping up a couple of stairs was like taking off for a jump. In fact, it almost exactly reproduced the propulsion.

Sue's methods were designed to replicate what dancers needed to do onstage. The motions would just be taken out of context and put in another, more controlled environment. This was the assurance the team gave me whenever I feared a new exercise or step. There wasn't anything they were suggesting that they weren't completely confident I could do while they encouraged and watched.

THE STRUCTURE OF the rehab resembled ballet more and more. After I had worked with Megan for a while, I could wear tights and ballet shoes in the studio and even look into the mirror and see that the figure staring back had begun to look like a dancer. As Megan had promised, I was becoming renewed.

I could actually bear to look and see if what I was doing resembled any form of classical ballet. I started to use the strength I had built on the stairs with Paula. Hamstrings and adductors that I couldn't feel previously I could now activate in exercises Megan gave me.

Each step in the ballet repertoire was added, one by one. A simple step, taken for granted when healthy, was a milestone. The first time I did one pirouette was a huge milestone. The first time I did a balancé (a waltzing step back and forth) was another milestone. Most steps caused pain at first. They felt stiff, mechanical. I would tentatively tiptoe through a step, never executing it more than 20 percent. Then, filled with fear, I would execute it as properly as I could. The movements were never at the level I expected of myself. But I had to let go of expectations. As hard as it was, I had to force myself to get over how it used to feel.

"It will never feel like it used to," Megan would tell me. "Maybe it will feel even better."

AS THE MONTHS crawled along, Megan built combinations from the steps I could do. The class structure was much like a normal model of a daily class, except each combination was tailored to my ability at present. The further along the rehab went, the faster the pace.

The birth of a step would be slow and methodical, then I could add on (more revolutions, a beat with the leg). While at first one pirouette had been a milestone, weeks later I was onto three, four, five turns.

I charged on, trying my best to ignore my tenacious inner demons. Certain steps were particularly hard to manage. A chassé, a skimming step where one foot pushes while the other replaces, was as rudimentary as any step in the ballet technique. Little boys and girls did this step with ease. But the torsion when my left foot was in the back, needing to plié to push off, was extremely limiting and uncomfortable. I would cheat and chassé facing front, which bore no resemblance to the step that Megan gave. But I couldn't bear weight on the foot in the angle the step required. Each day she would give it to me to execute, and each day she would troubleshoot it just as she had the day before. I knew how to fix it. I knew I needed to face more to the side. But that meant working into pain. And I didn't yet trust myself to work through it. Pain still meant danger to me.

Megan would sometimes test my abilities to do a step I hadn't yet done, and if it proved too difficult, she would leave it for weeks. Then, one day she would give it back to me with no warning at all. Having left it and built the strength required through another avenue, I would revisit it with little problem.

"You know you couldn't do this a couple weeks ago, right?" she would remind me.

SUE CARED DEEPLY about helping me find hope. My mental state was my driving force, she believed. I knew this to be true. But I still didn't see that hope. I literally couldn't say the word "when." When I am back dancing . . . When I perform again . . . It was always "if." If I dance again . . . If I perform again . . . I knew I needed to manifest happiness. But the "what if" persisted.

On Friday afternoons Sue and I would recap the week's work.

"See!" she would say, trying to make me realize that I had done what I couldn't do previously, "You did a tombé pas de bourrée today!"

I looked back at her stone-faced.

"I'll have to do a lot more than a tombé pas de bourrée onstage."

THERE WERE DAYS when I would become incapable of cooperating with myself or anyone around me. The anger would well up again, and Megan was usually on the receiving end.

Suddenly, nothing was positive, everything was grief-stricken.

Managing these moods was exhausting, for myself and for Megan.

As reluctant as I was to waste Megan's time with my emotions, it was all interconnected. If I couldn't properly communicate everything that was holding me back, then no true progress could be made.

ONE DAY, IN class with Megan, I tried to push on, but something was holding me back. I tried to plié. I tried to keep going. But I started to lose the willpower. It was one of those days when I didn't have the fight in me. I couldn't deal with the continual management of my body, begging for it to cooperate with me.

Afterward, Megan asked what was bothering me. I choked up trying to explain it. I told her I instinctively resisted working through the pain. The conflict was debilitating and was preventing me, mentally and physically, from being able to work productively. And I was tired of it.

"What do you think about a cortisone injection?" Megan asked.

"I know we haven't done one yet and it's up our sleeve as an option. Maybe now is the time for it."

"Let's talk to Sue," I said, "and see what she thinks."

I dashed through the hallway full of dancers, my head down, hiding my tears. Sue's office was empty. I began to sob. I couldn't control it.

I crawled onto the treatment table and continued to sob as we waited for Sue. Megan's face was a study in worry and concern.

"Oh dear," Sue said as she closed the door and asked what had happened.

I could barely get the words out.

"It was pinching all day. I tried to push on with class, but something was holding me back and telling me not to even attempt at pushing through it."

Then it all came out. The angst that I dealt with by myself and hadn't revealed to them. For the first time, I told them everything. It wasn't a choice. I could no longer hold it back.

I explained everything that I had been dealing with for the entire time I had been in Melbourne. I explained every insecurity, doubt, fear, apprehension. I said I didn't have the fight in me anymore. I didn't have the strength to push on, continually managing the pain. I was alone here in Melbourne. The city offered a place of refuge and escape so I could heal, away from the tapping fingers on my shoulder asking me when I would be back and why it was taking so long. And although everyone in the building supported me, the reality was that I was doing this alone. I had left the comforts of friends and a life in New York. I'd left it all, unaware of how much time I would eventually need to heal. And I didn't just need physical healing. Emotionally I had come stripped to nothing. And I was building everything back up again, but with people whom I didn't deeply know and with whom I didn't feel comfortable showing my true colors. I had to walk down the hallway with a face on, a mask of strength and cordiality, when in fact, inside I had never felt so low in my entire life. I had been fighting for so long. So, so long.

I told them, "Most days I don't have it in me, but I come in day after day, to fight and push on. I try not to waste your time, so I hide my feelings within myself. Then, when the day is over, I go home alone every night. The problems that you, the team, deal with during the day, I deal with every waking hour. I carry this struggle with me from the time I wake up until I finally can sleep at day's end.

"I can't even fathom what has happened to me. It's almost as if I can't recognize where I am or who I am. I think, 'How did I get here? How has so much time passed and I am still living this struggle? When will I feel, if ever, that the universe is working with me again?'"

I said that I knew they believed that I would do it. That I would come out the other end. They had been telling me this for months. That the work I was doing was paying off. But I just couldn't believe them. I had been disappointed so many times before. By a botched first surgery. A perpetually swollen ankle from a procedure that I didn't even need. A second surgery to remedy the first. And setback after setback. I was brought here, to rely on them, because everything else was lost. And I secretly believed that everyone around me was slowly losing hope and giving up.

I sobbed uncontrollably. They just watched and listened. Sue and Megan are both mothers outside of the workplace, and their maternal instincts kicked into gear.

"We have been waiting for this since the beginning," Sue said. "Now is when the honest work starts."

"I didn't want to waste your time with my emotional drama," I told her. "We are here to do a job."

"But this is all part of the job. Your mental health as well as your physical health."

One of Sue's greatest strengths is her decisiveness in times of crisis.

"I don't think you need a cortisone shot," she said. "I think you need rest. Let's calm it down so you have better control of it. You had been stressing before but still coped. Just now you aren't coping, so we need to pull back a bit.

"But more importantly, what will give you peace of mind? What can we do to convince you that you are doing this? That this is actually working?"

"Nothing," I dryly replied. "I'll believe it when I'm back onstage. But for now I believe in the work we're doing. I don't doubt the progress made until today. But I have no guarantee for tomorrow. Or what the eventual outcome will be."

I had gotten it all out. Although it was cathartic, I felt defeated. Lost. But there were two women sitting across from me who supported me and were there to listen and continue the fight, because they believed in it. Believed in me and the outcome.

I went home after that and crawled into bed. Drained. Speechless. Megan was so fearful that I might seriously harm myself that she drove to my apartment and called me to say that she wasn't going to intrude on my private space but wanted me to know she was nearby. Though I was unaware of it at the time, she stayed there, hoping to send good energy to me, for the next two hours.

Alone in my apartment, I realized there was nothing else to do but recharge. I was on empty and I needed to have something to give for tomorrow. Because tomorrow I would head back in and continue the fight, right where I left off.

Though my outpouring seemed to me like a setback, Sue was right. That was when the real work started. By telling them everything I was feeling, I had helped myself over the finish line. In reaching the bottom, I had nowhere to go but up.

CHAPTER 52

After that, every day in the studio I was doing just a bit more than the day before. We built. The milestones became more definitive. Seven months after the start of rehab, the team collectively agreed that I was ready to jump without the support of the barre. The strength I had built prepared me for this kind of test. So I jumped, very small at first and only twice at a time, but we finally tested out the pressure the foot was put under when I took off and landed from the floor. It took all my courage and trust to believe I could ease into the air and land without incident. My first jumps were a defining moment. From there I inched my way higher and higher into the air. These were at last milestones I wanted to celebrate.

I BEGAN PREPARING for jumps that were demanded of me in certain classical repertoire. Double saut de basque. Double assemblé. And what felt like the longest to finally reach, double tour. Again I had to trust that I wouldn't hurt myself if I tried it. I was shocked when I landed without incident. These were major tickings of boxes.

* * *

ALTHOUGH I COULD see the milestones, they were never good enough. And Megan learned to accept that.

One day, after I had done a series of double tours, I said to her, "I'm still not satisfied with my grand allégro."

Megan looked at me in disbelief. She laughed, having witnessed the obsessive dissection I put myself under.

AS THE WORK progressed, the hair that I had so eagerly shaved off before I came to Melbourne was growing back. I was returning to my self. The shaved, swollen, desperate person was now the dancer in the mirror in front of me.

THOUGH I WAS grateful to have those first few months surrounded only by my team, as time marched on, the dancers of The Australian Ballet became an additional and vital support system. Together we did exercises in the mornings and soaked our feet in ice buckets at day's end. I could join them in the common room, sit down and have a chat or a laugh, or even just sit silently. I became one of them as I sought solace to heal.

Some were aware of how much support they were giving me: Brooke, Amanda, Rohan, Amber. Others—Bene, Coco, Adam, Andy—just had to be there to make me feel comforted. They never pried. They never asked if there was "any hope." They just let me be. And because of that I felt safe enough to open up to them and become an unofficial Aussie. I wasn't alone after all.

ONE DAY IN August 2016, some weeks after I had unburdened myself, Sue was treating me on the massage table. I'd had a good class that day, and for many days before it. I lay on the table, relieved that another day's work was behind me, yapping away about nothing particularly important. She was actively flushing out my calves, creating an upward motion to release the tension.

Sue had observed my dancing the day before. She would intermittently come into the studio and sit on the floor in the front of the room, as discreetly as possible, to study my movement. This was the best, most concrete way to determine where I actually was in the process; how much progress had been made and where the weaknesses still were. She would sit there, silent, inspecting not just the foot but the entire body functioning as a whole.

As she massaged, she said, "After seeing you yesterday, I want you back onstage in October." She looked at me, smiling, a gaze of complete matter-of-factness.

I looked at her dumbfounded. "You mean in two months?"

"Yes." She smiled back. "Can you still not see that you are going to get back onstage?"

The incremental easing into each dance step was over. She had been pumping me up for a while. Reinforcing the positives of my work and studiously troubleshooting the weaknesses still to be conquered.

I had regarded her positive reinforcement as just her way of trying to get me to believe that I was making my recovery. I knew what I had done previously. And I knew what I had done that day. But I couldn't, or wouldn't, let myself jump ahead to the future. So her words went in one ear and shot out the other.

I climbed off the massage table and headed home. Sue reminded me of the October goal once more as I walked out. I laughed it off, making light of it. It was just another way for Sue to pump me up.

MY MIND WANDERED on the tram ride home. Sue could profess all she wanted, but I wasn't setting myself up for disappointment. There had been too many of those previously.

I unwound from the day's work on the balcony of my apartment. Earphones on, a cigarette rolled, playing the music I was obsessed with at the time. Beethoven's Seventh Symphony, Third Movement. It offered optimism. Strength. Positivity. I looked up at the sky, the light settling down over the roofs of Melbourne, the first, brightest star coming into view. I gazed beyond the world beneath me and my own struggles and into the vastness of the darkening sky. Sue's words came back into my mind.

Two months.

From two *years*, down to two *months*.

Oh my God, I thought. *I'm going to get back onstage.*

As the Third Movement pulsed in my ears, the tears flowed freely. Finally they were tears of joy, not pain. The pain was over. I could feel it. I cried because I had done it. *We* had done it. I thought of the work over the last months, slogging through day by day, step-by-step of the same routine, maintaining our determination in spite of everything. We had built ever so slowly and incrementally and finally produced the outcome we so desperately wanted.

All I could do was look up at the sky in gratitude, indebted to the universe for giving me this new opportunity to dance. I put my hands in the air, palms facing upward, as I rejoiced. I clasped my hands, crying, "Thank you." Then I repeated it, over and over.

That night I smoked my last cigarette. Smoking was no longer an option, now that I was a dancer again.

THE FOLLOWING DAY, after a deep, restful sleep, I came into the studio with a new perspective. Finally I had seen the light in my darkness.

Before our class started, I told Megan the news. "Sue wants me onstage in two months," I said.

"I know. She told me."

She looked at me. After a pause, she said, "For two days I've felt uneasy about something. I've been nervous but couldn't put my finger on what it was, that it's because I'm starting to let you go. It's time for you to fly and our time is almost up."

That moment truly was approaching, closer and more realistic than ever before. But the most powerful thing was that I knew it now. I knew I was returning to the stage. Awakened and reborn.

TAKING THE TRAM into the ballet center on my last day, I forced myself to look out the window instead of burying myself in a book, and to take in every stop, building, street that I had now passed five days a week for nearly a year. This had been my refuge. This city where I hid and healed. And somehow, I was heading in for the final time. The rehab was officially coming to an end.

THERE WAS A last set of stairs to my metronome in the concrete bunker. And for my last exercise, the leg extension igniting the burn of my quads that never got any easier.

But I knew that I would be doing the exercises I had learned for the rest of my career. Until I retire, I will be leg-extension-ing, J-Lo-ing, calf raising, side lying, step-upping, Nobby's landing. I will find a set of stairs in any city I dance in, and skip up them to my metronome.

MEGAN AND I worked one last time. It was business as usual: Megan giving me corrections when she felt I was open enough for them. Me trying to drop my armor and listen to her as I slogged through the steps, most of which were comfortable by now, some of which were still tricky. I pushed on anyway, thinking back a month and knowing that thankfully they were better than before and would be still better tomorrow. Emma Lippa, a Russian pianist (who for years had played during class and rehearsals at Bolshoi) heightened my artistic drive with her weighted, orchestral playing. She motivated me. Made me want to *dance*, and not simply *work*.

An hour later, I was cooked. I couldn't even muster the last à la seconde turns Megan gave me. "Get up on your hip," she said. I had no more juice in me to even do that. So without a grand finale, some sort of gesture that encapsulated the last many months of work, we finished. I sat on a chair by the mirrors. I was done. It was complete. I was ready to be released into the world.

Emma stood up from the piano bench. Megan knelt on the floor next to me.

"My congratulations," Emma said to Megan. "You have moved an enormous rock. Every day I would walk by the studio and there you two were, working, working. You have made an enormous effort."

Megan covered her face and started to cry. Through her tears she said, "I just hope that what I did helped you in some way. I so desperately wanted to help."

I couldn't hold back my tears either.

"Megan," I said, "you don't need to question whether it has worked or not because the proof is in what I am able to do now. Look at what I can do. And look at where I was when I arrived in Melbourne. That is the proof that it has worked."

She said, "I know it hasn't always been the easiest working relationship for us. And I've tried to adapt myself to what you needed. I stepped back when I thought you needed space and then would choose my words carefully when it came time to say something. But I just hope it was all the right approach. It has been such a gift to work with you and see your progress and witness what you can achieve."

I listened to her. She had gone through a lot with me throughout the year. The stress it put on her. The worry. Our work together had been just as much of a struggle for her as it was for me.

I told her, "I want you to know that you were always saying the right thing. That the friction between us came from my struggle to open myself up to your corrections. The battle was with my ego, not with you. I struggled to let my armor down and let you in. But I think back on the time spent here, and where I was at the beginning, with socks on, lying on a foam roller. And where I am now; jumping and gearing up to dance for an audience after two and a half years. And I think . . ." I couldn't get the words out. There were just too many emotions.

Finally I settled for saying, "Fuck . . . We did it, man. We really, really did it."

LATER THAT DAY, Sue, Paula, Megan, and I headed for a celebratory toast; to put a final mark on the work now behind us. We sat around the table and raised our glasses. It was my turn to thank them one last time. After a while, the administrative staff of The Australian Ballet showed up to celebrate with us. Soon we were all completely drunk, and reminiscing about the months of grinding but miraculous work.

I knew they were uncomfortable with the word "indebted." But I *was* indebted to them. They gave my life back to me. Again, I raised my glass to them and the experience we had behind us.

CHAPTER 53

In December 2016, I was about to take class at the State Theatre in Melbourne with the dancers of The Australian Ballet, with whom I would be performing short excerpts from the classical repertoire in seven days. When I stepped onto the stage for the first time in more than two years, it stopped me in my tracks. I couldn't walk beyond the edge of the wings to start a warm-up before class. I gazed around me. At the theater and its red seats; the vastness of the house encompassing three balconies. The proscenium separating the audience from the performer. The sharp division of the fourth wall. Then, the beating heart of any theater, which everything revolves around: the sacred area of the stage. Work lights on, absent the sets and lighting that audiences witness, but still as magical. Barres set up onstage for daily class. The piano, down stage right, with a light clipped to its lid. I hadn't ever felt so grateful to be on a stage and have the privilege to dance on it.

I couldn't contain my elation. I told the dancers around me what the day had brought.

"Can you take a picture for me?" I asked. "Today is the first day I'm dancing on a stage in over two years."

I was so moved to see them react with joy. They had a sense

of what I'd been through, for they had witnessed much of the arduous process.

I WARMED UP quietly, looking out to the vast theater where audiences sit. There was no one there now, just two thousand empty red seats. I was physically shaky. A slight tremble inside me. Before class started, I closed my eyes and took a couple of deep, slow, meditative breaths. I felt the ground under my feet, planting myself firmly to the floor. I opened my eyes again, ready to commence. And so, as in the studio, it started with pliés.

An accompanist named Bryan was playing the piano for class. Having suffered a concussion after falling off his bike, he knew the long road back to his art well. Through every step of my rehabilitation he had congratulated me.

"Great to see you jumping around, mate!"

"Great to see you rehearsing, mate!"

And today, he came up and hugged me.

"Great to see you onstage again, mate!"

And just as the four-count introduction began, I couldn't suppress my tears. It was overwhelming. I was back on a stage. A space I thought I would never return to. I bent and stretched my legs, coordinating their action to my arms.

I felt the power of the stage. I had weathered the unimaginable for more than two years, in the depths of depression and doubt. It was as if everything had unraveled around me, and through the year I had collected all the pieces slowly and laboriously and, with the help and support of my team, put them back together again in a new way. All of that brought me there, standing at the barre, crying, listening to Bryan playing and looking out into a vast, empty theater.

* * *

TWO DAYS LATER I was onstage for class again, this time looking into the wings impatiently. My parents were arriving from Phoenix for the week. I hadn't seen them the entire time I'd been in Melbourne. They knew little of my life here, my process, my daily routine. During that time they could only imagine my surroundings and the people who were helping me back to life. So when this show was scheduled, they had planned their trip "to thank the team." They were as indebted as I was to the entire Australian Ballet.

Pushing through center work, I kept glancing to the wings to see if they had arrived yet. Finally, two familiar figures appeared in the dimness of the overhead work lights. Midexercise, I stopped and raced over to them. They had just landed after their twenty-hour trip, delirious but happy. We embraced and held each other tightly, quietly crying. Tears of joy. All they could say through their tears was "We love you so much. We love you so much."

I knew my parents would have enjoyed seeing Melbourne, but they were more interested in what resided within the walls of the ballet center. Many members of the company welcomed them with the Aussie hospitality that I had come to know, including David McAllister, the Artistic Director, who from the beginning had fully supported my need to come there and work with his team.

Before the injury, I would have disappeared into the building early in the morning, leaving my parents to their own devices for the day, only to emerge early in the evening, tired, in need of dinner and a bath. Sensing their desire to watch the entire daily routine, I instead brought them with me for every move I made. I was happy to have them by my side. Grateful to see familiar faces after my year of solitude. And when the workday had finished, we headed back to my apartment to cook and talk. I had decided to open up to them. I had shut out most of the people closest to me in the last two years. But this was a new time. I could explain more clearly what had happened to me. And rightly express the gratitude I now felt having come out the other end.

I JOKED WITH friends that I had a "recital," like in my jazz days when my parents patiently sat through recitals that were hours long. This was a different kind of show and a huge milestone in my return to performing life.

The idea wasn't mine. Sue and Megan wanted to replicate an actual performance, and with the company just across the road performing their season at the theater in the evenings, idle stage time was available. The show would be midday, midweek, when the stage wasn't being used by the company. Megan coordinated everything. Repertoire. Partners. Audience. A proper rehearsal period leading to performance day.

The entire administration was invited to sit in, along with invited donors, the team, The Australian Ballet School, some dancers, and my parents.

With an audience, I felt the inklings of being a performer again. Nerves, adrenaline, the desire to present and perform. I wore baby-blue tights and a white T-shirt, by special request of Megan (her favorite outfit of mine). Brooke Lockett, the friend who was the catalyst for my coming to Australia, was one of my partners. Robyn Hendricks, a newly promoted Principal, was my other ballerina. They donated their time, aiding me in my return. Their connection with me onstage, through the two pas de deux we were performing, would get me through the show. Looking into their eyes gave me comfort, confidence.

As I was warming up, with curtain raised and audience in their seats, I walked around the stage. I gazed into the house, those two-thousand-plus red seats looking back at me, about three hundred filled with people. I envisioned how I wanted this show to go. I wanted to remain in my body. I wanted to rely on the strength gained over the last fourteen months. I didn't want to revert back to old habits. Previously, in the adrenaline rush of a show, that pressure I had craved taxed my body and led to injury. I hoped this had changed, that the strength and mental control would prove successful. I focused on this as I started.

But there is a point of no return, as I had felt before. When you are in live performance, there is no stopping, going back, redoing. So I assured myself that my years of experience would aid in my discovery of the stage yet again. And once I started, it was over in a moment's blink.

EVERYTHING WENT AS I wished. It was certainly the biggest test yet. My body held up. Nothing too painful or startling. But that unique feeling that only a performance can produce came flooding back. I was portraying again. Expressing again. I wasn't in a studio analyzing my quadratus femoris.

I was dancing.

I WAS FINALLY ready to leave Melbourne. Ready to return to New York. Ready to explore again. To "officially" dance onstage. And after the "recital," Sue, Megan, Paula, and I hugged our good-byes. They stood there. The last image I have of that Melbourne time is of the three of them standing together, watching my very last steps away from them.

CHAPTER 54

I had mixed emotions bidding Melbourne goodbye. I didn't want to leave the safety of the team. But it was time to return to ABT at last. I walked into my first rehearsal. I looked around with a new set of eyes, with a sense of clarity and calm and peace. No wasteful insecurities ran through my mind. I had taken a long journey to get to this place. I was ready to rehearse *Giselle* with Gillian Murphy, with Kevin guiding us along in the front of the room.

There wasn't new choreography to learn or a new vocabulary to pick up. This ballet is embedded in my muscle memory; I had danced it in venues throughout the world with many different partners and companies. But it was Gillian's first time to dance the role of Giselle with ABT, and I hadn't touched the role of Albrecht since the last time I danced with the company, nearly three years before. My one looming question: how will it *feel* to perform? I had missed what should have been the prime of my career. All I knew for sure was that I felt like the proverbial phoenix risen from the ashes.

In my first entrance, I was to run onstage, dashing forward to a musical crescendo. When the music sounded—music that was so familiar, calling up so many memories—I welled up instantly. I ran into the middle of the studio but couldn't continue. I stopped midmovement. The pianist stopped. I covered my eyes.

"I'm sorry," I said as Kevin, Gillian, and Emily, the rehearsal pianist, looked on. "I just never thought I would have the chance to dance this again."

I dried my eyes. I saw that they felt this with me. They knew the struggle I had endured and what it meant to return to the studio and have the privilege to rehearse again. There is no deeper gratitude than when something is taken away from you and you regain it through the help and guidance of others and, most significantly, your own sheer will. This was how it felt to stand once again in the studio and be able to push my instrument to the demands that Albrecht asked of me. And to look forward to the evening when I could share the fight and the resolution with the New York audience that knew me best.

AS THE REHEARSAL moved on, I rediscovered the role. Given my recent experiences, it couldn't help but feel totally different. I had been stripped bare, and now, gone were the affectations, the practiced gestures, the mannerisms that had seeped in with years of dancing. I didn't need those external crutches to lean on. I could just stand there, *as* Albrecht, not trying to *be* Albrecht.

Kevin and I were inspired to work with each other once more. There were details to iron out for sure; cleaner glissades, matching port de bras. But the character portrayal drove it all. If I didn't have that, nothing would come across convincingly. At times, I would stand there, watching Gillian as Giselle, feeling like I was doing nothing. But in fact I was doing everything. Because I just had to *be* there. I had been told that years before, but now, for the first time, it changed the game for me. I had never felt Albrecht before. But "before" meant nothing. It was a different lifetime.

* * *

A BODY OF WORK

IN THE BUILDUP to my first major performance at the Metropolitan Opera House and my return to the New York stage, I had to master the physical demands required of Albrecht in the second act of the ballet. He jumped in ways I knew well but hadn't tested since my recovery. Late in the ballet, Albrecht executes a series of entrechats sixes, legs quickly and compactly fluttering in the air, then landing only to propel upward again. That push on my tendon would be the ultimate test of how much it could handle. But I had fourteen months of building strength in that tendon behind me. The stairs I trudged up and down relentlessly allowed me to put pressure on it. I was liberated by the control I felt. The Australian team had taught me exactly how to approach the physical climb toward the goal; from day one of rehearsals until the evening of the performance. Every day built on the next, and rest was as important as the effort.

I was a different dancer, though. Again, I could *feel* it. I wasn't tempted to be an executor anymore, who goes from step to step hoping each one would work or that a pirouette would result in multiples, wowing the audience. I always knew those tricks didn't matter, but now I was confident enough to know I didn't need to prove my worth in that way.

The day before the performance, Gillian and I, in costume, prepared to rehearse in a studio far below the Met stage. Clinton Luckett ran the rehearsal, Barbara Bilach (by far one of the greatest pianists I have rehearsed with) played, and Megan, having arrived the day before from Melbourne, sat quietly in the front corner of the room. I didn't want to perform for her, show her what I had accomplished since she last saw me. I just wanted her to see me rehearse.

Nothing to prove, I told myself.

Though I intended only to try out a few steps, we ended up dancing the entire second act from start to finish. It went as I wanted it to: calm, controlled, open to honest interpretation.

I executed all the jumps, turns, and lifts as I had previously, no excessive exertion of energy. It wasn't until the end, being left alone after Giselle departs to her grave, that I realized what I had just done and in front of whom. I was able to do it all. I started to cry. Quickly, I left the studio, sweat-stained and in costume, to take a moment alone. But I couldn't stop. So I reentered, letting the tears flow freely and happily. I glanced across the vast studio and saw Megan wiping away her own tears. I walked toward her and we tightly held each other, sobbing. She had seen me when I was unable to execute a bend of my foot. And now we cried together because of what I could do a year and a half later.

MY ENTIRE FAMILY descended on New York to see my return to the stage. They were so deeply indebted to the team in Australia that they had brought them to New York for the performance. The evening before the show, we all convened in a restaurant close to the Met and toasted the ensuing moment. I looked around the table at everyone there. No one was missing. My closet supporters surrounded me. Sue; Paula; Megan; Mom; Dad; my sister-in-law, Kristina; and my brother, Brian, with whom I'd become deeply connected now that we were adults.

After I left them, familiar feelings crept in. Even though I felt like a completely different artist, approaching a major role for the first time, those familiar doubts accompanied me through my preshow routine: morning class, home, eat, sleep, shower, shave, to the theater. In the quiet of my dressing room, tears flowed as I read pages of well wishes from the entire Australian Ballet. Flowers were delivered. Bottles of champagne. Support from everywhere. While my makeup was being applied, I thought of the team watching me. I thought of my first entrance in front of the New York audience. I thought of the final bows. My tears came so rapidly that, for a moment, the makeup artist couldn't put the eyeliner on.

I made final preparations in my dressing room. Putting my tights on, final spray on my hair, the walk to the stage from my dressing room, the arrival of the rest of the cast. These preparations and rituals that I hadn't experienced for years.

Then the call to "places." Suddenly, unexpectedly, the company applauded me, their excitement as obvious as my own. Kevin approached and we hugged, tears in our eyes. With the curtain still closed, the overture started, and the stage lights imbued the scenery with the dim light of morning.

I stood onstage alone. A completely different person than before. I closed my eyes. Took a slow, meditative breath, then opened them and took in the sight of the vast Met stage.

I was ready.

In the wings full of dancers, I prepared my props: cloak, horn, and sword. I climbed up the stairs to the ramp and waited for my music. The final chords, then I bolted on stage, feeling so raw, so liberated, so open. The audience's applause felt as if they were welcoming me back home. A warmth pervaded the entire performance from that moment on. Gillian gave everything she had in her; she glowed from the moment we met onstage, finishing each line and gesture with delicacy and meaning.

Of course, I couldn't help but obsess about imperfections even though I knew it would take time to regain my "stage legs," the feeling of assurance that comes with experience onstage. One can prepare as much as possible for a show, but it is the show that produces true progress. Still I was beyond belittling myself over one missed pirouette in my variation. That wasn't the goal. All I cared about was communicating to the audience a true depth of portrayal.

I dove into the story as I had never before. And when Giselle finally returns to her grave in the final scene, I bowed my head, eyes closed, as she vanished. Lying by her grave, I opened them again. The vast Met stage was all but empty. It was now just me and the audience. Sharing this return together. Sweat-drenched and spent, I walked slowly to the center of the stage, then toward the audience, as the curtain descended, to the last quiet chords of the score.

Minutes later, after numerous company bows and curtain calls with Gillian, I stepped out in front of that vast gold curtain to bow alone. The audience stood and roared. I bowed through tears of appreciation. I clasped my hands together, closed my eyes, and bowed my head. There was nothing else for me to do but feel thankful for every bit of my past experience. The team. The work. The grit. The fear. The obstacles. The rebirth.

THE NEXT MORNING I walked into a quiet studio for class in the basement of the Met Opera House. A few dancers were already warming their bodies for the start of another day of rehearsals. My fatigue weighted me. But I welcomed it as a reward. A reward for the exertion of the night before.

I took my spot at the barre and began the first movements to bring my body to attention. It was as if the return to the stage and the audience I danced in front of hadn't happened. Time and duty marched on. This was the moment I had waited for. The beginning of class. When the show is over, the expectation of it in the past.

I had entered the studio one more time to work as I had on countless days, over the course of so many years before. I was again that creature of the studio, where the real work and the true glory of this art exist and thrive. The stage is a sacred space full of nerves, stress, triumph, and failure. But the studio is where the progress is made. The nuances found. The execution toiled over. Again and again.

The never-ending process: from my fifteen-year-old self training late into the night with Mr. Han, as he gave me the foundations of my technique, to Guillaume and Kevin, planting the roots needed to develop myself as an artist. Then Yuri, shaping every inch of my physicality. Then Sasha, showing me the fullest reaches of my instrument. One added onto the other. Year after year. Each offering a different approach but speaking the same language of ballet, in their own studios around the globe. Each adding one layer and then another to who I am, and what I might yet become.

I was there, after that journey to the edge, because of them. But also because of my sheer will to fight. The sweat, effort, stress, doubt; toiling away in a worn studio, whether in Australia, Russia, or New York.

As class continued, the room now filled with the company's dancers, the prescribed exercises unfolded one by one. We were like soldiers, executing our routine drills to the melody of the piano. As always, I felt the power of the music deep within me. I began to sweat, reaching that tipping point when endorphins flow. In the center, we turned, waltzed, jumped; each combination revving us up even more, beyond the fatigue, and into another day.

During grand allegro, our engines revved to full throttle, we set off into a diagonal of suspended jumps, hurling ourselves from one end of the studio to another with no sense of caution, each trying to find that moment, aloft, when time stands still. I had become so accustomed to being cautious when I jumped, so fearful of that sharp pinch of pain it induced. But now, there was no pain.

Positioned in the studio's corner, I braced myself, like a runner at the starting line, then launched into the force of my preparation. A deep intake of breath. I propelled myself into the air.

ACKNOWLEDGMENTS

Little did I know that, when writing this book, it would eventually evolve into an entire team of people helping me iron out, develop, edit, strikethrough, and organize. This entire undertaking was aided and accomplished through the patience of those mentioned here.

Trish Todd, my editor at Touchstone, eagerly took on the book and remained loyal past any formal due date. Her patience and reassurance that this wasn't a colossal mistake on my part (or hers) was what kept me pushing forward, giving me the needed time to let it fully bloom. She gave me confidence when I had none, and her voice saying, "Butt in chair!" is forever imprinted in my memory.

Elizabeth Kaye helped me transform my entire jumble of words into something cohesive and legible. She went beyond any form of expectation or obligation. And through her deep love of dancers and our art form, she stayed with me until the very last word, culling endlessly through the material. It was the perfect scenario for a first-time writer to be working with a seasoned one who understood my passions.

My agent, David Kuhn, supported this project from an idea into something to shake hands about and get to work on. I will always appreciate his honesty and insight. And also, his team: Becky Sweren and Nate Muscato.

ACKNOWLEDGMENTS

Kaitlin Olson, Trish's assistant, helped with many a logistic, printing 520 pages of material and shipping it to far reaches of the world, among many other crazy but necessary requests, never once objecting.

Thank you to:

Daniel Mendelsohn and Michael Kaiser, for reading certain excerpts and giving insight as to what needed fleshing out.

Dianna Mesion, my producing manager (who knows me better than I know myself), for diving in later on in the process, reading the book in its entirety, and especially ironing out the photos. WPE!

Jamieson Baker and Alex Kovacs at Untitled, who believed in the book and charged forward with Dianna to get it out into the world.

Shida Carr, for devoting her time and expertise to promoting the finished copy.

Roslyn Sulcas, for planting the seed and telling me to write my experiences down, as "you never know what could come of it."

Lastly, my parents, for never insisting on a read but when given a draft, checking to make sure certain passages were accurate, all the while learning more about a son they already knew.

INDEX

INDEX

411

INDEX

David Hallberg is a Principal Dancer with American Ballet Theatre in New York. He was the first American to join the Bolshoi Ballet in Moscow as a Principal Dancer. He continues to dance around the world and is a Resident Guest Artist with The Australian Ballet. He started the David Hallberg Scholarship, mentoring young boys aspiring to a career in ballet, and the Innovation Initiative, a platform for emerging choreographers, both at American Ballet Theatre.